The Leadership of
Civilization Building

Administrative Ideas and Realities

Superficial Administrative Ideas Held by Most Leaders	Administrative Reality
1. The management process is: Plan, Organize, Motivate, and Control.	1. The administrative process is: Diagnose, Theorize, Decide, Accomplish, and Review.
2. I have the authority here to govern other individuals.	2. Other individuals here must give me my authority to govern them.
3. I'm in charge; I have the power.	3. My power is derived from the consent of others.
4. I can fire anybody, anytime.	4. Anybody can leave me, anytime.
5. My job is to get the job done.	5. My job is to help others get the job done.
6. What we need is knowledge.	6. What we need is wisdom.
7. I have to lead everyone— I am the leader.	7. Everyone is a leader.
8. I am superior to others.	8. Others are equal to me.
9. The basic organizing principle of the human race is A over B over C over D etc. [A>B>C>D . . .] which is an Authoritarian Hierarchy (Authoritarianism and Totalitarianism); it provides no checks or balances in governance with minimum societal incentives.	9. The basic organizing principle of the human race is A (Administrators) over B (Bureaucrats) over C (Citizens) over A (Administrators) [A>B>C>A . . .] which is a Participative Heterarchy (Freedom and Democracy); it provides checks and balances in governance with maximum societal incentives.
10. "Governors" (leaders) have responsibility and authority—ultimately.	10. "People" (constituents) have responsibility and authority—ultimately.

The Leadership of Civilization Building

ADMINISTRATIVE AND CIVILIZATION THEORY,
SYMBOLIC DIALOGUE, AND CITIZEN SKILLS
FOR THE 21ST CENTURY

Richard J. Spady and Richard S. Kirby
In Collaboration with Cecil H. Bell, Jr.

Forum Foundation
Seattle, WA

Spady, Richard J.

 The leadership of civilization building : administrative and civilization theory, symbolic dialogue, and citizen skills for the 21st century / Richard J. Spady and Richard S. Kirby in collaboration with Cecil H. Bell, Jr. -- 1st ed.

 p. cm.

 Includes index.

 ISBN: 0-9700534-9-5

 1. Political science--Philosophy. 2. Civilization-- Philosophy. 3. Civics. 4. Leadership. I. Spady, Richard J. II. Kirby, Richard S. III. Title.

 JA71.S63 2001   320'.01
                        QBI01-200161

Published by the Forum Foundation
4426 Second Ave. NE
Seattle, WA 98105-6191
Phone (206) 634-0420
Fax (206) 633-3561
Typeset by Hargrave Design in association with Niche Press
Printed in the United States of America

Contents

Dedication

This book is dedicated to our families:

From Dick Spady, to Lou and to our children—John, Jim, Walt, Carol, Doug, and also in memory of my mother, Elsie E. Schmeer.

From Richard Kirby to Deborah and Alana.

And to our former colleague/mentor/scholar in this research, Dr. Stuart C. Dodd (1900-1975), and to our collaborator in this book, Dr. Cecil H. Bell, Jr.

This book is also dedicated to those citizens of the world who share with us a common quest: to work toward a better civilization. This is a goal that we, and those who follow us, can pursue with love throughout our future history together.

Acknowledgments

Nearly all of us can reach back in memory to a teacher who had a profound impact on our own learning. As principal author of this work, I (RJS) wish first to acknowledge the contribution to this book of the scholarship of Dr. Theodore Barnowe, professor of administrative theory and organizational behavior at the University of Washington Graduate School of Business Administration.

Professor Barnowe was one of those gifted teachers who filled his students with his own enthusiasm for the potential of the discipline to make important contributions to the successful functioning of organizations. In one course Professor Barnowe in 1970 challenged the students to write a term paper in which they were to "*just take anything in management theory and make it sound rational.*" It was from this broad challenge that the first rudimentary administrative theories presented here were conceived, and it was only with significant and meaningful contributions from the following individuals that they emerged three decades later:

- Our colleague, the late Dr. Stuart C. Dodd, Forum Foundation board member, UW Professor emeritus and a pioneer in sociology, whose social theories and insights helped cross-fertilize this work.

- Dr. Cecil H. Bell, Jr., former associate professor and chairman of the Department of Management and Organization at UW's School of Business, co-founder of the Forum Foundation, president of the Stuart C. Dodd Institute for Social Innovation, collaborator on this work, and my advisor while I was in the Graduate School of Business.

- The Rev. Dr. Richard S. Kirby, co-author of this book, executive director of the Stuart C. Dodd Institute for Social Innovation and chair of the World Network of Religious Futurists, who in recent years has begun to integrate the administrative theories presented here into his leadership and ethics classes at UW's School of Business Administration and into society at large as an international lecturer.

- The Rev. Dr. William D. Ellington (Theology), co-founder of the Forum Foundation; the Rev. Dr. William B. Cate (Social Ethics), president emeritus of the Church Council of Greater Seattle (1970-1990); and Dr. Jan Cate (Values and Ethics). All are current board members of the Forum Foundation.

- Others of the Forum Foundation's board of directors and their spouses, who over a period of many years worked, discussed, and challenged my theories and papers, and helped guide me through the labyrinth of social science research.

- Dr. Almas Chukin, former charge d'affaires for Russia's newly independent state, Kyrgyz Republic, who first invited me to his home country to lecture about administrative theory in 1991.

- Dr. Tatyana Tsyrlina, professor of education, Russia's Kursk State Pedagogical University, who translated our books, and who uses the Fast Forum® communication technique in Russia as part of her work with the Stuart C. Dodd Institute for Social Innovation.

- Dr. Nikolai Nikandrov, president of the Russian Academy of Education and Dr. Boris Bim-Bad, president, Russia's Open University in Moscow, for their encouragement and support of our theories in Russia.

- The Rev. Dr. Ken Bedell (Sociology), president of EPIC, Inc. (Ecumenical Programs In Communication) and Vice President for Administration, Forum Foundation.

- Jim La Rue for his help in artwork and layout and Jessie Kinnear Kenton for editing our earlier books on *The Search for Enlightened Leadership Volume 1, Applying New Administrative Theory* (1996) and *Volume 2 Many-To-Many Communication* (1998).

- Niche Press for its editorial suggestions.

Richard J. Spady
President, Forum Foundation
August, 2001

I have been a friend and colleague of Dick Spady's since 1970. I provided discussion, encouragement, and support to him as he developed his ideas about administrative theory and Zeitgeist Communication. I have always believed these ideas are important and sound. When he asked me to collaborate on this book, I went along for the ride because I found that any journey with Dick Spady is a high adventure. Also, working with Richard Kirby has been a delight. Richard brought a powerful intellect and historical understanding of civilization building that greatly strengthened the book.

Cecil Bell,
Vice President, Forum Foundation
August, 2001

I wish to acknowledge the wisdom and support of many kinds offered by Dr. Cecil H. Bell, Jr.; and I must express my gratitude to Dick Spady, President of the Forum Foundation, for his leadership in our five years of collaboration and for the opportunity of co-authoring this text. In addition, I would like to record my appreciation of several generations of students in the University of Washington Business School, for their valuable feedback as we have tested and refined our theories in the classroom.

Richard Kirby
Executive Director, Stuart C. Dodd
Institute for Social Innovation
August, 2001

P.S. from Richard Spady:

My collaborator and co-founder of the Forum Foundation, Cecil Bell, is fond of saying that he merely "went along for the ride." The truth is, he is a rigorous scholar, and, with Richard Kirby, is the one teacher who has helped us focus our work more than any other. As a late-life graduate student and practitioner of administrative theory and a life-long learner, I am eternally grateful for the learning climate created by Cecil and the University of Washington in Seattle.

Foreword

Designers or architects of civilization are rare. Builders of civilization are even more rare. Thinkers about civilization do not lie thick on the ground, neither in the realms of business, nor government, nor society.

Nevertheless there is a hunger within every human mind for the habitation, the safe harbor of civilization.

The notion of a civilized society or simply a state or place of civilization is one that the human mind naturally understands. It would appear, as social philosophers increasingly understand, that we are made for civilization.

Jean Jacques Rousseau in his famous book *La Contrat Sociale* (*The Social Contract*) states that a human being is "born free but is everywhere in chains." These chains are not merely chains of imprisonment or starvation, but chains of squalor and degradation. These chains reveal a widespread impoverishment of culture. This perhaps is also what Thomas Hobbes, the 16th-17th Century political writer had in mind in his book *Leviathan*. His famous words described human life as typically "nasty, brutish, horrible and short." His words still describe what millions feel is an apparent "life-sentence." Life is not a gift but a punishment: condemnation to living in a world whose civilization is rudimentary and sometimes altogether absent.

Likewise Olaf Stapledon (1886-1950) in his books on *Philosophy and Living* spoke of his desire to study the causes of the "tragic disorder in our terrestrial hive." The social disorder of civilization's absence seems indicative of a wider, perhaps a cosmic disorder. But builders of civilization act to *reverse* this grim syndrome of social entropy, deterioration, violence and the increase of misery.

In the history of culture, it has been a rare event for theorists of civilization to discover new truth about this great subject. For theorists of civilization investigate how people can live together not only in harmony and productivity, not only in brotherhood and freedom, but in a state of civilized being which harmonizes the artistic, scientific, economic and spiritual elements of social being.

Civilization exalts human social nature, and causes social being and human nature itself to evolve towards higher levels of consciousness and happiness. Landmarks in the history of civilization definition include St. Augustine of Hippo. This 5th Century North African bishop was one of the most eminent Christian theologians in his or any other time. It was he who wrote the *City of God* in the twilight of the period that we call "ancient" or "Patristic" times. This was at the dawn of the Middle Ages.

Indeed he wrote his great books even as the Vandals were destroying the great empire of Rome, in the twilight of which St. Augustine lived.

With the coming of the Renaissance and the Reformation as the second Christian millennium got under way, science, religion and civilization began once again to form a harmonious triad. The founders of the modern scientific revolution, Descartes, Bacon, and their colleagues in political and scientific realms, understood the revolution of scientific thought that grew out of the Renaissance to be a civilizing influence. They were concerned with the higher truth not only of physics and astronomy but also of society.

The Industrial Revolution occupied parts of the late 18th Century, and much of the 19th Century. The emerging power of new technologies to change the world was seen as truly remarkable by many people in those eras, and the one that immediately followed. The early years of the Industrial Revolution were also the years of the birth of new political ideals and whole new countries such as the United States. To the social philosophers of the late 18th and 19th centuries, these changes were momentous advances (or so they seemed) in human affairs. They were accomplishments that seemed like signals or heralds of a triumphant new period of human history. This would be the beginning of sustained and ever-increasing "progress." It seemed to these thinkers, and in due course to political and social leaders also, that the 20th Century would be one of unhindered progress. This would be the greatest century known to humanity.

So began the social philosophy of the 20th Century, in a mood of vast hope, eager expectation of benevolent scientific-technological breakthrough, and the lively believe in — at last! — sustained progress for humanity and human society.

Shortly after the century began (with wars in parts of the world such as South Africa), the Titanic, the "unsinkable," the sign of triumphant technology and human unconquerable ingenuity, sank on its maiden voyage. Perhaps progress was not inevitable. Perhaps science did have limits.

Then came the apocalyptic event of the First World War. Nations were bled almost to death, genocide appeared, new forms of weaponry such as mustard gas were deployed, and unnumbered millions of the youth of humanity were killed in a futile, horrific war. This led to the great economic depressions of the 20's and 30's, and then the Second World War, followed by the Cold War. Once again, it turned out science was not only not inevitably progressive, but not even inevitably benign. The appearance of atomic and hydrogen bombs left mid-century humanity with a chronic subliminal fear of science at its worst as a threat, not as an angelic presence.

Science-technology had made the 20th Century into the cruelest and most murderous in all known history.

It was as if the idea of "progress," sadly, was a philosophy of evolution that perished on the battlefields of the First and Second World Wars. As Bryan Appleyard says in his book, *Understanding the Present*, science was humbled and its humbling needs to continue.

But philosophers and theologians studying the theory of science are reasoning that the picture is not wholly gloomy. For what is generally known as "science" is only one of many possible social endeavors leading to knowledge and technological applications. Perhaps the spiritual core of science was lost during the time of the Industrial Revolution, but it is now being regained. We still can believe in "progress," but in a more humble and gentle way, and with the hope of a better, wiser science and a healing technology.

Richard J. Spady and Richard S. Kirby are introducing new truth about the theory AND the practice of civilization. Appropriately, as a new century dawns, this book, *The Leadership of Civilization Building*, offers an enlightened approach to leadership. This innovative text in civic innovation offers the students, the teachers and the citizens of the 21st Century practical tools of understanding civilization, including civic action. The authors present a curriculum that will allow persons all over the world to develop their own power as citizens. As a result all citizens are shown how to become architects and builders of the civilization of tomorrow.

In Section One, *Theory Building*, Spady and Kirby present new administrative and civilization theories. They dethrone hierarchical, authoritarian approaches to all kinds of management or administration in society, in business, in government and in churches. They install in their place a "democracy of the intellect" and a democracy of leadership. Their theories imply a resultant quantum leap in the efficiency and financial potency of all organizations and citizens. Their theories constitute an empowerment of employees, administrators and CEOs, elected and "duly appointed" government officials, teachers, artists, scientists, pastors, and all those who work in groups.

In Section Two, namely *Technology Building*, the authors have announced a breakthrough in social science with a description and utilization of the Fast Forum® Technique, Symbolic Dialogue, Social Audits, Opinionnaire®, Viewspaper®, and the Future Molding Game™. They are building on contemporary realizations that *human being* is radically, intrinsically, and necessarily *interpersonal* being. These realizations are based partly on insights drawn from such varied fields as anthropology, philosophy, socio-biology, religion, and quantum mechanics.

Spady and Kirby also present the necessary *social technology* for multiple simultaneous human communications to take place effectively. In this way, they are enabling leaders, governors, managers, and citizens of tomorrow to be able to communicate more and more intelligently and effectively with one another through symbolic dialogue. Their work makes it possible for the *collective intelligence of communication systems* to become more and more potent, financially productive, and progressively intelligent leading toward wisdom.

There is a special value in the work of the authors in empowering *young people.* The authors offer groupware and socialware application models that implement Eric Erikson's work on "psycho-social education." This approach is a potential landmark for pedagogy and youth leadership approaches to democracy in schools and among young people in all nations. New administrative theory supports an early and exciting civic role for young people. Today's and tomorrow's teachers can use the social technologies presented by Spady and Kirby. For what? To call youth to high service and to summon them to moral and emotional maturity! Young people can be encouraged to exercise their energies in the service of an idealism that will not fail. Youth leaders, their teachers, and their groups are being "called up" now. They can be enrolled in the service of a great cause. They too are among the leaders of the building of the civilization of tomorrow. For that is a civilization, a culture, a way of being human in societies, which they themselves must inhabit. Spady and Kirby provide instruments of communication and inspiration with which young people can be designers, as well as recipients, of the culture of the near future.

Likewise, at the other end of life's journey, the book provides fuel for the more gentle energies of *senior citizens* to awaken their wisdom and rally together to support each other in refashioning and reconceiving the philosophy and the story of old age.

In this book the authors gather up their thinking about the civilization of tomorrow and present key elements of what must be called civilization theory. These theories include the definition of civilization and an explanation of its implication for citizens everywhere. Indeed one of the great tasks of the book is to equip persons everywhere to understand their responsibilities, their rights, and their powers as citizens.

For it is not only officials who are the architects of the civilization of tomorrow, but also civilized people everywhere. It is the achievement of this work that it invites persons everywhere to play a major and ever growing part in the civilizing of their own civilization, and in advancing everywhere the theory of the citizen. They offer a fresh and imaginative analysis of the meaning of citizenship in a high-tech (but high touch), multi-media, global-scientific world. The authors have thus broken new ground in achieving a new definition of democracy in a world of Many-To-Many Communication. They help us imagine and construct together a world where government can indeed be "of the people, by the people, and for the people."

Rev. William D. Ellington, Ph.D.
Co-Founder/Board Member,
Forum Foundation
Rev. William B. Cate, Ph.D.
Board Member, Forum Foundation

Preface

Citizens—cities—civilization builders and teachers: awake! Our book is dedicated to you—the present and future citizens of the USA, of all nations, of the world. It is a call to you, a call to wise vision. Where there is no vision, the people perish. [Proverbs 29:18, KJV]

This book is a manual for creative civilization builders. It is also a textbook. A leader's/teacher's guide will be issued to support it.

Our purpose is to equip civilization builders. In this book we give a *vision* of cost-effective civilization building to builders of civilization, such as political, business, educational, and religious leaders. We provide an introduction to the tools—conceptual and social—to do that building.

Our aim is to help leaders and their constituents to "talk" symbolically together. On what subject? On the *improvement* of organizations, institutions, and society as a whole.

Our theme is that a better civilization is not only desirable, but also attainable. We believe this is not only true ethically and spiritually, but also as a civic, economic, educational, and political project.

We have many readers in mind. Some of our intended audiences are: governors, political leaders, public officials, political scientists; students and teachers of civilization and sociology; students, teachers, and practitioners of management and administration; religious and moral leaders, all churches, and religious communities and laity; and parents.

We plan that our text will be read wherever "civics" and/or futures issues are studied—in schools from grade school through graduate school and in business, law, and ministry schools everywhere.

We intend that our text will be read by professionals in politics and government, whether *officials*—such as governors, county executives, mayors, legislators and congresspersons and their aides; or *teachers* of political science/philosophy, civics—and their students.

Our book offers solutions (theories), not just diagnoses of problems.

We describe and prescribe a civilized future—thus we offset the gloom of pessimistic future-trend books.

We offer skills, vision, and strategies to citizens, not just governors. We encourage people to *make* trends, not just observe them as some authors do.

A major purpose of the book is to inspire the use of Fast Forum® and symbolic dialogue program models or applications in governments, organizations, schools, the community, and churches. Students of administration and civilization in business schools, public planning, education, and seminaries can read it as a textbook to help clarify their own emerging theories of organizational dynamics and leadership.

The book aims to give people a sense of being in control of their own future. We desire to help citizens in all lands grow into being the creators of their own civic destiny. Thus we hope that this is an empowering book, for it is a book about civic power. It aims to offer civic inspiration.

We hope to enable these *new social processes of communication* to mature and become embedded in public policy. Our current civic necessity is what we call *building working social models* of Many-To-Many communication. These practical social technologies such as the Citizen Councilor Network and Psycho-Social Education are vital civic experiments for the cities and citizens of the 21st century. They will enable every interested person, every citizen who wishes to do so, to contribute to civilization building. They will mobilize his or her opinions and energies toward the vision of the highest good for society. This is what we call the Zeitgeist ("Spirit-of-the-Time"). For it is this which is the "Supreme Governor" of society.

Richard J. Spady
Richard S. Kirby
Seattle, August, 2001

I

· ·

Theory
Building

Introduction
to Civilization
Building

Major Themes of the Book

Welcome to the world of deliberate civilization building! The leadership of civilization building is an inspired act to which we invite citizens everywhere. In this Introduction we take you through some of the key ideas in the book that follows. We invite you to think of it as like warming up your muscles before a workout or a sports game.

A Great Achievement

Civilization, and its constituent *culture*, is one of the great achievements of humanity. It is a high achievement which comes out of barbarism and advances to the life of *homo sapiens*. The story of civilization is a tale with a past, present, and future. This is a story of the journey of the human race. It starts from the simplest hunter-gatherer societies; it advances to the deliberate pursuit of maximally civilized nations and associations.

A Textbook for 21st Century Citizenship

We call the process guiding this journey's latest stage *Civilization Building*. Our books offer a manual, a handbook, and a curriculum for those who take a leadership role in the building of the civilization of the near and far future. Thus we present in the following pages a textbook for 21st Century citizenship.

Leaders Are Everywhere!

This does not mean "Leaders" with a capital "L" but all those who want to help the task of Civilization Building. These leaders of Civilization Building might be regular workers and citizens. They could be movie stars, elected politicians, innovative thinkers, and Five-Star Generals. And they might be students, teens, and senior citizens, the unemployed, prison inmates, and the chronically ill, as well as celebrities. *Citizen Skills* for the 21st Century are for all human beings.

An Epic Story

All of us who are alive today, were alive in all our yesterdays, and will be in all of our tomorrows are part of this epic story of the journey of the human race.

The journey towards civilization started, perhaps in a cave; it may end among the stars. Around a million years ago the human neo-cortex formed over evolutionary eons. Pre-historic man and woman together squinted up at the stars and wondered. These wisps of thought must have been distilled from eons of earlier wonder. They finally coalesced in a swirl of consciousness and burst into history's most violent storm. It is a storm that still rages today: a storm in the human mind. It is like a persistent, tempestuous search. It continues to ask the most searching questions for those who live, as we all must, in an interdependent society. Examples are:

Who am I?

Where did I come from?

Where do I fit in?

What is my role in life?

What are we doing here?

What's it all about?

Where am I going?

What should we, what can we, what must we do?

Are we alone in an impersonal universe?

These are spiritual questions, which reach beyond the known into the unknown, beyond the personal into the transpersonal.

What Are We Doing Here; Where Are We Going?

Indeed, these questions of an individual's "identity" and a group's calling may be among the most important religious questions of the age. From that earliest cave dwelling, with man and woman working together, people first organized themselves into the basic and most enduring of all human leadership institutions: the family. Instinctively, they knew that together, through their "organization," they could achieve more than either could ever do alone, because "organizations" are synergistic and can amplify human effort. It was then that humankind asked not only *"Where am I going?"* but also, *"Where do I want to go?"* and *"How can I get there?"* The appearance of the human family as a natural social unit also led to the "I" questions being resolvable only in "we" questions. *In other words, the meaning of life is social.*

The Search for Civilization: an End of Pain?

So began the search for civilization. The human quest to discover and actualize the archetype of civilization was not only a search for beauty and love. It was also an anguished search for an end to chronic, apparently meaningless suffering. Thus was philosophy born. This was the search for the way out from the prison of pain, loneliness, and war.

The birth of society was followed by the birth of the study of society. Later this became sociology, social science, and social innovation. Civilization building occurs as civilization builders apply social innovation to social problems and as the builders awaken the genius of society and societies. Civilization building occurs as an answer to the organizational and societal quest of people working together to improve their future and that of the human race.

The Administrative Process

People create organizations and institutions to collaborate toward, and indeed to accomplish their objectives together. Accordingly, every organization is involved in the administrative process.

Humankind has learned much about the dynamics of administration in the last few decades, just as it has learned much in psychology, sociology, education, and the physical sciences. Unfortunately most managers of organizations and institutions today, public and private, are still using management theories that are both erroneous and outdated. Leaders often *create* as many "human" problems through their inadequate management styles as they *solve* in their preoccupation with physical, social, economic, political, and other problems.

The Ultimate Source of Power and Authority

One major problem we have identified standing in the way of building better organizations, institutions, and, ultimately, civilization, is inadequate understanding of the nature of the administrative process of leading and governing. Another is a misunderstanding, or a forgotten understanding, of the ultimate source of power and authority.

This ultimate source of power to govern is vested in the people being governed. Thus, it is no accident that the preambles of both the Constitution of the United States and the United Nations Charter begin with the same powerful phrase, *"We the people."*

Great Civic Values

The preambles to these historic documents are history's clue to the ultimate source of power and authority. We believe this to be true of all organizations and institutions, public and private, everywhere in the world. Great civic values are operating here; they have engendered such civic ideals as the principles of freedom, equality, democracy, and justice. They are embodied in the Declaration of Independence, the Constitution, and the Bill of Rights. They enable the American people, working together as a people, "one nation under God, indivisible," to enhance their various communities. They also allow Americans to participate, simultaneously, in the larger integrating activity of civilization building in other parts of the world. They point to a way of life in which members of the human race can work together as "global" citizens.

Communicate Their Vision of the Common Good

What is the responsibility of all citizens in their schools, churches, neighborhoods, cities, counties, states, and governments, and in their private organizations and workplaces today? It is to discover and communicate their vision of the common good! This is an inalienable right and equally a responsibility! When people communicate their vision coherently and with growing consensus, then the vision itself begins to steer society toward that objective—naturally. This is how our conceptions of "civilization" grow and improve.

Many-To-Many (MTM) Communication

Today, we're all familiar with "one-to-one," and "one-to-many" communication (one person mails a letter to another, or sends e-mail to one or many persons simultaneously). The world, though, is moving rapidly toward a need for what we call Many-To-Many (MTM) Communication. (This will be developed in Section Two.) Here, the "many" must be able to communicate to each other and respond to the ideas of their leaders and others *symbolically* (i.e., not physically) in order to understand the values of themselves, their leaders, and others. This is all done in a process that increases everyone's own self-awareness about the world around them.

The Question for All of Us, Leaders and Constituents Alike, is:

How can citizens and constituents be enabled to communicate with each other and with their leaders constructively? *How* can we enable and inspire "the people" to be involved in their own governance and their own "pursuit of happiness" in ways that result in a significant increase in the authority and legitimacy of their political, economic, and cultural organizations and institutions in the world?

We believe a solution to this problem will be found in "Many-To-Many Communication" technology in the context of civilization building.

Here at Seattle's Forum Foundation the essence of 30 years of research in pure and applied social science (other than the 10 administrative and three civilization theories, which follow), brings the following realization.

Big Meetings—the Achilles' Heel of the Democratic Process

Big meetings at often-remote distances for people are the Achilles' Heel of the democratic process in a society, public and private.

People no longer have the time and energy to go to big meetings—especially at remote distances. Or, if they do attend, the logistics at such meetings are such that only a few people can talk and most people can only listen. This causes frustration, giving rise to the emotions and exhaustion that come from cumbersome efforts to gain consensus. For example, efforts to pass controversial resolutions using Robert's Rules of Order are often highly frustrating experiences. As a result, people drop out of such meetings, prompting remarks such as, "Look at the apathy among the people; they are not coming to our important meetings."

In fact, a popular complaint among leaders nearly everywhere today is, "People are apathetic!"

Our own analysis indicates otherwise; people simply get exhausted from their previous efforts to be responsible. They remember their frustration and exhaustion trying to get their ideas across in their organizations and institutions, and finally say to themselves, "These meetings are just not worth my time." So, they drop out. Well, that's not apathy.

How to Get the Attention of the Leaders

Freedom of speech, freedom of the press, freedom to petition, and the right peaceably to assemble are all hollow rights if people *cannot be heard.* And today citizens believe that organizational, institutional, and governmental processes are such that they *cannot be heard.* Indeed, good and dedicated people give indications of this every day. For example, they do this when they choose to march in the street or otherwise demonstrate. This is how they attract attention to a perceived injustice or worthy cause. They too often feel obliged to choose this method rather than use the normal institutional representative processes. There is a grave danger in the use of such dramatic, confrontational, and "show biz" techniques to access the public agenda—if carried to extremes. A backlash and public cry for "law and order" may result in a call for even greater authoritarianism than currently exists. This could lead to dictatorship—the most depraved corruption of governance.

Universal Administrative Theories

Up to now, we believe no one has provided a comprehensive set of universal administrative theories. Such theories should be able to conceptualize the realities of administering human affairs. They should theoretically apply in most if not all contexts. They should be tools to help as we navigate, individually and simultaneously collectively and corporately, through life.

Maximum Contribution to World Society

Thus we introduce here the set of general administrative theories presented in Section One. We believe they are applicable in all human organizations. As practitioners and scholars, we have tried to craft them with the best values and knowledge of social science. We invite our readers to put them to work now for civilization building. You too can lift them up to help create new organizational and societal contexts, to train creative leaders of society. You can help leaders and their constituents achieve their maximum contribution to world society.

The Art of Successful Governance

Perhaps governance will always remain an art and not a science. But we should at least try to identify those principles and dynamics that can be understood and applied by every leader. Every individual citizen can also understand these principles. We need only first, to be interested, and second, to make the effort to understand!

We hope, too, that our collective works will help inform the enigmatic question of human purpose and destiny. For we, the human family, are on the move. We are heading from barbarian atrocities and wars of the past and present, to a future "civilization." This is the highest purpose of our textbook. For it is a text for the builders of the "Civilization of Tomorrow."

How to Collaborate! The Key to Civilization Building

Civilization Building succeeds—we repeat—as humankind learns how to collaborate. Collaboration is the way to grow. Collaboration is the way to enable the exercise of individual, societal, economic, religious, and political responsibilities. Collaboration is the means to achieve organizational and institutional objectives in local, regional, state, national and international arenas, both public and private, governmental and non-governmental. Collaboration is the vehicle for building civilization so as to make it finer, more widespread, more enduring, more profound.

The Definition of Civilization Building

Religious leaders know that in every human heart there lies the hope of finding, or contributing to, true civilization. Yet few people, even academic social scientists and politicians, have tried to define or study civilization. As we enter the Third Millennium, there is a great need for leaders—indeed for all citizens—to understand civilization well enough to know its history, and to share in its ongoing creation and improvement. Our definition of civilization building is: *the dynamic, historical processes of human innovation and social evolution that improve the survivability of the human race and the success of the human species through its enlightened organizations and institutions.*

We believe that a person's civic identity is one of the deepest components of human nature. It is nothing less than the link between who we are and the civilization we build for ourselves.

Inspired Citizens of the World in Pursuit of Happiness!

This book, the fruit of social science research sponsored by Seattle's Forum Foundation since 1970, presents a set of theories, challenges, and techniques for the administrators and citizens of the future that we hope will provide vital energy for 21st Century citizenship and governance in the world. *Inspired citizens of the world in pursuit of happiness!*

For the most part this book is a rewrite of our previous books: *The Search for Enlightened Leadership, Volume 1: Applying New Administrative Theory* (1996) *and Volume 2: Many-To-Many Communication, A Breakthrough in Social Science* (1998), by Spady and Bell. The exception is that this book contains the Civilization Theories in complete form rather than in an intuitive form as was presented in the two prior books. Thus, our past research in administrative theory has brought us now to the science of civilization building.

Our late colleague, Dr. Stuart C. Dodd wrote:

"The first aim of science is the description of our world. Science seeks a system of categories that will capture the essential aspects of the entities under study. The second aim of science is the explanation of the origin of the entities. Science seeks to know the causes of the entities under study. The third aim of science is the prediction of the future. Science searches for

accurate methods of predicting future events and structures of interest. The fourth aim of science is a general understanding. Science attempts to find basic structures and processes that model the behavior of entities at all levels and times. These four aims of science have been guides for my work in cosmic modeling." [1]

Section One of this book presents our ideas on Administrative and Civilization Theory. Section Two presents our ideas on Many-To-Many Communication and Zeitgeist Communication and discusses a technology we have developed called the Fast Forum® Technique.

My Personal Quest: Richard J. Spady's Story

My co-author, Richard Kirby, and collaborator, Cecil Bell, asked me to write this story. They felt it was important to do so to help set the context for the research presented in this book. Many of my mentors have been religious and are listed here. However, the substantive content in this book is not religious; it's about administrative theory and Zeitgeist Communication.

I didn't start out with the idea of being a "civilization builder." Rather, like most persons in the world do at some times in their lives, I was simply trying to volunteer and be of help where I could.

In 1965 I was asked to serve as Seattle District Lay Leader of The Methodist Church by the Rev. Joe A. Harding, the new Seattle District Superintendent.[2] The district had about 44 churches and 25,000 members in what is approximately King County. When I visited churches I would ask people basically, "What is the problem in the church? What is the problem in society?" What I heard people saying in response was, "We have no way to constructively contribute our opinions that is 1) *inherently beneficial* to us as individuals—through a process that itself has a payoff for our time and energy, 2) that's good for the church—which we love, and 3) that's good for the society as a whole—we are not out on an island by ourselves, we are part of something bigger."

Methodists traditionally have been very interested in social concerns—especially education. At the time we were going to big meetings of 200-300 people using Robert's Rules of Order to pass resolutions. It wasn't working well. Someone would grab the mike, sometimes getting emotional, and off he or she would go on a personal tangent about an idea strongly held. It's probably a common experience of most people. We all have opinions, and some are very strongly emotional and important to us. But the process itself was often frustrating both to leaders and to people participating. It was decided to do some social experimenting.

We had an executive committee of The Seattle District Board of Laity of about 20 men and women who conducted church affairs at the district level. We met monthly. But about every four months we held a forum among ourselves. However, we were not primarily interested in the issues—we were more interested in experimenting with the process itself. Sometimes we had a panel of experts, and sometimes we didn't. Sometimes we would do "this"; sometimes "that." Our question? How can individuals in church and society be heard? It seemed that freedom of speech, religion, the press, and peaceable assembly were not working. People felt *unable to be heard*. Big meetings at often remote distances and typical legislative processes using Robert's Rules of Order to pass resolutions posed barriers to communication among people in their normal societal contexts.

Race Relations

In the spring of 1968 we held our last forum before I left office. The issue was, "How can we reduce racial tensions in Seattle"? This was right after the racial riots in the Watts district of Los Angeles. Several good ideas emerged from that dialogue. I decided to try to implement them in Bellevue, Washington where I lived. It was a growing suburb located just east and across Lake Washington from Seattle.

I met with the mayor, the superintendent of public schools, religious, chamber of commerce, and community leaders. The result was that a new group was formed, The Eastside Inter-Racial Clearing House. It conducted a very low key, people-to-people program. People interested were able to participate merely by phoning the sponsor's offices at the Eastside YMCA. Participants were matched with others from different racial groups in Seattle for dialogue. They would meet in a picnic, recreational, or informal dinner setting and talk about the problems of race. About 400 people participated during the summer.

In the fall the clearing house board asked themselves, "What can we do now constructively in race relations"? We decided to conduct a series of Family Inter-racial Dialogues in which three black families and three white families would meet every Friday evening three weeks running from 7:00 PM to 9:30 PM.[3] However, these dialogues differed from the way the Church Council of Greater Seattle had conducted similar forums the previous two years. First, we involved *total* families. The youth who were too young to talk were in a gymnasium playing together under supervision, while the adults and older youth were in a nearby room at the East-Madison YMCA, the

Seattle Rotary Boy's Club, or at a Bellevue school facility. Perhaps the play of the youngest children was not so important to black youngsters who see lots of whites, but may have been very important to white youngsters who would seldom get a chance to play with blacks. Second, we used the "Fast Forum®" technique that, as we understood it at that time, had emerged from our experimental forums conducted in the church.

At the end of the last Friday evening dialogue of the first group, I stopped the meeting 30 minutes before they were scheduled to leave. I said, "We have been talking about the problems of race for over six hours. Now it's time to take stock of where we are." Then I gave everyone a 3x5 card. "Please print legibly on one side of the card what you think is the main problem in race relations or something that should be done to improve race relations, as briefly and concisely as possible." After doing this, all the cards were given to me, and I numbered them consecutively. Then I gave all the cards back to the group together with a response sheet containing three columns labeled yes, no, abstain. I gave the instruction, "Please read the card you have and try to determine the writer's *overall meaning*. If you can identify with the idea, completely, without reservation, mark your response sheet 'yes.' If you cannot identify with the idea, also without reservation, mark 'no.' If you cannot give it a clear yes or a clear no—mark your response sheet 'abstain.'"

Then they began reading the cards and responding to each card in turn. They sat in a circle, and as they completed responding to a card, they passed it on to their left and would get cards from their right. There was only silence as everyone contemplated the ideas. It was all over in 30 minutes; people put on their hats and coats and left. The following week we met for a farewell potluck dinner.

I took my family home and hurried to my dining room table to tabulate the responses. I could hardly wait. I tallied individual responses by the categories of youth/adult and black/white and transferred the totals to the back of each statement card. I then reordered them with the largest number of total "yes" cards at the top. After I had studied the category results and total results on each statement card in turn, I said to myself, "I think I understand how these people feel about race." "No," I said to myself, "it's a stronger feeling than that—I believe I *know* how they feel about race." Well, it was an interesting idea, but I dropped the thought from my mind.

The following Friday night the second group completed its third and final dialogue. This was a new group; I didn't know anyone. However, they all knew I was coming to administer their summing up of their dialogues. I repeated the process in the group. At home I tabulated all responses by the categories of youth/adult and black/white, ranked the cards with the most number of yes answers on top, read each in turn, and then studied the responses on the back of each card. When I was through I said to myself again, "I think I understand how these people feel about race." "No," I said, "it's a stronger feeling than that—I believe I *know* how they feel about race." Well, it was an interesting idea, but it still didn't ring any bells. I dropped the idea from my mind a second time.

But when it happened to me again after tabulating the responses of the third group, I remember sitting up straight in my chair with my eyes wide open and asking myself, "Why do I keep having this feeling of objectivity? I don't just think I know how these people feel about the problems of race—I believe I really *know* how they feel about race." Thereafter, I watched for this phenomenon. It happened again on the fourth group, the fifth group and on to the end. By that time I was highly frustrated. I felt something very important was happening to me in my awareness of the subtle ideas being considered, but I didn't have a clue as to what it was.

After nearly a month of full concentration on the problem, I concluded that the reason this phenomenon was observed was for the same reason that an electron microscope can "resolve" or see more than an optical microscope looking at the same field—*the unit of measurement is shorter.* For example, the unit of measurement of an optical microscope is the wavelength of visible light, but that of the electron microscope is the electron. Many electrons go to make up the wavelength of visible light. I named the phenomenon "Social Resolving Power."

How does this relate to people?

When people get together in big groups to convey their thinking, they first ask, "How are we going to proceed?" Most of the time they fall into using Robert's Rules of Order as used in legislatures and in congress because it's probably the democratic process with which they are most familiar. But that process has its own problems. The more controversial an issue is, the more likely it will just barely pass by a small majority after several amendments. Then this resolution, this single unit of measurement, will often go out in a press release announcing in banner headlines, "The xxx conference of xxx organization says such and such." And the more controversial it is, the more likely the proclamation will be printed as "news" by the media. The process is awkward and clumsy, and at times downright misleading, because while it conveys the majority opinion, it usually doesn't convey the minority opinion or the degree of consensus. Was it passed by 51% or 95%? That makes a difference. The result is often confusion and hard feelings from such press releases.

In contradistinction, the Fast Forum® Technique (see Section Two) reports individuals' responses to many different statements or questions. Primarily it presents the number of respondents answering yes, no, or abstain to every question, but it provides other responses too. In addition, respondents can be categorized by demographic characteristics such as gender, age, or ethnic origin. These more detailed analyses of the same data result in greater Social Resolving Power and enable a "symbolic dialogue" to occur between and among the people in those categories as they study the feedback information.

We then presented the ideas generated by the dialogue groups to over 500 Bellevue church members from various churches in the form of a "survey." The church responses were either yes, no, or abstain. Immediately, a new problem arose. What does it mean, for example, if 228 people respond yes, 153 respond no, and 207 abstain? The numbers were so vast it was hard to comprehend the data. On the other hand if I talked about "standard deviation" and "variance," people would turn me off like a light. I reasoned that the most widely understood mathematical symbol was the percentage, %.

After much struggle, I emerged with a new statistical symbol that solved the problem. We called it the "Polarization-Consensus Rating". The Polarization Rating is a measure of the *weight* given to the item; it is the percentage of people participating who answered either yes *or* no out of the total number of respondents. People who abstained were not "polarized" thus they were not included. The Consensus Rating is the percentage positive of those who were polarized, that is, the percentage of yes votes out of the total polarized votes.

Graduate School of Business Administration

However, it was in the tabulation of these data that I learned how boring it is to count someone else's "X's" on a piece of paper. It put me to sleep. I realized the process would never work unless results could be tabulated accurately, swiftly, and economically. The only thing I knew that could do this was the computer, but I didn't know anything about the computer. So I went back to square one. I decided to become an inactive partner in my business,[4] and in the Fall of 1968 I enrolled in the Graduate School of Business Administration at the University of Washington, concentrating in the field of Administrative Theory and Organizational Behavior.

Two weeks into my first class on administrative theory it hit me that what I had perceived as a church problem—the inability to communicate—was not primarily a church problem; *it was a universal organizational problem.* It was bigger than a church problem. By then I was hooked—obsessed with the problem—and I still am to this day.

One day Professor Cecil Bell lectured saying, "In an organization a kind of—

Zeitgeist—will emerge— which is the prevailing beliefs of the people involved." Little did I know then that this innocent, academic statement would later set a new course in my life toward civilization building.

In an advanced course in Management Theory from Dr. Ted Barnowe, the class was given a term paper assignment to, "Just take anything in management theory and make it sound rational." I thought it was a fun assignment. I came out with eight theories about organization dynamics and governance. Most were a paragraph long; one was just one sentence long. Each was then explained in two or three pages as I told the professor why I thought each dynamic was true. The term project focused my thinking. When I was through, I read my own paper and concluded, "*If* these dynamics are true, to function properly a human organization or institution *must* have an effective feedback communication system." I called this the "Zeitgeist ('Spirit-of-the-Time') Principle." Most organizations and societies today have no such system.

Zeitgeist Communication has an exact definition. It is that field primarily concerned with communicating ideas, and opinions about those ideas, *across and upward* in organizations and society. This is in contradistinction to newspaper, radio, TV, magazines, books, lectures, speeches, sermons and the like—all one-to-many communication systems. Zeitgeist Communication can create a process of "symbolic dialogue" between representatives/leaders and constituents. This is in contrast to most other mass communication media that are all primarily one-way *downward* communication systems. I decided then that I wanted to devote much of my energy to improve administration and communication in organizations and institutions.

The Academic Computer Center, University of Washington

In 1970 I contracted with the University of Washington Academic Computer Center to write a computer program that would provide me with the communication technology I needed to tabulate data. As a theoretician, I knew where to go but didn't know how to get there. The computer programmer[5] knew how to get there but didn't know where to go. We designed and crafted the first Fast Forum® computer program; it has been updated six times since then. Now I had the technology to analyze large quantities of data, accurately, swiftly, and economically in a way that most people could comprehend.

The Forum Foundation

I established the Forum Foundation in 1970 as a non-profit Washington State corporation dedicated to educational research in administrative theory and communication methodology. My co-founders were Dr. Cecil Bell, my University of Washington advisor, the Rev. Dr. William Ellington, and a Board of Directors. Several years later I gifted the Fast Forum computer program to the Forum Foundation.

Now I had the organization I needed to continue and expand my research into administrative theory and Zeitgeist Communication.

Futures Research

From 1971 to 1990 I served as a volunteer on the staff of the Church Council of Greater Seattle that had 17 judicatories and over 300 local churches. I had the portfolio of "Futures Research" which we defined from the beginning *not as forecasting* but rather as the search for ways to *influence* the sociological and technological future. It was more a process of "*forthtelling.*" In this study of 1) people and 2) organizations we honed our research theories and technology. The Rev. William B. Cate, Ph.D., was president-director of the Church Council of Greater Seattle and the closest thing I, as a self-employed person, had to a "boss" during this period. It was here in the Seattle religious community that we continued our research. Progress was slow but we continued to learn.

My portfolio in Futures Research at the Church Council gave me the opportunity to develop my interest in computer technology for Many-To-Many Communication. I was able also to associate with people who were speculating about the future.

At a national United Methodist communication conference in the early 1980s, I met the Rev. Kenneth B. Bedell, Ph.D. Dr. Bedell had written the first book on the use of computers in The United Methodist Church. We became friends. The following year the Church Computer Users Network (CCUN) was established as a grassroots group from the church. He was elected the first president of CCUN, and I was elected Vice President. We established the first "Circuit Writer" national network for United Methodist Communications (UMCom).[6] This was a valuable and learning-filled association that continues to today.

I also participated in the founding of the Religious Futurists Network (RFN). This was formed as an outgrowth of the "First Global Conference on the Future," co-sponsored by the World Future Society in Toronto in 1980. I attended as the official representative of the Church Council of Greater Seattle. The Religious Futurists Network later became the World Network of Religious Futurists. I was one of the original members. Fortunately, this membership allowed me to get to know the Rev. Dr. Richard S. Kirby of London who was subsequently elected as the international chair of the organization.

Stuart C. Dodd, Professor Emeritus, University of Washington

In the early 1970s I met Dr. Stuart C. Dodd, Professor Emeritus of Sociology at the University of Washington. He was 14 years head of the Washington State Public Opinion Laboratory at the university. He was the leading authority on typical polling in the northwest states.[7] We met at meetings of the Evergreen Chapter of the World Future Society.[8] This chapter wrote a letter to Gov. Dan Evans and suggested a futures study for Washington State patterned after the Hawaii 2000 project. The result was the "Alternatives for Washington" project that is still considered a classic in citizen participation programming.

Stuart Dodd was a genius and yet as common as an old shoe. He treated everyone with consideration and respect; he was always just a warm, friendly human being. Dr. Dodd served on the board of the Forum Foundation from 1973 to his death in 1975 and did much to focus our research today. I recall the first time I met with him in his office and described our administrative theories and research. As I was leaving with my hand on the doorknob, he said, "Dick, don't ever let anyone tell you that what you are doing is not important." I replied, "Thank you. I won't." His support and encouragement have been everything to me. Someday, I vowed, I will find someone with the scholarship and mathematical skills to pick up the traces of his ideas and run with them. All of his files are in the University of Washington archives just waiting to be studied—they are a social science gold mine for the human race.[9]

Founding the Stuart C. Dodd Institute for Social Innovation

I learned long ago that if something needs to get done, one has to get organized to do it. So in 1997 I helped organize the Stuart C. Dodd Institute for Social Innovation. It is a 501 (c) (3) non-profit, tax-exempt organization to encourage scholarly, interdisciplinary research in the archives of Stuart C. Dodd. Here is the story behind the Institute.

An institute to continue the work of Dr. Dodd had been a dream of mine for many years. But Dodd's work on mathematical cosmology is not for the faint of heart; few people can understand it, much less move it forward. My acquaintance with the Rev. Dr. Richard S. Kirby through the World Network of Religious Futurists told me he might be the person for the job.

I visited Dr. Kirby in London in 1994. He had finished his Masters of Divinity studies at General Theological Seminary of the Episcopal Church, New York (USA) in 1985 and his Ph.D. in Theology studies at King's College, London from 1987-

1992. Richard Kirby is an outstanding scholar. I judged he had the capacity to pick up the traces left in the archives of Stuart Dodd.

Dr. Kirby was open to my proposal, and he wanted to return to the United States. I offered him a home and office in Seattle (owned by my business firm and dedicated to public service) and invited him to be the Stuart C. Dodd Chair in Social Innovation at the Forum Foundation. He accepted, came to Seattle in 1995, and is now an American citizen.[10] When the Stuart C. Dodd Institute for Social Innovation was formed in 1997, Richard Kirby became its first Executive Director.

He has been instrumental in furthering my understanding about civilization building. I invited him to become my co-author as we worked together on this book after Cecil Bell indicated he preferred to be a collaborator.

Russia

In July 1990 the Goodwill Games were held in Seattle. More than 1,000 Russians were hosted by Rotary International's Seattle District 5030. I am a member of the Bellevue, Washington Overlake Rotary Club.[11] I hosted one young man from Kyrgyzstan, Marat Akylbekov. On a hunch, I gave him a copy of our most recent unpublished manuscript on Administrative Theory when he returned home. In April 1991 I received a letter from Dr. Almas Chukin who was a professor of economics at Kyrgyze State University. He had read the frontispiece of the manuscript (the same as in this book). He wrote, "Everything in the left-hand column is the philosophy of the communists. We need to understand what is in the right-hand column. Please come to Kyrgyzstan and lecture."

Days after Gorbachev was restored to power following the 1991 Russian coup against him, I flew to Moscow and then on to Krygyzstan. My wife and I and personal interpreter, Leo Pavloff, were treated like royalty during our month-long trip because by that time Dr. Chukin was employed by the State Ministry of Economics. I met with many people; they were all friendly. They liked America and were extremely interested in democracy. Returning on the trans-Siberian railroad to Moscow, we passed within 30 miles of where my father had been born in Norka, Russia near where the railroad crosses the Volga River.[12]

At the end of 1991 I was invited to make a presentation at a conference on "Moral Education" at the University of Georgia (USA) where I met Dr. Tatyana Tsyrlina, professor of education at Kursk State Pedagogical University in Russia. She subsequently invited me over the years to two educational conferences in Moscow and one in Kursk. In 1996 she introduced me to Dr. Arthur K. Ellis, Director, International

Center for Curriculum Studies at Seattle Pacific University. We, Dr. Cecil Bell and I, had just finished writing our first book on *The Search For Enlightened Leadership, A New View of Administrative Theory* (1996). Dr. Ellis arranged for me to go to Moscow with him in May, 1997 where I led a day-long workshop for university administrators hosted by Dr. Boris Bim-Bad, president of Russia's Open University. I was asked to write a condensation of the book. This was published in *Magister*, an international psychological-educational journal of Russia, by Dr. Nikolai Nikandrov, who attended the conference and currently is the president of the Russian Academy of Education.

Professor Tatyana Tsyrlina has become an associate of the Forum Foundation and the Stuart C. Dodd Institute for Social Innovation and also an organizer of a Rotary club in Kursk with my help. We have provided her with the technology to tabulate data in Russia using the Fast Forum® technique. She has done some creative research in Russia including data tabulation from women's groups throughout Russia on the issue of "sex trafficking" (white slavery). This was done through video conferencing made possible by George Soros. We continue to learn from these experiences. See her report in Chapter 5.

Social Principles and The Book of Resolutions of The United Methodist Church

But one of the greatest influences in civilization building for me has come from two remarkable religious documents of The United Methodist Church: the *Social Principles* and *The Book of Resolutions*. The 2000 edition of *The Book of Resolutions* contains 338 public policy statements concerning The Natural World, The Nurturing Community, The Social Community, The Economic Community, The Political Community, and The World Community, all based on the Social Creed. It is a reference book that is revised every four years by the General Conference, the highest governing body of the church. When I read it, I am highly influenced by it because I know it is my corporate church trying to give me, the church, and our society a moral sense of direction in today's complex world. "John Wesley (founder of the church) believed that the living core of the Christian faith *was revealed in Scripture, illumined by tradition, vivified in personal experience, and confirmed by reason.*"[13] This is known as the Wesleyan Quadrilateral. Since our tradition is as Protestants, we are taught in our theology that our responsibility is directly to God through Christ and there is no other person or institution between us (including the church). That is very powerful theology because it means I am free, as every member of the church is free, to disagree with any part of the *Social Principles* or *Book of Resolutions and not be ostracized from the church.* Why? Because it is not the corporate church that has the primary responsibility to effect this world in the direction of our theology, i.e., civilization building. *It is each individual member* who has that responsibility. That all translates directly in the secular world to the equal responsibility of a citizen in the world.

The journey of a thousand miles begins with a single step. These are some of the milestones in my journey. We welcome you to step with us now toward civilization building by looking at what some sages of the past have said in *Pointers from History*.

Toward The Solution: Pointers from History

The following quotations have inspired our search for greater understanding in the areas of administrative theory and governance, Many-To-Many Communication, and civilization building. We believe they contain great truth. They gave us insight into the problems to be confronted as we try to advance the process of civilization building. We hope you will find them valuable as well.

> Man is a being in search of meaning.
>
> > Plato

> The minds of men are mirrors to one another…. Philosophy is common sense, methodized, and collected…. The end of all moral speculations is to teach us our duty.
>
> > David Hume,
> > *18th Century Scottish philosopher*

> When in the course of human events, it becomes necessary to dissolve the political bands which have connected them with another, and to assume, among the Powers of the earth, the separate and equal station to which the Laws of Nature and Nature's God entitle them, a decent respect to the opinions of mankind requires that they should declare the causes which impel them to the separation.
>
> > Thomas Jefferson,
> > *The Declaration of Independence,*
> > *July 4, 1776*

The art of human collaboration seems to have disappeared during
two centuries of quite remarkable material progress. The various
nations seem to have lost all capacity for international cooperation in
the necessary tasks of civilization. The internal condition of the
nation is not greatly better; it seems that only a threat from without,
an unmistakable emergency, can momentarily quiet the struggle of
rival groups ... . How can humanity's capacity of spontaneous cooperation be restored? It is in this area that leadership is most required, a leadership that has nothing to do with political 'isms' or
eloquent speeches. What is wanted is knowledge, a type of knowledge that has escaped us in two hundred years of prosperous development. How to substitute human responsibility for futile strife and
hatreds.

> Elton Mayo,
> Harvard Professor sometimes called the "father of
> the human relations movement," in the preface of
> the classic *Management and the Worker* by
> Roethlisberger and Dickson published in 1939.

The capacity to exercise a relatively high degree of imagination, ingenuity, and creativity in the solution of organizational problems is
widely, not narrowly, distributed in the population [Theory Y].

> Douglas McGregor,
> *The Human Side of Enterprise*
> (McGraw-Hill Book Co, New York, 1960), page 48.

It is not essential that everyone participate ... . The essence ... is
that participation should be an available option.

> John W. Gardner,
> Godkin Lectures, Harvard University, reported in
> *Christian Science Monitor*, April 16, 1969.

The ultimate disease of our time is valuelessness ... rootlessness, emptiness, helplessness, the lack of something to believe in and to be devoted to.

> Abraham H. Maslow,
> *Religions, Values, and Experiences* (New York: The Viking Press, Inc., 1970), p. 82.

Science is the world of what is. Ethics is the world of what ought to be. ... [There are those who are] in love with the aristocracy of the intellect. And that is a belief that can only destroy the civilization that we know. If we are anything, we must be a democracy of the intellect. We must not perish by the distance between people and government, between people and power.

> Dr. Jacob Bronowski,
> *The Ascent of Man* (1973), award-winning book (page 435) and TV series.

As human systems and organizations grow ever larger, more complex, and more impersonal—in our schools, in our communities, in our churches, in our governments, and in our industries and commerce—the individual shrinks toward facelessness, hopelessness, powerlessness, and frustration.

> Dr. Stuart C. Dodd,
> Professor Emeritus of Sociology, University of Washington,"Citizen Counselor Proposal," with Richard J. Spady, *The Seattle Times*, November 10, 1974.

I would urge all of us as futurists ... to devote some of our energies to finding new ways to destandardize, deconcentrate, descale, delimit, and democratize planning.

> Alvin Toffler,
> Closing address, 2nd General Assembly, World Future Society, Washington, DC, June 1975.

No society can function as a society unless it gives the individual member *social status* and *function*, and unless the decisive social power is *legitimate* power. Status, function, legitimacy: [are] the essentials of the new order. (Emphasis added by Tarrant)

> Peter Drucker,
> *Drucker: The Man Who Invented The Corporate Society* by John J. Tarrant (Warner Books, 1976), page 25.

The need [for leadership] was never so great. A chronic crisis of governance—that is, the pervasive incapacity of governments and other social institutions to cope with the expectations of their constituents—is now an overwhelming fact worldwide.

> Harlan Cleveland,
> "Learning the Art of Leadership" reprinted from *Twin Cities* magazine, August, 1980.

We believe that the reduction of the citizen to an object of protagonists, private and public, is one of the greatest dangers to democracy. A prevalent notion is that the great mass of the people cannot understand and cannot form an independent judgment upon any matter; they cannot be educated, in the sense of developing their intellectual powers, but they can be bamboozled. The reiteration of slogans, the distortion of the news, the great storm of propaganda that beats upon the citizen twenty-four hours a day all his life long may mean either that democracy must fall a prey to the loudest and most persistent protagonists or that the people must save themselves by strengthening their minds so that they can appraise the issues themselves. There can be little argument about the proposition that the task of the future is the creation of a community. Community seems to depend on communication. This requirement is not met by improvements in transportation or in mail, telephone, telegraph, or radio services. These technological advances are frightening, rather than reassuring, and disruptive, rather than unifying, in such a world as we have today. The only civilization in which a free man would be willing to live is one that conceives of history as one long conversation

leading to clarification and understanding. Such a civilization pre-
supposes communication; it does not require agreement.

Robert Maynard Hutchins,
"The Great Conversation," 1984, Editor-in-Chief,
*Great Books of the Western World, Encyclopedia
Britannica,* vol 1, excerpts page 13 through 58.

Managers do things right. Leaders do the right thing.

Warren Bennis and Burt Nanus,
LEADERS, Harper & Row, New York, 1985.

Our children long for realistic maps of a future they can be proud of.
Where are the cartographers of human purpose?

Dr. Carl Sagan,
Prominent astronomer and scientist, "People
Digest,*" Dayton Daily News and Journal Herald,*
page 29, November 21, 1987.

The present tumult in our world is the natural and understandable
result of a vigorous intelligence moving out of the savagery of our
life form's childhood. Instead of humanity's demise, our era seems to
be filled with evidence that we were meant to survive and evolve
much further.

Gene Roddenberry,
Creator of *Star Trek,* "A Letter to the Next Generation," *TIME,* April 18, page 1, 1988.

But the more careful rationales for citizenship seem to agree in their
emphasis on two ideals: democratic citizens draw conclusions about
public affairs through critical, rational deliberation, and they participate in community life to sustain or enhance realization of democratic ideals.

Fred M. Newman,
University of Wisconsin-Madison, "Rational
Deliberation and Social Participation? Why
Bother?" Presented to the annual meeting of the

College and University Faculty Assembly of the
National Council for the Social Studies, Phoenix,
Arizona, November 18, 1994.

We are living through the birth pangs of a new civilization whose institutions are not yet in place …. We need to create a whole new
structure of government capable of making intelligent, democratic
decisions necessary for our survival in a Third Wave, 21st Century
America …. The time has come for us to imagine completely novel
alternatives through the widest consultation and peaceful public participation … to reconstitute America.

Alvin Toffler,
Creating a New Civilization (Turner Publishing,
Inc., Atlanta, 1995), pgs. 82 and 90.

Through public policies, government is involved with every technology in a variety of roles. As a result, the president of the United States
becomes the nation's systems manager…. Since every technological
choice poses ethical questions, outcomes are shaped more by the
moral vision of political leaders and the electorate than by the technical content …. To achieve the goals of a humane, democratic society,
large numbers of people need to make thoughtful, realistic choices
…. We need to know who we are, where we are, and then decide on
where we want to go …. Finally, we need to admit that facing the future is as much ideological as it is technological. The bedrock values
that define the nation's behavior depend on people taking responsibility. We are not just consumers of technology. In a high-tech world,
we are producers, managers, investors, and sometime innocent by-
standers and victims. We are voters. Unknowingly perhaps, we are all
stewards of our natural inheritance and responsible for what we leave
our progeny. We are citizens of the world.

Edward Wenk, Jr.,
Professor Emeritus of Engineering, University of
Washington, *Making Waves* (University of Illinois
Press, Urbana and Chicago; 1995), pg. 198, 230,
237, 240.

Americans are thus beneficiaries of a miraculous confluence, the intertwining of democracy and technology, the "Double Helix ...." If information for governance is lacking, the nation may have the necessary propulsion but an inadequate capacity to steer .... For democracy to survive, the social capacity for responsive and accountable management of technology requires a new learning curve built not on business administration nor on technical virtuosity, but on human qualities of moral vision .... Last, preserving liberty requires intense public participation. Democracy is everyone's business .... As a moral compass, two institutions not previously mentioned seemed fit for that gigantic task, the universities and religious institutions.

> Edward Wenk, Jr.
> *The Double Helix* (Ablex Publishing Corp., 1999),
> pages 1-12.

Through historical circumstance, we are all heirs to the awesome opportunity and critical responsibility to become authors, guides, and actors in the future of human evolution.

> August T. Jaccaci and Susan B. Gault,
> *CEO, Chief Evolutionary Officer* (Butterworth-
> Heinemann Publications, 1999), page 5.

Perhaps the most important factor in all these recent advances [in biotechnology], particularly as they continue to unfold, is the responsibility we have concerning education. It is the public, through the power of the vote, that ultimately decides what programs, scientific or other, merit funding. Without education, a rift will emerge between the voters and the scientific community. The latter may hold in their hands the answers to all of the great genetic questions, but the voters will hold the cards. Voters will not pay for something that they do not understand.[14]

> Leroy Hood,
> Founding chair, and William H. Gates III Scholar,
> Dept. of Molecular Biology, University of Washington, Foundation for the Future Seminar, Bellevue WA, 1999.

Our current notions of business and trade are a fertile garden for re-thinking the human future ....

Because the ever-increasing power of global business is arguably the greatest planetary force of combined human creativity with the greatest potential for successfully weaving the web of peaceful human unification, what synthesizing focus for business might we imagine? ...To pull all this thinking together into a final consideration for CEOs [Chief Evolutionary Officers], I suggest that we focus our imaginations on a business dedicated to creation of the largest working tool and guiding story that the planetary culture can have and now sorely needs: a new cosmology .... Imagine that every living human, all of us together, could find engaging mutual creative endeavor. Imagine that we could tell each is a gift of grace from and to the whole glorious and eternal purpose of evolution, and of the universe. This cosmological story has been within us all along waiting to emerge ....

Love is the unitive power and presence common to all religious and spiritual beliefs that gives them their deepest potential to heal, nurture, and to glorify with joy the human soul and spirit.

> August T. Jaccaci and Susan B. Gault,
> *CEO Chief Evolutionary Officer,* page 179.

But as world events reflect, we remain far from mastering the art of human relations. We have invented no technology that will guide us to the destinations that matter most.

> Madeleine Albright,
> Former Secretary of State, at the commencement
> address of the University of California, Berkeley,
> 2000. Reported in *USA Today,* June 2, 2000,
> page 19A.

Policy development for sustainable development may get its strongest push from community action. Over time, this can build the constituency needed to tackle sustainability issues on the scale of nations and the international community.

The grassroots approach to sustainable development also entails a powerful partnership with science. Because the issues at hand tend to have large technical components, scientists are called upon to diagnose problems and define the range of policy options. Stakeholders [i.e., citizens] choose among problems and make policy recommendations. Solutions are based on intensive dialogue between experts and stakeholders. Civic science joins expert knowledge to sustainable development projects and policies (Schmandt 1998). Holistic scientific inquiry serving community goals can pave the road to sustainable development.

> Jurgen Schmandt,
> "From Idea to Action: The Role of Policy," *Sustainable Development, The Challenge of Transition* (Cambridge University Press, 2000, UK), page 219.

Man is scientifically a giant, ethically a pygmy ....
Religion without science is lame; Science without religion is blind.

> Attributed to Albert Einstein

1

. . . .

General
Administrative
Theories

In this section we present the 10 administrative theories from our research findings as briefly and concisely as possible. Each is followed by an expanded explanation. These theories also form a paradigm. Joel A. Barker states:

> *Paradigms are sets of rules and regulations that do two things. First they establish boundaries .... Second, these rules and regulations then go on to tell you how to be successful by solving problems within these boundaries .... Paradigms filter incoming experience. We are viewing the world through our paradigms all the time. We constantly select from the world that data that best fits our rules and regulations and try to ignore the rest. As a result, what may be perfectly obvious to a person with one paradigm, may be totally imperceptible to someone with a different paradigm. I call this phenomenon, the Paradigm Effect .... Sometimes your paradigm can become the paradigm—the only way to do something. And when you are confronted by an alternative idea, you reject it out of hand. Now that can lead to a nasty disorder. I call that disorder Paradigm Paralysis. Paradigm paralysis is a disease of certainty.* "[15]

We have been formulating and measuring these theories since 1970 and first published articles on them in 1980, 1984, and 1986, as well as a prepublication manuscript titled *Administrative Theory* in 1986.[16]

From our experiences and scholarship these new general theories seem true. We hope that you, the reader and final judge, will agree and use these theories to help form your own paradigm of the basic principles of administration and governance that apply in an increasingly complex, dangerous, but hopeful world. In the words of the cartoon character Pogo, "We have met the enemy, and he is us." Hopefully, these theories will provide a better grasp of how to administer "us" and avoid the effects of "Paradigm Paralysis" in the future. We invite you to become "Paradigm Pioneers" with Barker and with us in a search together for more effective administration in all organizations and in the processes of governance everywhere in the world.

The 10 natural dynamics of governance and administration are listed below. These dynamics constitute our view of administrative theory.

1. The Basic Attitude—An implied administrative imperative.
2. The Theory of Learning—The source of individual creativity.
3. The Theory of Leadership—The source of organizational creativity.
4. The Theory of Authority—The source of organizational power.
5. The Theory of Politics—The source of collaboration and action.
6. The Self-Fulfilling Prophecy—The generator of theories and the determinant of individual and organizational capacities.
7. The Administrative Process—A definition.
8. The Helping Professions—A definition.
9. The Zeitgeist Principle—Discovering the Supreme Governor.
10. The Natural Factors—A new paradigm shift toward civilization building.

The Basic Attitude in Civilization Building

One must always treat all persons with dignity, consideration and respect. We can reject or not agree with anything said, but we must always respect another person's right to say it. The process is LISTEN to the other person, WEIGH what is said, and then do one of three things with the idea or information received: ACCEPT it, REJECT it, or MODIFY it, i.e., accept that which fits, and ignore the rest—*but always with consideration and respect for the other person, and his or her views—in order to protect best one's own freedom to speak.*

The Basic Attitude is an administrative imperative; it is a given. If an individual does not possess this basic attitude in today's world culture, it is unlikely that he or she will truly be successful as a "governor."

A governor is anyone who governs someone else: parents govern children, teachers govern students, principals govern teachers and students, managers, supervisors, bosses, leaders, police officers, military officers, administrators, public officials, heads of state and the like are all "governors." We must always have respect for others, *and be willing to listen to them rather than simply trying to control them.* That leads to all sorts of difficulties.

We must learn how to reject the ideas of another person without in any way rejecting or diminishing the person himself or herself. This is the modern-day idea, "I'm OK, you're OK"; it is the biblical idea, "Love thy neighbor as thyself" which is in both Jewish and Christian scriptures.[17] It is the same idea, just millennia apart. This basic attitudinal relationship is required among all of us who wish to exercise the individual, organizational, and societal responsibilities that transcend our vocational "work-a-day-world," and reach into our avocation and "life work" of civilization building.

As human beings, we must learn to collaborate in order to reach our organizational and societal objectives—which is civilization building! The principal authority for the Theory of the Basic Attitude comes from the mandate in both the old and new testaments, "Love thy neighbor as thyself."

Our culture is rooted in Judeo-Christian religious concepts, and a basic tenet of the Christian religion is, "Everyone is unique and is just as important before God, *but no more* than anyone else." This principle also underscores the idea of "equality of citizenship" found in the Declaration of Independence and reflected in the now famous phrase, *"We hold these truths to be self-evident, that all men are created equal."*

As a nation of people that takes seriously its democratic and religious traditions, it is imperative to adopt this "basic attitude" of universal respect based upon equality in all our relationships with each other. This helps people search together, as citizens, for ways to implement national and international objectives as well as the more limited objectives in organizations and institutions that vitalize our society.

One of the characteristics of a great people is to be able to handle diversity and differences of opinion in a constructive manner. This was once exemplified by the preaching of the Rev. Jesse Jackson in the pulpit of the Rev. Jerry Falwell in September 1985 in efforts to find common ground to end South Africa's policy of apartheid (racial separation). "We do not want to call and talk about each other, but talk with each other and agree to agree, or agree to disagree, and to be civil and in search of common ground," Jackson told parishioners on a Sunday at Falwell's Thomas Road Baptist Church. In response Falwell stated, "We may not agree on many of the political and social issues, but we agree on this," referring to apartheid. "We have the right to agree and disagree and to do it charitably and lovingly," said Falwell. This is the attitude the human race everywhere must foster in the search together to build civilization.

Years ago, the late Gene Roddenberry, creator of Star Trek, alluded to his deep belief in the "basic attitude." He stated:

> "One obstacle to adulthood needs to be solved immediately: We must learn not just to accept differences between ourselves and our ideas, but to enthusiastically welcome and enjoy them. Diversity contains as many treasures as those waiting for us on other worlds. We will find it impossible to fear diversity and to enter the future at the same time."[18]

Bigotry

Society is now well aware of racism and sexism. But most of us are little aware of some of the other faces of "social bigotry." These are but a few examples:

- *"You can't participate because you're not white"* (racism).
- *"You can't participate because you're not male"* (sexism).
- *"You're too old or too young"* (ageism).
- *"You lack expertise and credentials"* (elitism).
- *"You're not ordained"* (religious elitism).
- *"You can't participate because you're from another class"* (classism).
- *"You can't participate because you haven't been elected or duly appointed"* (roleism).

Of all the forms of social bigotry, one of the least recognized and most insidious is "roleism." It is insidious because hardly anyone thinks of it as social bigotry. But consider:

Roleism denies the political importance of the ordinary individual and interested citizen. It obscures the political right of every citizen to provide his or her thinking and leadership. Unfortunately, roleism is pervasive among public officials and legislators who have become protective of their "turf and perks." Roleism is a major barrier to social progress. It prevents people from contributing their best thinking to organizations and society, and to doing their part as citizens in civilization building.

There are many barriers to human participation. Together, they serve to violate the trust people must have in order to vitalize their political, cultural, business organizations, institutions, and civilization of which they are a part.

The Theory of Learning

When an individual is exposed to a problem or is asked a question, the individual is thrust into the dynamics of the Socratic Method, one of history's proven learning techniques. It has four steps: *awareness, frustration, insight, and verification.* In the process an individual not only learns something new but literally becomes someone new psychologically speaking. This ability to learn through the dynamics of the Socratic Method is a universal human ability.

Creativity is a process that brings a new idea into an individual's mind. It is the ability to learn, and it is a universal human capability.

Socrates didn't tell his students the answers to problems. He posed questions instead and sent them to ferret out the answers themselves. In the process, they became aware of the problem (i.e., Socrates' question) and experienced frustration (apparently a necessary prerequisite of success), achieved insight—and learned—and became new persons psychologically speaking. If true, and we believe it is, *the implication is that individual intelligence can be developed merely by asking people questions.*

Consider this example:

You warn a friend about his liquor consumption. *"You're drinking too much,"* you say. *"You could lose your health, and you may lose your job, your family, and your self-esteem."*

Your friend says, *"I'm OK. I know what I am doing."*

One day your friend wakes up in the gutter, and thinks to himself, *"My God, how did I get here"*? Your friend has just taken the first step to solving the problem; it began with awareness of the problem.

"Awareness" goes a long way toward solving problems in our lives, our organizations, our society, and it goes to the heart of civilization building. Awareness does not come easily, though, because thinking is hard. You must think about the problem, ponder about the problem, and worry about the problem. Without this kind of focus on the problem, you are unlikely to generate enough "psychic voltage" to give light to it. It is this struggling and frustration that sets the stage for the most important step—insight, which wells up from within you.

The first three steps (awareness, frustration, and insight) are personal. They form a relationship between individuals and their problems in the world. No one else is involved. However, the fourth step, *verification*, is a group effort. Here morality and values and "right" or "wrong" answers of the individual are best tested anonymously against the responses of others who are participating in solving the problem. Secondary insights are then gained; these insights enable the individual to continue to learn. All of this is done without putting anyone in a "win-lose" situation—that makes it an ideal learning climate.

What are the implications of this dynamic? It means we must enable people (including young people) to make lots of real decisions about lots of real problems in life; in the process of doing that, they will *learn* through the dynamics of the Socratic

Method. When an individual learns "X" amount, the organization and society of which he or she is a part learns exactly the same amount, and all move toward being better able to solve problems in the future. The principal authority for the Theory of Learning is Socrates.

We are impressed with the writings of Rollo May and with the cover explaining his book *The Meaning of Anxiety.*

Dr. May challenges the current belief that "mental health is living without anxiety," and adds that living without anxiety in our world of the atom bomb reveals a radical misperception of reality. He then asserts the theory that anxiety is essential to the human condition, that confrontation with anxiety can relieve us from boredom, sharpen our sensitivity, and create the tension that is necessary to preserve human existence.

Throughout this seminal work there runs the motif of anxiety in relation to intelligence, creativity, and originality, themes that have been barely touched in contemporary research. Dr. May points out that anxiety is a phenomenon of increased intelligence—anxiety is the shadow of intellect.

Finally, "*Not only can anxiety paralyze, but it can be the impetus for our most positive change. Anxiety is the best teacher, for it is only by confronting and coping with anxiety that self-realization occurs.*"[19]

We agree that anxiety may be a precursor to creativity and a necessary step leading to "awareness" in the Socratic Method.

Insight through the Socratic method is a process that comes to individuals of all ages everywhere as they struggle with their own problems and dream their own dreams. One of the most charming stories we have heard in this regard was in an address given by a highly regarded local journalist, Brent Northup, in Bellevue, Washington. At the graduation ceremony of a small elementary school, Northup opened by telling the children that summertime was dream month. He challenged them to write stories, make up poems, and draw pictures and just see what comes out. He asked the children if they knew where to find their dream. He held up a pen and told them that buried within the ink they could find their dream. He then said that after you find your dream, you should plant it, put an idea on top of it, and surround it with warm feelings. "Don't ignore your dream," he advised, "or it will disappear, and then when you are 30 or 40 years old you will still be looking for it." He was then asked, "How do you know when you find your dream?" The answer was simple and true. "Your eyes light up and you smile."

If we accept that all original thinking and all new ideas come from the mind of some individual at some time and some place, then the importance of a "creative climate" in organizations and institutions everywhere that permits individuals to participate with their thinking is better appreciated. The role of administrators (governors) should be understood not as directors or authoritarian figures, but as members of the "helping professions" (similar to teaching, counseling, and the ministry) in which governors help their charges develop their own creative thinking abilities through the Socratic Method.

Our Social Failure

Given the dynamics of the Theory of Learning, one can understand the magnitude of our failure as a nation and society to provide all people, young and old, with regular opportunities to participate with their opinions—and thus learn!

Enabling citizens to contribute their own thinking and opinions in the public agenda is diminished in the presence of paternalism and the realities of the "self-fulfilling prophecy." Governors (parents, teachers, counselors, ministers, public officials, managers, leaders and others) must abandon their often "wet blanket" approach and be more flexible. They must let their charges face real problems in life themselves, provide a creative climate in which to do it, and be willing to enable their charges to make choices in order to express their own thinking and leadership and grow in their own individual capacities. As their charges learn to fly with their own wings, they will not only learn something new, they will become someone new—*new beings, happier, with improved individual and community mental health, spiritually and politically renewed!* The process will build "social capital."[20]

The Theory of Leadership

Leadership—like creativity, the ability to learn—is a universal human attribute. Leadership is a function and not a quality reserved for the titled head of an organization. To develop leadership properly, all decisions in an organization or institution should be made at the lowest level possible, consistent with two basic premises. First, adequate information is available with which to make a valid decision. Second, adequate resources are available to implement the decision reached. If either adequate information or resources is not available, the decision should be moved up one level higher in the organization or institution until both valid information and adequate resources to implement the decision are available.

The Theory of Leadership is the source of organizational creativity, the process that brings new ideas into an organization or institution's "mind."

Adopting a conscious policy to decentralize decision-making in organizations and institutions in which higher levels assign problems to lower levels produces enormous amounts of leadership. As individuals are assigned problems, they are thrust into the dynamics of the Socratic method and the creative-thinking process; they cannot avoid it. They become aware of the problem, experience frustration in solving it, achieve insight, and learn. The organization and society of which the individual is a part then move toward better problem resolution in the future. And all people involved become engaged in an overall process of civilization building.

Conversely, the leadership style that insists upon centralized decision-making invites abuses. A frequent example is exhaustion of the leader. It can be argued that the "one man band" organization is the weakest. The strongest organization is one in which anyone, from top to bottom, could leave and the work would continue with little or no interruption. The best governors and administrators seldom "tell" subordinates what to do, but rather provide a creative climate and processes in which people tell themselves what to do to most effectively accomplish their organizational tasks and objectives. Leadership by self-direction and self-motivation to the maximum extent possible for all people in organizations, institutions, and society is the goal. This is democracy in action!

Again, to develop leadership properly, all decisions in an organization or institution should be made at the lowest level possible, consistent with two basic premises: First, there must be adequate information with which to make valid decisions. Second, there must be adequate resources to implement the decision reached. If either is unavailable, the decision should be moved one level up, where both are available to make effective decision-making possible.

But the question arises, "Can a person at the bottom be a leader? By definition there is no one to lead." Yes there is. Even the individual at the bottom level of a bureaucracy or a society has to "lead" himself or herself through the labyrinth of addressing organizational and societal problems and then to use his or her own time and resources to solve those problems. This conforms with everyday experience. One need only look around. How many people can be observed who in their workplace are perhaps at the bottom of the organizational hierarchy yet in their private lives are pillars of leadership in churches, communities, volunteer organizations and the like? What do all human beings on earth do from the time they get up in the morning until the time they go to bed at night? They try to bring some kind of order out of the chaos that is often going on around them in their lives. That is leadership—a positive force— and a universal human attribute.

If we want people to collaborate, and to participate vitally, we must recognize that the quality of "leadership" in our theory is not something reserved exclusively for the titular heads of organizations. It is, in reality, a quality that infuses all people from the highest to the lowest "rank" in every organization.

We must nurture those creative techniques that both encourage and permit people at all levels to contribute their most important human contribution—their ability to think and to lead. After all, without them the organization would not exist. It is important, in the utilization of this universal human quality of leadership in organizations, that there be a way to pose real problems in life at the lowest levels possible.

People must be brought into planning processes at all levels through new theories and communication techniques that enable them to participate with their opinions within their time and energy levels. As Douglas McGregor wrote in *The Human Side of Enterprise:* "The capacity to exercise a relatively high degree of imagination, ingenuity, and creativity in the solution of organizational problems is widely, not narrowly, distributed in the population."

What is the source of wisdom? Because there is so much knowledge in the world today, it is a truism to say that most people, including ourselves, are just plain ignorant about most things, and anybody who is considered to be an "expert" in anything is indeed fortunate. So within a culture where "becoming an expert" is a process of knowing more and more about less and less, the implications are that the answers people seek in the increasingly interdependent, complex future are not likely to be found in any one person or small group of people, but are more likely to be found somewhere among all of us in the totality of our knowledge and experiences. Does that mean "expertise" is not needed? Not at all. There is a need for more, not less, but in addition, there is a need to differentiate between "knowledge" and "wisdom." William Cowper, an 18th century English poet, captured one subtlety of this difference in his insightful work: *"Knowledge is proud that it knows so much. Wisdom is humble that it knows not more."*

Thus, it is necessary to learn how knowledge can be distilled to produce the wisdom needed for making organizational and societal policy decisions. This will become a whole new organizational and cultural skill requiring its own expertise after the administrative theory has been worked through. And who is the main repository of this wisdom? The people are—people in organizations and people in society and people in the world. *Most of the knowledge in the world is in books in libraries and in computer data banks, but most of the wisdom in the world is in the minds of people walking the earth. We need to learn how to reach it.*

We like the insights of Erik H. Erikson, preeminently recognized psychologist, and his wife Joan: "*What is real wisdom? It comes from life experience, well digested. It's not what comes from reading great books. When it comes to understanding life, experiential learning is the only worthwhile kind; everything else is hearsay.*[21]

Along a similar theme which points to the wisdom of the people, George Gallup wrote: "*In conducting thousands of surveys on almost every conceivable issue for nearly half a century, I have learned three significant things about our fellow citizens. One is that the judgment of the American people is extraordinarily sound. Another is that the public is nearly always ahead of its leaders. The third is that the electorate has become better educated and more sophisticated politically than ever before.*[22]

Our more limited research experience verifies Mr. Gallup's conclusions. When people are trusted and enabled to be responsible in their organizations and society by their leaders, they use good judgment, they are rational, they are wise.

Conclusion

Centralization of decision-making (i.e., authoritarianism and totalitarianism) actually suppresses the "leadership" function in an organization or institution.

Many believe that authoritarianism provides the strongest "leadership," but that is not the case. That is, centralization strategies to "control" or "take charge" and the like tend to suppress "leadership" in general. This is why decentralization, freedom, and participative democratic processes are the wave of the future for the human race in public and private organizations, institutions, and governments. Such processes simply provide *at all levels* a more effective "leadership" function, which is a universal human capability, and are thus more effective and efficient.

Furthermore, the decentralization process takes nothing away from the administrator or official at the top. In fact it strengthens his or her role since "authority" begins to flow upward naturally and makes the overall role of governing easier and more effective.

There are extremely important and direct links between administrative theory and economics and politics. "Administration" cuts across and transcends economics and politics. Freedom is required for effective leadership by stakeholders in a democratic context in solving vast, complex, organizational, institutional, and societal problems. Also, the fundamental issue is not "capitalism versus communism in nationalism"; the issue is "freedom versus totalitarianism in civilization building."

What does this all imply for the future of military and other dictatorships in third world countries and other highly centralized and authoritarian nations? It is extremely important for them that they begin to adapt themselves to becoming more free and open societies. Fortunately, this is what all people in all nations in the world will tend to do naturally. Dictators and authoritarian leaders cannot prevail. Time itself will see them fall due to the liberating energies of these natural, worldwide, cultural trends toward freedom. Therefore, it is better for them to embrace the trends and help shape their countries constructively by using their power to make the transition to democracy peacefully.

The Theory of Authority

"Those who govern derive their power from the consent of the governed."[23] "Authority lies always with him to whom it applies…. Authority is another name for the willingness and capacity of individuals to submit to the necessities of cooperative systems."[24] "…It is the governed who determine the governing of men."[25]

The Theory of Authority clarifies the source of power in all organizations.

This theory is probably the most widely misunderstood of all the theories presented in this book. Through the years most people have believed that "authority lies in the office," i.e., in the president, in the governor, in the public official, in the general or admiral, in the policeman, in the owner or administrator, in the manager, in the supervisor, in the boss and the like. This view prevailed among scholars for years.

Then as insights came to those contemplating the problem this view changed. The nature of authority was realized to be more complex than originally perceived. The view expanded to recognize that the authority of leaders resides in their "task," or again later, in their "knowledge," in their "charisma," i.e., their personal ability to instill confidence in their constituents, or in the "situational ethic" where the situation places special requirements on the leader, e.g., during a war. While all of the above are not without truth, the evidence of our studies, experiences, and research suggests that a more definitive and accurate description of the seat of "authority" and power in all organizations, public and private (and applying to all persons from parents to heads of state) is: "those who govern derive their power and authority from the consent of the governed." This basic principle is stated in the Declaration of Independence.

We hold these truths to be self-evident, that all men are created equal; that they are endowed by their Creator with certain unalienable rights; that among these are life, liberty, and the pursuit of happiness. That, to secure these rights, governments are instituted among men, deriving their just powers from the consent of the governed. [26]

Chester Barnard, a transitional writer in the field, has best analyzed "authority." Mr. Barnard was not a professional scholar but a student and practitioner of administrative theory and organizational behavior. He had 18 years' experience as Chief Operating Officer of the New Jersey Bell Telephone Company and 20 years as President of the Pennsylvania Bell Company. He was able to blend theory with practice and write about it. This is a characteristic uncommon among authors of today but is characteristic of our own Forum Foundation research. Barnard is generally recognized among telephone company historians for significant differences in his administrative style from other regional telephone company executives. He came from the same mold as Theodore Vail, the earlier organizing genius of AT&T itself.

Barnard's statement is most accurate: *Authority lies always with him to whom it applies. Authority is just another way of talking about the willingness of people to submit to collaborative systems.*[27]

Barnard's propositions were verified by the research of Alexander Leighton, psychologist, anthropologist, and naval reservist who studied Japanese-American citizens interned during World War II. The significance of Leighton's work seems to have been missed by most scholars. Leighton concluded in his book, *The Governing of Men:* "It is the governed who determine the governing of men." [28]

Barnard's view that, "Authority always lies with him to whom it applies," and Leighton's conclusion that, "It is the governed who determine the governing of men," and Jefferson's declaration that, "governments are instituted among men, deriving their just powers from the consent of the governed," have important meaning to all "governors."

It means if children are not willing to be "parented," then parents cannot "parent" them; if students are not willing to be taught by a teacher, then the teacher cannot teach; if students (or teachers) are not willing to be "principaled" by a principal, then the principal cannot "principal" them; if employees are not willing to be managed by an employer, then the employer cannot manage them; if bureaucrats are not willing to be administered by an administrator, then the administrator cannot administer them; if soldiers and sailors are not willing to be commanded, then a commander cannot command; and if citizens of a nation are not willing to be led by a government, then a government cannot lead them (be they kings, tyrants, or dictators and the like).

If the people of the United States were not willing to be governed by the President and the Congress, then the President and the Congress could not govern them, Constitution or no Constitution, army or no army! All of the power of the President and the Congress is derived, like that of all leaders everywhere, merely by the willingness of the people in their constituency to be governed by them. This principle applies to all governors—be they parents of children to the heads of state everywhere.

A case in point was the transfer of power in the Philippines from President Ferdinand Marcos to Corazon Aquino in February, 1986. While Marcos tried to maintain his "legal" power as constitutional president, such power could not prevail against the unwillingness of the people to be governed. Other examples come from the popular uprisings in Czechoslovakia and other eastern European nations as they moved from the centralism of communism toward democracy.

While it may appear upon cursory analysis that individuals can be "coerced" or "forced" to comply with their governors (as in ruthless dictatorships), it is the individuals themselves who hold the final key and ultimate power to continue or terminate the governing relationship by simply withholding their consent. Children leave home or school, employees quit their jobs, and martyrs die to oppose perceived injustice or tyranny. As history shows, the ruthless dictator never knows when the time will come that the people will exercise their own ultimate power and rebel. The mood of the world is changing rapidly today and people increasingly are becoming more aware of their human rights—they will prevail. Zdenek Janicek, a brewery worker in Czechoslovakia, after reciting part of the Declaration of Independence to his co-workers said, "Americans understood these rights more than 200 years ago. We are only now learning to believe that we are entitled to the same rights."[29]

There are other important related concepts. For example, owners of businesses contribute importantly to success in a free enterprise system by their willingness to invest in capital. Their main contribution to resources is only one part of the total resources required, however—material goods. The most important resource of every organization and institution is its people! Ultimate power and authority rest with people. It is desirable that people be provided opportunities to give their continual consent to be governed in the organizations and institutions in which they exist. This applies whether they are children, students, employees, consumers, or citizens. It would seem that all governors would welcome such information for it would allow them to self-correct when needed and thus, with improved collaboration from their charges, *expand* their *authority* to govern.

In the role of consumer, for example, people hold a special "economic sovereignty" over business organizations or nations that supply them with goods and services. With a wave of their magic wand, by the simple casting of their dollar "votes" in free markets, they can withhold their "consent" and thus alter the course of "future economic history" for each business or nation. For example, look at the world's reaction to South Africa's policy on apartheid.

Similarly, military officers are taught the foundations of their legal authority and legal responsibility, stemming from the Constitution, through the President, Secretary of Defense, regulations, and orders and through the chain of command as "officials of the United States." But they are also taught the fundamentals of personal moral responsibility and moral authority, which in certain circumstances might transcend their legal responsibilities and legal authority. On occasion they might have to judge on the spot whether to obey or refuse to obey an "illegal" command.[30] This is recognition that, as Thoreau believed, the "sovereignty" and "authority" of the individual is of a higher form than that of the state and thus of any organization or institution formed by or functioning within the state.

In other words, the ultimate source of power and authority (sovereignty) everywhere—in governments, armies, police, businesses, communities, churches, families, parents, groups, and public and private organizations—is held by the individuals who comprise it, the people—citizens, soldiers, customers, workers, members, parishioners, students, children and the like. That is to say, people always hold the strategic, long-range, lever of power in their organizations and institutions stemming from their individual and corporate moral responsibility and moral authority. Governors hold only the tactical, legal, short-range, lever of power stemming from their legal responsibility and legal authority to govern. Unfortunately, this is not widely understood. The confusion and inappropriate organizational and societal strategies practiced today by managers and officials result from their failure to recognize this basic relationship and the fundamental importance of the individual citizen.

People have the final power and authority in all organizations of which they are a part. When their moral authority is exercised, they ignore the consequences that their "legal governors" might use in retaliation. Moral authority is perhaps the only force that is able to transcend all "legal authority," whenever and wherever it confronts it, either individually or corporately. It is not just rhetoric that the Constitution of the United States and the preamble to the United Nations' Charter both begin, *"We the People."* It is history's clue to the ultimate source of power and authority in all organizations everywhere in the world. This has been a long, hard, lesson to learn and one that petty organizational, corporate and institutional tyrants as well as military dictators of developing nations had better heed in the future. This power and authority is available to create a new and better future for mankind in our nation and the world in a process of—*Civilization Building.*

The Trend Toward Democracy

The world is moving increasingly toward democracy. This movement is driven by natural, psycho-social, world cultural forces that are occurring that cannot be stopped, only guided.

The extent to which a nation's leaders learn how to use dissent constructively is a measure of the nation's potential for greatness. Totalitarianism, authoritarianism, and closed, bureaucratic systems are doomed to fail. It is democracy that is the historical wave of the future from the groundswell of history in both public and private organizations and institutions.

Because of natural dynamics, societies move from kings, dictators and authoritarianism toward democracy and freedom. Democracies simply work better. A democratic open society provides for dissent, for the opportunity for all to participate in the shaping of the common future. It is simply more efficient and politically viable than a closed, centralized, authoritarian, dictatorial system. In a democracy, authority flows continually and more readily upward from the people to their political leaders, who can then govern more effectively, efficiently, and economically. Such is an *inspirational society in pursuit of happiness."*

The Theory
of Politics

A political relationship is defined as one between or among equals, and progress in a political relationship comes only from agreement, or failing that, from compromise through collaboration; otherwise there is stalemate. Progress in a political relationship is best reached by increasing interaction and improving communication, and thus understanding, between or among the participants. It is a misnomer to consider any human organization as "non-political," and it is a political right of people to be enabled by their governors to participate viably in their organizations, institutions, and governments.

The American culture is rooted in Judeo-Christian religious concepts, and a basic tenet of the Christian religion is, "Everyone is unique and is just as important before God—*but no more*—than anyone else." This tenet from our nation's religious heritage helped form the basic proposition of "equality of citizenship" stated in the Declaration of Independence as, "*We hold these truths to be self-evident, that all men are created equal.*"

The Declaration of Independence is a spiritual and philosophical document containing the fundamental principles upon which this country and its Constitution were founded. The struggle to achieve these principles is still being played out today in the continuing cultural efforts to overcome barriers to participation such as racism, sexism, ageism, elitism, and other "isms" that deny the political rights of people. The social turmoil that periodically surfaces is derived from the on-going attempts to get the Constitution, the laws derived from it in our society, and the everyday life experiences of people into synchronization with the "administrative reality" of the Declaration of Independence. For these reasons, all relationships among human beings should be considered fundamentally political, i.e., between or among equals as we are defining it.

Webster's Dictionary defines equal as "One not inferior or superior to another" and political rights as "Those rights implying participation, either direct or indirect, in the establishment or administration of the government."

It is commonly thought that human relationships among people in military organizations, governments, bureaucracies, businesses, and other such hierarchical organizations are non-political, i.e., not a relationship among equals. They are all considered to be hierarchical and built upon a management system in which there are superior/subordinate relationships. But this is not fundamentally true (in the spiritual sense of the Declaration of Independence); it only seems true (in the sense of the legal system and the everyday experiences of people).

People normally conduct themselves in their public and private "legal roles" as if the superior/subordinate relationship were really true. Because of this, most human organizations, including those of business, church, and state, upon which the people depend for their very economic, spiritual, and societal survival, often flounder from a lack of overall direction and "leadership." The confusion comes from not knowing fundamentally who is really "in charge." As explained in the Theory of Authority, the people are in charge. For example, The Constitution of the State of Washington reads:

"Article I

DECLARATION OF RIGHTS

1 POLITICAL POWER. *All political power is inherent in the people, and governments derive their just powers from the consent of the governed, and are established to protect and maintain individual rights."* People in all institutions and in society have the ultimate power and authority over their own relationships of all kinds. We all need to understand this.

In our "real life work" of civilization building, we are all citizens and equal in our nation and in the world. According to the Declaration of Independence, all human beings are equal; our fundamental relationships among all citizens should reflect this great political and philosophical truth.

However, this equality does not manifest itself throughout our work-a-day world. For there we are invariably subordinate to someone in our various organizational and societal "role" assignments—to our "bosses," to public officials, to the police officer, to our parents, to our teachers, and the like. No one is immune.

In spite of the prevalence of superior/subordinate relationships, it is a misnomer to consider any human relationship in any organization or institution as being "non-political." Fundamentally, all organizations are political, a relationship among equals—including even governmental, military, and police organizations. It is only in the organizational "work-a-day roles" that we each play that "superior/subordinate" relationships appear. But notice that the governor in the relationship does not have the power to prevent a subordinate from leaving if the subordinate is intent on doing so, and is willing to disregard any consequences—including death in the case of martyrs.

These role assignments, from the highest to the lowest, have evolved historically from cultural efforts as a people to collaborate toward organizational and societal objectives as accomplished through legal and societal systems.

Citizenship is a job for life. We are all sometimes "unemployed" in our vocational work-a-day world, e.g., during periods of growing up as children, while studying to learn new skills as students, when we lose our "jobs" as individuals and must seek new work, when retired and other such examples. However, as citizens we can never be "unemployed" in our life work of civilization building. Every citizen in the world is gainfully employed in this task from life to death. That is the administrative reality which leaders and citizens everywhere must realize. *Each person simultaneously is a citizen of his or her own country and of the world.* And we do not have a retirement age for citizen participation or activism.

Examples of Political Relationships

The most foundational "political relationship" in the history of the world is the family. It exists in the smallest organization—a husband and wife. In addition to their love and family relationship, theirs is basically a political relationship between equals. If they cannot agree on how to conduct the affairs of their family, then one or both of them must be willing to compromise. They must collaborate in order to achieve progress toward their family goals. If neither is willing to collaborate, they will become polarized. We call this process "estrangement." If it continues further without abatement, and with growing intensity, the process leads to rupture in the political relationship, which we call "divorce."

The next more complex form of political relationship in a society is that which exists between or among members of a partnership. They each have one vote. If partners cannot agree, or are not willing to collaborate with their differences, they cannot make progress in their relationship, because it is basically political in nature, that is, they are equal in power legally. If their differences continue without interruption, they will become further polarized, leading to a rupture in their political relationship, which we call "dissolving the partnership."

The next higher and more complex form of political relationship in our society is that which exists among legislative-type persons, for example: members of community or church committees, boards, agencies, city or county councils, school boards, state legislators, and members of Congress. These persons are either elected or appointed to their positions, and apart from their persuasiveness and influence, each such committee person or "legislator," is equal in power in that each has one vote. This is the law. If committee members or legislators cannot agree on how to make progress in their political relationship, and if they are not willing to collaborate, in spite of their differences, they cannot get anything done, i.e., they will become stalemated and polarized. If this disagreement continues without abatement, they may become increasingly polarized. And because they are "political leaders," large numbers of their constituents often share their views and become polarized too. If the process continues without abatement and gains in intensity, it will lead to an open rupture in the political relationship. Depending upon the level of intensity of the rupture in the political relationship involved, it is called: apathy, uncooperativeness, resistance, militancy, civil disobedience, rioting, or rebellion.

The apathy of people in their organizations and institutions is really the first sign of a rupture in the political relationships among equals that exists between leaders and their constituents. Apathy is an unmistakable sign of an organization's or an institution's poor "mental health" and should be considered a serious condition requiring the attention of leaders to reverse the trend. It is usually the result of an inadequate administrative style by leaders who are unable to communicate viably with their constituents. This condition stems, primarily, not from the indifference of followers, but from the inadequate administrative theory held by leaders who are unable to conceptualize correctly the administrative reality of the situation. Such leaders neglect or disdain the great truth that leaders and followers are fundamentally equal. As a result most such leaders do not develop adequate feedback communication systems with their constituents.

Finally, the highest ranking and most complex form of political relationship that exists in the world is that of statesmanship among nations. This occurs between or among statespersons within the family of nations. If they, as equal members from sovereign nations, cannot agree on how to conduct the affairs of the world, then neither they nor the world will be able to progress in their relationships. They must be willing to collaborate in spite of their differences. Otherwise there will be stalemate. If they are not willing to collaborate, they may become further polarized. Because they are the political leaders of nations of people, their constituents will often become further polarized too. If the process continues without abatement and gains in intensity, it may lead to an open rupture called war (or at a lesser scale, cold war, "covert" war actions or activities, "ideological warfare," sabotage, terrorism and the like).

Increasing Understanding and Collaboration

Thus, in a political relationship, which we defined as any relationship among people, the only way to make progress and avoid stalemate is through agreement reached best by collaboration or compromise. Otherwise polarization and possibly rupture will follow. The principal way to reduce polarization in a political relationship is to increase interaction and improve communication between or among the participants and thus increase understanding. This is best accomplished merely by talking but always done with the "Basic Attitude" as a guide to personal conduct, including a strong willingness to listen with an honest attempt to understand and intent to reach agreement.

Rensis Likert, former Director of the Institute for Social Research and Professor of Psychology and Sociology at the University of Michigan, was preeminent in the field of social science research. He writes, "Of all the tasks of management, managing the human component is the central and most important task because all else depends upon how well it is done." Beginning research on a science-based system of management, which he initially proposed in *New Patterns of Management* (1961), and described more fully in his book *The Human Organization* (1967). Likert identified four basic management styles, System 1 through System 4.

- System 1 was "Exploitative Authoritative," i.e., kings, tyrants, and dictators.
- System 2 was "Benevolent Authoritative," i.e., benevolent kings, tyrants, and dictators.
- System 3 was "Consultative," i.e., closed relationships but with open communication.
- System 4 was "Participative Group," i.e., open, reciprocal relationships.

Likert studied the operating characteristics of these four management styles. In general, results over a large number of characteristics showed System 1 to be a negative, poor, and ineffective management style and showed System 4 to be a positive, good, and effective management style.

The character of communication was vastly different in the four systems. For example, "Amount of interaction and communication aimed at achieving organization's objectives" ranged from:

- System 1 "Very little"
- System 2 "Little"
- System 3 "Quite a bit" and
- System 4 "Much with both individuals and groups."

In "Direction of Information Flow" results ranged from:

- System 1 "Downward"
- System 2 "Mostly downward"
- System 3 "Down and up" and
- System 4 "Down, up, and with peers."

In "Downward communication (the extent to which communications are accepted by subordinates)" results ranged from:

- System 1 "Viewed with great suspicion"
- System 2 "May or may not be viewed with suspicion"
- System 3 "Often accepted but at times viewed with suspicion. May or may not be openly questioned"
- System 4 "Generally accepted, but if not, openly and candidly questioned".[31]

Likert concluded that management systems are more productive and have lower costs and more favorable attitudes as they move toward System 4 (Participative Group) than do those systems moving toward System 1 (Exploitative).[32] *He stated, "These three variables, overlapping group structure (i.e., the "Linking-Pin" concept), group decision making, and the principle of supportive relationships can be considered to be causal."*[33] *That is, effective coordination, excellent communication in group decision-making, and high capacity among units to influence and motivate each other are causal.*

Therefore, with increased interaction and improved communication comes the best hope for understanding, collaboration, and eventual agreement. This applies in every political relationship, ranging from that between or among a husband and wife, individual citizens, parishioners, partners, and legislators, to that among the statespersons of the nations of the world. This also applies to the political relationships between or among citizens of the world who are equals and who are participating simultaneously in a process of civilization building in an organization as well as culturally in an institution, in a government, and in the world.

The Self-Fulfilling Prophecy

- All human beings are prophetic! They make prophecies about future events and outcomes. The way in which an individual (or family, group, organization, institution, community, state, nation, society, or civilization) perceives a situation, perceives "self," or perceives others (the prophecy), will determine the perceiver's reaction to the situation, "self," or others encountered in its environment. The reactions themselves, in turn, tend to direct events subsequently encountered toward reinforcing and confirming the original perception, i.e., they tend to be self-fulfilling.

- Perceptions of self are gained from one's past experiences, especially past successes or failures, and the "mirror" of the reactions of others. Positive perceptions of self provide the motivation for human beings and organizations to learn and grow in their abilities and capacities.

- Desired capacities are best achieved initially by acting as if they were present.

The Self-Fulfilling Prophecy is a generator of theories and is the determinant of individual and organizational capacity.

"The most beautiful quotation from Blake that I know," writes author Jacob Bronowski, "is a remark in which he says, 'Every honest man is a prophet'."[34] The theory of the self-fulfilling prophecy is the most widely known of all the general administrative theories which we have identified. Most people will conjure up something very close to reality when hearing the words, "self-fulfilling prophecy."

Years ago Dr. Arthur W. Combs, preeminent national educator stated:

"What we do is really predicated upon what we believe. So it's these beliefs, attitudes, opinions, values, and opinions of people that we have to learn to take a look at. That is to say, what we do [our behavior], is really predicated upon what we believe [our perceptions and prophecies]. So it's these beliefs, attitudes, opinions, values, and perceptions of people [their prophecies] that we have to learn to look at, if we really hope to predict their behavior [or our own]." [35]

If people perceive threats, their initial reactions are either fight or flight. If "fight," the reaction is toward aggression, i.e., stands firm, does not avoid contact, is aggressive and will organize resistance, resists accommodation, rocks the boat, and the like. If "flight," the reaction is toward pacifism, i.e., one hides, avoids contact, is not aggressive, tries to accommodate, doesn't rock the boat. *No one reacts to "reality"—rather we all react to our "perceptions of reality."*

These dynamics of the perceptions of governors and leaders tend to determine the capacities of their charges and constituents, because they tend to be self-fulfilling. For example, when a leader prophesies that those led are "not able,"—then those led will be treated as if they are not able. Hence, the leader won't trust those led (because they are not able to be trusted), won't challenge those led, won't enable those led, all because the leader does not consider them able. And sure enough, at the end of the relationship, those led are usually not able, which fulfills the leader's prophecy and proves him or her "right." On the other hand, when the leader's attitude changes and he or she prophesies that a student (or other ward) is able, then those led will be treated as if they are able. Hence, the leader will trust those led (because they are able to be trusted), will challenge those led, will enable those led and so forth, all because the leader considers them able. And, sure enough, at the end of the relationship, those led are usually able, which again fulfills the leader's "prophecy" and proves him or her "right,"—because the leader had provided a *creative climate* of trust and confidence in which those led could grow psychologically.

The concept of the self-fulfilling prophecy is a phenomenon of great importance. Earliest attention that we know about was called to this in a speech by Dr. Fritz Roethlisberger, a Harvard professor and outstanding authority on human relations.[36] He identified the problems that superficial, negative, and incorrect ideas (theories) held by managers about people (i.e., their "prophecy") cause in human relationships, although he never used the phrase "Self-Fulfilling Prophecy." For examples of such ideas see the Frontispiece of this book, "Administrative Ideas and Realities."

The concept was further developed by Doug McGregor, author of *The Human Side of Enterprise*, but in terms of his now famous "Theory X" and "Theory Y."[37] For example, in Theory X (negative attitudes or "prophecies"), " . . . most people must be coerced, controlled, directed, threatened with punishment to get them to put forth adequate effort toward the achievement of organizational objectives." McGregor believed that new research in social science made possible a number of generalizations "which provide a modest beginning for new theory with respect to the management of human resources," that he referred to as "Theory Y." For example, in Theory Y (positive attitudes or "prophecies"), "The capacity to exercise a relatively high degree of imagination, ingenuity, and creativity in the solution of organizational problems is widely, not narrowly, distributed in the population."[38]

Thus, McGregor's research showed that these traditional characteristics of "good leadership" are widely held among people and not narrowly based among just a few organizational or societal "leaders," as then popularly and historically perceived.

McGregor concluded:

> *The purpose of this volume is not to entice management to choose sides over Theory X or Theory Y. It is, rather, to encourage the realization that theory is important, to urge management to examine its assumptions and make them explicit. In doing so it will open a door to the future. The possible result could be developments during the next few decades with respect to the human side of enterprise comparable to those that have occurred in technology during the past half-century. And, if we can learn how to realize the potential for collaboration inherent in the human resources of industry, we will provide a model for governments and nations which mankind sorely needs.*[39]

Individuals, groups, organizations, and institutions gain perceptions about themselves by observing past successes and failures. This is caused by what they have done, but mostly from the "mirror" of the reaction of others to them. The parent, teacher, counselor, minister, manager, or leader must "mirror" trust, confidence, warmth, and encouragement to his or her charges and also provide as much of a "creative climate" as possible to permit psychological growth. When this is permitted by governors, the recipient of this attitude perceives himself or herself in the same manner, and thus develops his or her own self-confidence and self-image and an ego strong enough to survive the failures in life which are inevitable to everyone. Failure in a creative climate is perceived merely as a stepping-stone along the way to achievement. Failure does not become a crushing defeat, but only another learning experience, i.e., awareness of what does not work. Successful experiences, no matter how small, and positive perceptions of self, therefore, provide the motivation for individuals, groups, and organizations to grow in their abilities and capacities and *to learn.*

If one desires attributes, personal characteristics, or capacities that are presently not within one's personality, then these can be best acquired initially merely by *acting* as if they were present. This is also directly related to the concepts of the Rev. Dr. Norman Vincent Peale in his book, *The Power of Positive Thinking.* The application of the self-fulfilling prophecy, in this situation, is slightly different. The individual prophesies for himself or herself, and then proceeds to fulfill his or her own prophecy. This is why it is best when you have to "do" something that before going out and doing it, you first get yourself "psyched up to do it" to the point where you prophesy to yourself, "I think I can." And then you go out and do it—and you probably can.

In one part of the Dale Carnegie Course, individuals learn how to become enthusiastic by standing in front of a mirror (and later the class) and forcefully, with fist slapping into hand, repeating over and over, "If you want to be enthusiastic, you have to act enthusiastic!" The psychology is: If you want to be enthusiastic, you have to act enthusiastic—and soon you become enthusiastic! Similarly, in an interview of Cary Grant by an audience, he was asked who he had most wanted to be when he started out. "I guess I just patterned myself on a kind of combination of Jack Buchanan—he was the reigning musical comedy star of those days—and Noel Coward. In other words, I pretended to be somebody I wanted to be until finally I became that person. Or he became me."

Thus, if we want a way to develop new and desirable attributes and capacities within ourselves that do not presently exist in our own view, then we should *act* as if we possessed the attribute or capacity, and soon we will possess it (from the point of view of others who will "mirror" back to us our actions). We will have become a new being. For example, if one wants to be a "loving father" (though one perceives oneself as not being a loving father), then one need only to act like a loving father (from one's point of view it's only an act and not real); soon one will become a loving father (from the point of view of one's children who will mirror back your lovingness). Similarly, if one wants to be compassionate, friendly, tolerant, without prejudice, kindly, open, sincere, interested, authentic, honest and so forth (though one perceives one's self not to have these characteristics), then one needs to act as if one possessed these, and soon one will become possessed of them (from the point of view of others who will mirror back your actions). This suggests, in turn, that if we want others to be understanding, compassionate, collaborative, loving, tolerant, kind and the like to us, *we must express these qualities to others through our own actions first.*

> *Love thy neighbor as thyself (Matthew 19:19) and the Golden Rule: Do*
> *unto others as you would have others do unto you.*

We cannot think of a better way for humanity to build toward a just and sustainable civilization together in the emerging future than through using this fundamental wisdom passed from our religious heritage.

The self-fulfilling prophecy is a very important dynamic in the conduct of human affairs. Many managers (governors), perhaps most, easily rationalize negative feedback information received from interactions, interviews, polls, letters, verbal complaints, demonstrations, and the like as being untypical of the people in their groups, organizations, or constituencies. This is especially true of governors imbued with the concept that "authority" stems from the top down. They tend to brush off such negative responses because usually, at first, there are so few. They tend to be reassured by what has often been called the "silent majority," who apparently are not complaining or "making trouble." It becomes easy to rationalize further and stereotype these "fringe" elements as agitators, extremists, right or left wingers, or just plain soreheads and definitely not a good type. Believing this to be true (their prophecy), they then treat such persons through their actions in this fashion, and sure enough, they usually turn out just the way it was predicted, i.e., as troublemakers—to fulfill the prophecy.

Another example is the businessman who receives a few complaints from customers which he brushes aside as untypical, since he hasn't heard from the "silent majority"—until one day he wakes up to find he is out of business. The general rule is: *Never trust a silent majority.* It is usually an ominous silence. Assume the complaints, feedback and the like are valid indicators of prevailing concerns among persons in the overall group. Be sensitive and act responsibly. If the complaints are not really justified, the "silent majority" will quickly respond and restore the correct tenor of things, but when there is no such response, it is an ominous silence. The truth is that individuals, families, groups, organizations, institutions, societies, and civilizations that have strong mental health *are not silent.* There is, instead, spontaneity, happiness, and joy that will not be contained.

While the concept of the Self-Fulfilling Prophecy is widely known and accepted, we have wondered why we, and others, have not thought of it earlier as the "generator of administrative theories." It seems obvious as one thinks it through. We suspect the reason is that this "perception ⟶ prophecy ⟶ reaction" phenomenon has been with us since the beginning of our first consciousness as human beings. It has been automatic—fight or flight!

We are further reminded of the "Theory of the Obvious." In the field of law the theory states, "It is so obvious, it does not have to be proved." However, in contradistinction, in the field of Gestalt psychology (involving the shape or structure of the interrelation of the parts of a system as a whole as being something more than the mere sum of the parts), this same theory states, in effect, "The obvious isn't always so obvious." In this case, the administrative reality appears to lie more with Gestalt psychology. New knowledge and understanding of ourselves as human beings, individually, organizationally, and socially, is frequently "not obvious."

The physical sciences are sometimes referred to as the "hard" sciences and implied to be harder and more rigorous than the social or "soft" sciences. Why then has humankind made far more progress in understanding the physical sciences than the social sciences? A reason might be that the data generated in research in the social sciences are more complex. After all, a single human being is complex. The study of the relationships of many human beings working together seems to be infinitely more complex and compounded. It becomes a lot like trying to take accurate measurements using a rubber ruler. It stretches and shrinks depending upon the observer, and researchers in social science keep getting conflicting measurements of what is "right" and what is "wrong."

Management (a Disenchantment)

In an interview conducted in May-June 1993 by T. George Harris, Peter Drucker said: *"I'm not comfortable with the word manager any more, because it implies subordinates. I find myself using executive more because it implies responsibility for an area, not necessarily dominion over people."*

Management Professors Warren Bennis and Burt Nanus, co-authors of *Leaders,* observed that a critical difference between managers and leaders is that, *"Managers do things right; leaders do the right thing."*[40]

This is a tremendous theoretical insight.

As our understanding of the dynamics of administrative theory has matured, we too have grown disenchanted with words like *manage, manager, management.* These concepts do not adequately describe the profession, and are out of touch with changes in the new, shape-shifting workplace.

Imagine a young, relatively inexperienced administrator who learns that beginning Monday morning he or she will become a *manager*, a *supervisor*, or a *boss.* The danger is that the words themselves contain subliminal implications about administrative style. That to "manage" one must rely on directing and controlling. And, given what we now know about Self-Fulfilling Prophecies and Theory X and Theory Y leadership, the young administrator is likely to create one management crisis after the other before learning that this may not be the best way to go about doing the job.

We prefer to use such terms as *administer, administrator,* and *administrative.* These words are more neutral, and imply a more creative and a less authoritarian administrative style.

The Administrative Process (a Definition)

The Administrative Process is: DIAGNOSE the problem, THEORIZE its solution, DECIDE what to do about it, ACCOMPLISH what was decided, and REVIEW what was done. It is an ongoing process.

This definition of the administrative process critiques the traditional view of the functions of management. It suggests that administration is best conducted by many people, not just a few. It highlights the need for effective communication processes in organizations.

Most older leaders of today have been taught that the management process is plan, organize, motivate, and control (or a derivative: plan, organize, coordinate, direct, and control as in the military). If an individual's concept of being a manager or boss or governor is that one must motivate, direct, or control others, the individual easily moves into an authoritarian management style, the most pervasive style in organizations and society today. This closes doors for two-way communication between leaders and people, feedback from people to people, and the organization begins to "fly blind" with leaders perceptually detached from their constituents. The situation is similar to a ship with defective radar traveling at high speed in dense fog through waters filled with icebergs—its chances of survival are not good.

On the other hand, an organization whose leaders enable constituents to participate viably with their ideas and opinions whenever possible receives accurate feedback. It is the same ship but with reliable radar. It perceives its environment accurately and can change course frequently to adapt to changes and avoid calamity.

In the new definition of the Administrative Process above, notice there is no mandate for leaders to motivate, direct, or control others. The old definition put the burden for leadership on leaders and/or the managers and left everyone else with the passive (and resented and resisted) role of being motivated, directed, and controlled. The new definition allows everyone to participate in the Administrative Process. It also implies that leadership is a responsibility that resides in everyone and not just in the titular head of the organization, as popularly believed.

Notice too in the new definition, that *all people* who are interested and involved should be enabled by their leaders to participate and exercise their leadership and influence through the *diagnosing, theorizing,* and *reviewing* functions when appropriate. At the same time, the normal prerogatives of legally elected or duly appointed organizational leaders/representatives charged with decision-making are retained by them. The organization's leaders can still make the final decisions, and the normal implementation of the decisions can still be accomplished by bureaucracies (if involved) as at present or can be expanded to include the people. This definition also looks at the Administrative Process as an ongoing, never-ending process. *The goal in a free and open democratic society is to achieve self-motivation and self-control by both individuals and organizations to the maximum extent possible.*

This new definition of the administrative process is best accomplished within a creative climate. This is set by a positive and helpful administrative style by those who govern. It should be noted that while "Diagnose" is the first step in the administrative process as we have defined it, it is also hooked directly to the self-fulfilling prophecy as we explained earlier. That is to say, people perceive a problem and contribute their perception (right or wrong) as their "diagnosis" of the problem and then continue right along in the administrative process step by step. Since individual citizens prophesy, it is imperative that they be enabled by their governors through policies of openness and involvement to communicate their opinions, concerns, values, ideas, and attitudes to their peers when appropriate and possible. It is only through these open democratic processes and the emerging interaction, that a prevailing consensus develops which helps to guide the state, organization, or institution toward organizational and societal solutions.

Professor Edgar Schein of MIT, author of *Organizational Psychology,* describes the historical development of assumptions about people (i.e., prophecies). Each of these assumptions was developed at a different historical time, and the first was "Rational-Economic Man" (Adam Smith, 1776). This prophecy assumed that, "Humankind is lazy, needs to be manipulated and controlled, is incapable of self-discipline; and economic incentives are the only motivators." These proved to be superficial, erroneous, and negative "Theory X" ideas.

Three more cultural management concepts were subsequently developed. These were "Social Man" (1940s; Mayo, Roethlisberger, Trist). This prophecy assumed that, "Social needs basically motivate people, finding meaning in work must be sought in social contexts, peer group forces are stronger than management incentives and controls, and the like." These assumptions were the beginning of positive, "Theory Y" ideas.

Later concepts followed. The next was "Self-Actualizing Man" (1960s; Maslow, McGregor, Herzberg, Combs). This prophecy assumed that, "The motives of humankind fall into hierarchies of needs beginning with survival, then safety and security, then social, then ego satisfaction, autonomy and independence, then 'self-actualization' for maximum use of self."

Schein explains that, given these assumptions (administrative theories and "prophecies"), managers developed different types of "implied managerial strategies" for each case. For example, managers imbued with the ideas of "Rational-Economic Man" initiated economic incentives and believed the authority of managers to lie in their offices. They interpreted the management process to be: plan, organize, motivate, and control. Managers imbued with the ideas of "Social Man" believed that attention should be given to people's social needs; feelings of acceptance and identity should concern managers; group incentives should prevail over individual incentives, and the like. The concepts held by managers of "Self-Actualizing Man" were similar to "Social Man," but added that motivations shifted to "intrinsic" (from the individual) rather than "extrinsic" (from the manager); authority shifted to the task; managers needed to be facilitators; and they needed to delegate as much as possible.

Schein concludes with his contemporary theory of "Complex Man." This prophecy assumes that, "Here the manager believes that humankind has a complex interaction between initial needs and organizational experiences thus responding to many strategies. Different people have different needs. These needs change over time. There is no one set of strategies suitable for managers that apply to all people at all times."

The implied managerial strategy for today, according to Schein is:

A manager [governor, leader, statesperson] should be a good diagnostician, inquire into problems, and value differences among people and the diagnostic processes that reveal those differences. Differences of opinion are not considered a threat but are rather an opportunity for better diagnosis of problems leading toward more effective decision-making.

This situation requires new and better communication processes in organizations. *Therefore, the discovery of new, vital, feedback communication techniques applicable in all human groups, communities, organizations, institutions, and societies in the world today holds the key to the release of a fabulous amount of human creativity.* This social energy is currently being wasted by most organizations and institutions here and elsewhere in the world, public and private. Most organizations have adopted inefficient, authoritarian management styles with little or no systematic feedback in their bureaucracies. These styles often suppress human creativity rather than encourage it. This has the effect of a "wet blanket." Such has not been a deliberate effort on the part of most leaders. It has merely evolved from the bureaucratic nature of organizations. The lack of practical techniques and viable administrative theories often leaves today's governors unable to conceptualize reality accurately. More appropriate managerial styles and more effective communication processes are thus required for successful governing.

The problem in management and administration in organizations today is not just a lack of good theory (why) and realizing that managers should be good diagnosticians as Schein suggests. In addition the problem is a lack of new communication techniques to enable managers (administrators, leaders, and governors) *to become good diagnosticians.* We face a problem of lack of methods for finding out people's opinions and ideas. Perhaps "creative technique" would best describe the process required to achieve insight into the problems that face us. These problems confront us individually and corporately as a people and as administrators (governors), both today and in the future. In Section Two of this book we present several new communication techniques and give examples of Many-To-Many feedback models and groupware technology in organizations that can enable managers and leaders to become better diagnosticians in today's complex world.

The Helping Professions*

Leaders (governors) are a part of the helping professions which include officials, administrators, teachers, counselors, ministers, nurses, parents and such other persons in personal interaction with followers, constituents, students, clients, parishioners, patients, children, citizens and other similar relationships. The characteristics of good and poor helpers are the same regardless of the profession.

*Based on research by Dr. Arthur W. Combs

Preeminent Educator/Psychologist Arthur W. Combs began a research program in the early 1960s to identify the characteristics of "good and poor" teachers and counselors. Later he expanded the research to include priests and nurses. He lumped all these occupations together into what he called the "helping professions," which he found had common characteristics regardless of the profession.

Dr. Combs was a perceptual (cognitive) psychologist; he represented a brand of psychology that assumes people act on the basis of what they perceive and what they believe. Combs said:

> The real characteristics of the helping professions, whether we are talking about counselors or teachers or Episcopal priests or whoever, the important thing about these people, the important characteristic is that all of these professions are dependent upon instantaneous response. The child says something, the teacher has to say something back; the client says something, the counselor has to reply; the parishioner says something to the priest, the priest has to reply. In each case all of these professions are dependent upon instantaneous response.
>
> Well, that's a neat problem. How can you have a profession that's dependent upon instantaneous response and be sure that the response is a good one? In other words, you don't have time to think about what's the right thing to do. But how can you be sure then that the immediate thing you do is likely to be a good one?
>
> In a human being, however, what we came to understand is that what determines the answer which comes out of the human being. . . is the person's system of beliefs. What he believes is what makes the difference with respect to how he behaves.[41]

Now we turn to the question: What are the characteristics of "good and poor" helpers? Dr. Combs identified the characteristics of helpers (leaders) to include the following:

The Characteristics of Good and Poor Helpers

POOR HELPERS (LEADERS)	GOOD HELPERS (LEADERS)
1. External data are important — order, neatness, forms, rules, procedures and so forth.	1. Internal data are important —are sensitive to the beliefs, opinions, attitudes, and values of people.
2. Are concerned about things.	2. Are concerned about people.
3. Feel people aren't trustworthy and able.	3. Feel people are trustworthy and able.
4. Violate the dignity and integrity of people.	4. Preserve the dignity and integrity of people.
5. Don't see themselves in positive ways.	5. See themselves in positive ways.
6. Have controlling purposes.	6. Have freeing purposes.
7. Have narrow purposes.	7. Have broad purposes.
8. Are self-concealing.	8. Are self-revealing.

Source: "Human Relationships," address given 1970 by Dr. Arthur W. Combs, DAS Conference, Washington Education Association, Seattle, Washington.

We believe what Dr. Combs actually discovered in his years of research were the characteristics of good and poor *leaders*, including teachers, counselors, officials, administrators, priests, nurses, parents, and others. Leader/follower relationships often require instantaneous response. And good leaders (and governors) demonstrate the characteristics described in the right-hand column in that they are concerned about people and internal data, feel people are trustworthy and able, preserve people's dignity and integrity, see themselves in positive ways, have freeing and broad purposes, and are self-revealing. It seems to us that leadership is one of the "helping professions," and a very important one.

The reality is that if one takes away the functions of teaching and counseling from any administrator—there isn't much left. John Gardner states a similar insight. "Every great leader is clearly teaching—and every great teacher is leading."[42]

Dr. Combs stated that,

"In a world where we no longer know the goals, where the goals have to be the development of intelligent persons who are skillful at problem-solving, we need a different kind of psychology. We need a psychology that will help us understand the internal life of human beings. To do this, teachers [leaders] have to turn their attention to values because the

beliefs, feelings, attitudes, and understandings that make up the perceptions and prophecies of people will determine the choices they make."

Combs believes that teachers (leaders) should help their students (constituents), "explore and discover their own values which is the important question." That is, "in the pedagogy of teaching, a teacher should not 'teach' values to students but rather should help students explore their own values." The same applies to leaders who should help their constituents explore their own values.

In an article titled, "What makes a Good Helper? A Person Centered Approach," Combs writes concerning his research:

"With respect to the counselor's self concept categories ... as a matter of fact, categories about self correlate so closely with one another as to suggest that only one, 'sees self as enough' may be so fundamental that more specific categories exist only as variations on the same theme. This suggests that [a self-perception of] 'personal adequacy' is perhaps the only description required for effective discrimination of teachers [leaders]."[43]

We are struck by how this key insight of Combs correlates highly with the research of Warren Bennis and Burt Nanus, coauthors of *Leaders* (1985). In an interview by American Express, Warren Bennis responded:

> *Four major themes did become apparent in our interviews. Our leaders embodied four areas of competency: attention through vision, the means to communicate vision, positive self-regard, and building trust with associates. Most of the best leaders have a positive self-image. This is not an ego thing. They are aware of their capabilities and have the confidence to share power with their colleagues. Positive self-regard allows leaders to be more tolerant of the mistakes and feelings of others .... The experiences of many of our country's top leaders have convinced me that leadership skills can be learned.* [44]

These insights of Combs and Bennis as to the characteristics of leaders are extremely important.

Unfortunately, while Combs was a nationally known educator and psychologist and widely known to those in the field of education, his work has not been as well known or utilized among scholars of administrative theory and organizational behavior. They might have been misled by research solely about "teachers."

Good theory is that which conveys a maximum of insightful knowledge in as few words as possible. No one in the field of administrative theory has yet lifted up and integrated the work of Dr. Combs into the discipline. It was for these reasons that we added "The Helping Profession (a Definition)" as an additional general administrative theory.

The Zeitgeist Principle

To work most effectively, human organizations and institutions (from the smallest —the family, to the largest—civilization itself) require a functional feedback communication capability. Feedback systems are necessary in order to apprehend the Zeitgeist, the Spirit-of-the-Time. This is best accomplished in most organizations by a democratic, open, participative, reliable, viable, anonymous, routine, and objective feedback communication system. Few organizations, institutions, governments, and societies in the world today have such an envisioning system. Organizations with such a system can perceive the Zeitgeist and envision better decisions for the future.

Society Seeks Its Self

It is well known among psychologists that an individual without a clear sense of direction cannot prosper. A person with a divided mind cannot easily find the way forward. Social psychologists and sociologists also know that a group (of any size) is also a kind of person. A group has a "mind," it has a temperament, it has character, it has personality; and it grows and changes.

In previous centuries, there existed a common language to discuss these issues of the nature of society. A few hundred years ago our ancestors could talk of the soul of society, without embarrassment or confusion. A couple of centuries ago they could discourse on the "genius" (presiding spirit) of society. As recently as 100 years ago, nations had a profound sense of their destiny and calling. The dark side of nationalism, which fanned the flames of two World Wars since the year 1900, is one of the factors that silenced conversation about the destiny or soul of nations. This is understandable—but we do not want to "throw out the baby with the bathwater."

On the other hand, the language of "soul" has not altogether vanished. It cannot go away, for it is intrinsic to social identity. Instead, beginning with the era of Carl G. Jung (1875-1961) and his followers, the language of "soul" has been replaced with the language of "self." It is more fashionable and acceptable for people to say that they are looking for their "self" (identity, calling) than that they are looking for their "soul." The latter word is considered, these days, to be too mystical or religious, too vague or metaphorical.

As always, what is true of the individual is true of society and any group. Because human nature is social, and because a group is the sum (and sometimes more than the sum) of the participating individuals, groups from families to nations are always unconsciously seeking their soul/self. We know this is true because of the wide currency of such sayings as, "The British have lost an Empire but not found a role (in the modern world)."

It is for this reason that the "*Zeitgeist* Principle" is important for the growth of society. For it respects the fact that a group—an organization, a club, a society, or a nation—needs to find its own understanding, its calling, if it is to activate its powers fully.

The *Zeitgeist* is the spirit of society at any moment, i.e., the " Spirit-of-the-Time." We could picture the Spirit of Society as like a sun hidden from the ordinary life of society by clouds of ignorance and other obstacles to knowledge. The social technology of Many-To-Many Communication helps an organization know itself. In finding its self, the organization finds its spirit, its calling in the moment, in the time of its inquiry.

For an organization to know itself it must at least know its own mind. This is where what we call "Zeitgeist Communication" comes in. It maximizes the communication within an organization, particularly the communication between the leaders of the organization and its constituents.

There has to be an impersonal quality to "Zeitgeist Communication." This is best accomplished in most organizations by a democratic, open, participative, reliable, viable, anonymous, routine, and objective feedback system.

To work properly, human organizations and institutions (from married couples to civilization itself) require a working system of "feedback" communication. Most organizations, institutions, and governments in the world today have no such system, often "flying blind."

"Zeitgeist Communication" solves this problem. It does so by setting up a *symbolic dialogue* between organizational leaders and their constituents. This is done rather than a physical dialogue (which is usually not possible) or a "virtual dialogue," e.g., one-to-many communication on Internet, which while possible, is too dynamic and doesn't allow appropriate reflection and interaction of leaders and constituents.

The Zeitgeist—the Supreme Governor

Zeitgeist is a German word that Webster defines as: "The spirit of the time; the general intellectual and moral state or the trend of the culture and taste characteristic of an era."[45] That is, the Zeitgeist is a blend of the prevailing intellectual factors (the factual, scientific world of "What Is") and moral factors (the opinions, values, ethics, and world of "What Ought To Be")—at a point in time. This organizational and societal consensus at a point in time is the source of moral authority and in turn is the supreme governor and a force capable of transcending legal authority when encountered. The interactive and iterative organizational and societal processes leading toward consensus thus provide a principal social force sufficiently strong to govern spontaneously. Such processes in an organization provide the moral authority necessary to govern while assuring the spontaneous collaboration of people toward legitimate organizational objectives, responsibly advocated by leaders.

Today in these times of tension and fast-moving events in our communities, states, nation, and the world, the problem in groups, organizations, communities, institutions, societies, and civilization itself is one of lack of technique and strategy. That is, *how* can we communicate ideas back and forth among individuals in peer groups so that through an interactive and iterative process a Zeitgeist will appear? This is a kind of jelling of opinions and ideas over time to achieve within a group or culture an individual and group awareness of organizational and societal consensus.

Administrative theory strives to conceptualize complex organizational human relationships. Studies indicate that when an individual or group is given a directive by a governor, the individual's or group's willingness to comply is directly proportional to the perception of the "suitability" of the directive by those governed. People collaborate when they perceive that a directive is suitable to their own and their organization's and society's purposes, i.e., in line with the Zeitgeist. People resist when they perceive a directive to be unsuitable.

Individuals will collaborate within broad zones of indifference to "legal" directives of their governors depending on their perception of the "fit" of the directive. If they perceive the legal directive to be unsuitable and against the Zeitgeist of the culture, they will resist or refuse to comply. This suggests that the Zeitgeist of the culture is itself a governor, in fact, is the supreme governor.

Again, the Zeitgeist of a culture is the source of moral authority. This is perhaps the only force that has the power to transcend or change all legal authority. This is true whenever moral authority confronts legal authority, either individually or corporately. Examples are when runaway children leave home because of perceived injustices, employees quit their jobs because of perceived inequities, and martyrs die for their causes. History is replete with the stories of individuals who in the exercise of their final, supreme, moral authority chose, in the most extreme examples, to martyr themselves to oppose tyranny or injustice as they perceived it. Other examples involve societies or groups that have rebelled or mutinied and exercised their final, supreme, moral authority to transcend the legal authority of political leaders and commanders over them. The American, French, Russian revolutions and others are such examples.

The founding fathers of this country, in perceiving the unsuitability of the directives from England, used their moral authority initially, and their military authority secondarily, to transcend and change the legal authority of the King. Following the turbulent periods after World War II, the people of France used their moral authority to change the legal authority of their constitutions several times as they perceived such changes were needed. Countless revolutions and uprisings in country after country through the years attest to the same Zeitgeist administrative principle.

Perhaps a hypothetical analogy will help illustrate the importance of the Zeitgeist of the culture as the source of moral authority and as the supreme governor. Assume that a military superior gives a command, "Shoot that man." What the subordinate would do in the next moment would depend upon his perception as to the suitability of the command against his own beliefs and that of his perception of the belief of his culture, the Zeitgeist. If he perceived an enemy soldier approaching him and his superior with a gun, intent to kill, and in a war setting, he would willingly cooperate and shoot instantly. An observer of the incident might report under oath in a courtroom, "The subordinate responded instantly, without thinking, and in blind obedience to the command and authority of his superior, shot and killed the intruder." We can all understand why such a statement might be made by an observer based upon direct personal observation that most people might agree was truthful. But the observer was wrong.

What actually happened was that first the soldier heard the command, then perceived its compatibility to his own beliefs and to the Zeitgeist of the culture of which he was a part, and then he shot the enemy—all in an instantaneous response. But if the perception of the subordinate had been different, for example, if he had perceived a man sitting before him, unarmed, tied to a chair, not threatening him or his superior, and in a peacetime setting, he would not have complied, i.e., not have collaborated nor given his authority to be governed by his superior even though he had a legal responsibility to do so. In this example, if the last condition were changed, that is, the incident occurred in a wartime setting, the subordinate might comply reluctantly, though most, if not all, would still refuse to comply with the "legal" command. In a more modern setting, assume that protesting students or citizens were unarmed and peaceably demonstrating, and that a command was given by political leaders to police or soldiers to "club them" or "shoot them." What would happen then would depend on the perceptions of the individual rank and file police or soldiers as to the suitability of the command. Soldiers and police cannot always be depended upon to follow "orders" if they are perceived as inappropriate or illegal by those expected to carry out the command. Thus, directives to subordinates and subsequent responses are related to the subordinates' perceptions of the "situational ethic" at the moment as defined by the Zeitgeist.

Though the subordinate had a legal responsibility to comply with the command of the superior who, in turn, was backed by the sovereignty of the state itself, the source of legal authority, the subordinate invoked his personal moral authority to transcend the legal command. If the subordinate's perception of the Zeitgeist, the supreme governor, is correct, he will be vindicated and the superior will be charged with giving an illegal command. If the subordinate's perception of the Zeitgeist is incorrect, he will be charged with disobeying orders. In either case *it is ultimately the*

Zeitgeist of the culture that provides the final moral standard to judge the proper course to follow. Whoever misjudges the Zeitgeist will suffer the consequences.

The tragic drama and final conclusion of the My Lai massacre and Army Lt. William L. Calley, Jr. in the Viet Nam War is an example. The trial of Lt. Col. Oliver North, Admiral Poindexter, and others in the Iran/Contra affair is another. The Zeitgeist of our culture highly influenced the final disposition of their charges. Another example, but on a larger scale, is the indictment of nine generals and admirals for the kidnapping, torturing, and killing of thousands of people during the "dirty war" against leftists in Argentina in the1970s. These military leaders made up three successive three-man juntas that ruled Argentina until President Raul Alfonsin's civilian government was elected in 1983 ending nearly eight years of military rule. Elsewhere, the verdict may not be in yet: history will be the final judge whether the students in China or the political leadership in China correctly gauged the Zeitgeist during the 1989 student dissent movement which resulted in military suppression and the Tiananmen Square massacre.

Another case in point is from a report from Prague, Czechoslovakia reported by the New York Times on November 27, 1989 concerning "another cheering rally of 500,000 people, who continued to demand democratic changes." The report concluded:

"In one of the most unexpected developments today, three members of the motorized police corps that clubbed demonstrators on Nov. 17 gave an emotional apology to the mass demonstration. 'I want to express profound apology that our leaders set us against the people of our own country,' said Ludwig Pinc, a police lieutenant. 'We want to accept the outstretched hand of students.' He said the police faced strict punishment if they did not follow orders, and he added that many police officers favored the call for democracy. 'We all can't be thrown into the same sack,'" Mr. Pinc said.[46]

A knowledge of the Zeitgeist, the supreme governor of a culture, therefore, is essential for both subordinates and superiors. It is essential for subordinates, for their very survival, to be able to predict the behavior of their governors and people in their culture and guide their own actions accordingly. It is essential for a superior for exactly the same reason, and also to know *how* and *when* to give directives that will be willingly (even enthusiastically) followed.

While the Zeitgeist of a culture often appears slow to change (requiring generations at times), it is always in a process of dynamic change and is capable, especially in this day of mass communications, of changing quickly. It is doubtful, for example, that President Roosevelt's request for a declaration of war against Japan and Germany would have found the nearly universal acceptance and authority that it did if it had been requested prior to the attack on Pearl Harbor. Another example was the dramatic change in public opinion that took place when President Truman sought election. Pollsters had predicted all along during the campaign that Governor Dewey would defeat President Truman. However, the American people changed their minds between the Friday before the election and Tuesday's election, and decided to retain President Truman. (See endnote for further details of this story.) [47]

Americans, and perhaps all societies, tend to be "culture bound" as a people and resist change. If we want maximum adaptability to cope with the stresses characteristic of this age in our governments, businesses, organizations, communities, churches and the like, we must experiment further and improve our knowledge of Zeitgeist Communication. Edmund Burke, a famous English 18th Century politician, demonstrated his awareness of the importance of this as follows:

"No men can act in effect who do not act in concert; no men can act in concert who do not act with confidence; no men can act in confidence who are not bound together with common opinions, common affections, and common interests."

When people lose touch with each other, as is so often the case today in big organizations, institutions, and nations, organizational chaos often follows. On the other hand, when people have a strong sense of participation, identification, and interaction with each other, organizational creativity, mental health, and effectiveness are enhanced. As a result, "social capital" is increased.

For these reasons, we refer to the Zeitgeist as the supreme governor. While the Zeitgeist is just a collection of ideas and opinions, *it is composed of the prevailing ideas and opinions.* Furthermore, its *vision* reflects the ways in which individuals, groups, organizations, institutions, societies, states, nations, or civilizations perceive themselves and toward which they ultimately move in a "self-fulfilling prophecy." Scientist Eldon Byrd said, "Thus, we are the creators of our own destiny rather than the victims of it." [48]

This organizational and societal consensus, this Zeitgeist, ranging from that within an individual up to that of civilization itself, is that from which we derive not only our laws but our constitutions as well. Our laws are merely a codification, an attempt to put into writing, what we must do as a people to conduct the public business. The Zeitgeist, the supreme governor, is really the prevailing ideas and beliefs of the people who comprise the culture from which the law itself is derived.

Apprehending the Zeitgeist

The best way for people to communicate with each other is face-to-face, eyeball-to-eyeball, which is the counseling relationship among human beings. This is not only a process where professionals counsel clients and provide therapy; everyone participates in this counseling process whenever one person talks with another. Far from being merely preparation for change, person-to-person communication *is dynamic change occurring itself.* But no individual today has the time and energy to talk with but a few of his or her peers in any but the smallest group or organization. At the same time that our population has grown, the culture has evolved to big meetings. And that's a problem.

The need of people everywhere today is to develop ways to communicate ideas and opinions about those ideas:

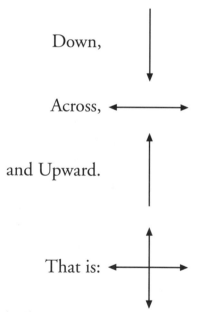

Down,

Across,

and Upward.

That is:

People in organizational, institutional, and societal contexts need to be enabled by their governors to communicate up, down, and across their organizational and societal structures. This needs to be done in interaction with their governors in order to make visible the functional leadership of the Zeitgeist, supreme governor of the culture. This must be accomplished by *symbolic dialogue* (in small groups of 4 to 12 persons) between leaders and constituents because they cannot meet physically. The dialogue is required so that constituents are enabled to contribute their opinions to the world around them. After all, it is their life, their organization, their society, their families, their children, their community, their taxes, their governments, and their future. They have a right to participate. Their participation provides the moral authority of people in the exercise of their moral responsibility in an ongoing process of organization, institution, and civilization building. How this can be done will be shown in Section Two of this book.

Zeitgeist Communication Defined

We are working to define a new field of communication that we have called Zeitgeist Communication. Zeitgeist Communication is defined as those dynamics concerned primarily with communicating ideas, and opinions about those ideas, across organizational and societal network structures and upward to the leaders/representatives. This is in contrast to most other communication media such as newspapers, radio, television, books, magazines, speeches, and sermons. They are all primarily, one-way, *downward*, communication systems. The aim of Zeitgeist Communication is to build viable feedback processes in organizations for people to apprehend the Zeitgeist.

The need of people everywhere in the world is to be able to make a positive and meaningful contribution to the decisions that affect their lives and futures, public and private. To do this, new organizational and societal contexts must be created by officials and leaders to enable people to make such contributions. People must consider these contexts to be meaningful also in their "life work" of civilization building. These new techniques must enable citizens (or organization members, constituents and the like) to participate meaningfully within their time and energy levels.

The Forum Foundation[49] has developed the Fast Forum® technique which uses an objective Opinionnaire® based on participation and administrative theory rather than an objective questionnaire based on statistical and mathematical theory. Different rules apply. The results of participant responses are presented in profile reports and can be summarized in a Viewspaper® when desired. A newspaper reports the news in the vitally important exercise of the people's rights of freedom of speech and of the press. On the other hand, profile and Viewspaper® reports communicate the views of a specific group of people participating, to themselves, to others interested, and to their organizational and societal leaders in the equally important exercise of their "Right to be Heard." This is a *symbolic dialogue* rather than a physical dialogue.[50]

All such communication is "advisory only" to organizational and societal officials who have the *legal* responsibility for decisions in our republic. However, organizational and societal members and citizens have the *moral* responsibility to participate with their views and opinions and can now do so using the Fast Forum® technique.

The Right to Be Heard

It is a sad state of affairs when those "in charge" (the people) feel they cannot be heard. No wonder so many organizations and institutions today (especially governments) flounder and appear leaderless. They are often perceptually detached from their "leader"—the people. Since this right to be heard was never enumerated or granted to the federal government by the Constitution, it is one of the implied rights still reserved to the people by the Ninth Amendment: *"The enumeration in the Constitution, of certain rights, shall not be construed to deny or disparage others retained by the people."* Thus, citizens need to be heard; they should not feel that the available political processes are inadequate and that their only recourse is to march in the streets, demonstrate, or worse yet, riot.

John W. Gardner stated, "the essence of participation theory is *not that everyone participate but that the right to participate viably is made available to everyone."* [51] Therefore, while it is not important that everyone participate, it *is* important that constituents be enabled to participate by their leaders if they wish to do so. For example, though we encourage everyone to vote in an election and it is desirable, that is not what is important. What is really important is that the viable opportunity to vote is made available to everyone.

The Zeitgeist Principle, a primary thesis of this book, proposes that a human organization will not work properly, the way most people would want their organization to function, unless ideas—and opinions about those ideas—flow downward from leaders, across networks among constituents, and back upward to leaders in a democratic, open, participative, reliable, viable, anonymous, routine, and objective communication system.

What is lacking in today's organizational, institutional, and cultural processes are: 1) general administrative theories to help conceptualize the new realities, 2) techniques of Many-To-Many Communication to implement the general administrative theories, and 3) computer programs to exploit the technology available that can be applied to some of our old organizational and societal problems. This is the search that inspired Buckminster Fuller, Marshall McCluhan, Peter Drucker, Rensis Likert and many others.

> *It may be too early to come to grips with 'technology' as a specific human and social dimension and as the way man does and makes,* writes Drucker. *I have, I realize, not gotten much beyond specific examples and generalities and certainly nowhere near a 'general theory;' neither of course have*

Bucky Fuller and Marshall McCluhan. The work on technology and culture is still to be done. [52]

What all of us have missed is Professor Elton Mayo's call for a new "type of knowledge."

How can humanity's capacity of spontaneous co-operation be restored? It is in this area that leadership is most required, a leadership that has nothing to do with political 'isms' or eloquent speeches. What is wanted is knowledge, a type of knowledge that has escaped us in 200 years of prosperous development: How to substitute human responsibility for futile strife and hatreds." [53]

The Natural Factors of Governance, Administration, and Communication

When organizations or institutions have a democratic, open, participative, reliable, viable, anonymous, routine, and objective feedback communication system that enables its members, constituents, or citizens to participate meaningfully within their time and energy levels with their opinions in interaction to queries from their leaders/ representatives in symbolic dialogue, three "natural" and favorable administrative dynamics spontaneously tend to occur.

First, diagnosis (the first step in the administrative process) of organizational and institutional problems is improved, leading to more effective decision-making in the future.

Second, learning (through the dynamics of the Socratic Method) is improved for individuals participating, the organization, and society, and all move toward being better able to solve system problems in the future.

Third, peace prospects are improved in organizations and institutions because democratic, open, participative, reliable, viable, anonymous, routine, and objective communication processes are therapeutic in nature and tend toward a reduction of tensions and a resolution of conflicts in the future.

There is an organizational concept that we have come to call the "natural factors." Whenever anyone organizes anything, he or she should try to utilize as many "natural factors" as possible. Natural factors might include tasks and role assignments which are considered by those participating as being, for example: fun, interesting, meaningful, constructive, inspiring, important, profitable, personally supporting, mentally healthful, physically healthful, prestigious, and power-giving. These are energy-giving rather than energy-depleting tasks and role assignments. Governors should also try to organize assignments in such a way that people are enabled to accomplish their tasks and roles spontaneously with a minimum of direction from superiors. Natural factors are important in achieving this kind of organizational climate. As we have said, the most desirable and efficient organizational and cultural climates are those in which people are self-motivated and self-controlled in constructive interdependence to the maximum extent possible.

People should be enabled to perform their organizational tasks and role assignments naturally, i.e., no one should have to tell people or leaders "what to do"; they should just tend to do it because it is the natural, spontaneous thing to do. It's like paddling a canoe. It's a lot easier if you plan your trip so that you find yourself going downstream, rather than find yourself trying to go upstream against a stiff current. There is a lot of difference in the expenditure of energy and the likelihood of success. In addition, the threat of disaster if you suddenly lose your paddle is significantly different.

These natural factors are performed by people for intrinsic personal reasons. Natural factors tend to provide *the organizational dynamics that move the organization spontaneously toward solving its problems and anticipating or adapting to changes in its internal or external environments.* Since administrative theory itself is defined as the search for those same dynamics, we have come full circle.

We believe that when an organization, institution, or society has a democratic, open, participative, reliable, viable, anonymous, routine, and objective communication system (and most organizations and institutions in our society and in the world today do not have such a system), natural favorable organizational dynamics occur. These tend to move the organization, institution, or society toward solving its problems, and anticipating or adapting to changes in its internal or external environment. At least three natural organizational dynamics occur in the presence of such a feedback communication system.

Diagnosis of Problems is Improved

When an organization establishes a routine feedback communication system, the data generated provide a diagnostic tool to decision making. Theoretically, better diagnosis of system and organizational problems leads to better theories and decisions in the administrative process of Diagnose, Theorize, Decide, Accomplish, and Review as defined earlier in the Administrative Process.

For example, when leaders of large organizations or bureaucracies have a reliable feedback communication system, they may perceive that their colleagues or constituents want to go through "Door A" on some issue. The leaders may know, however, through their knowledge or expertise, that the better course of action is through "Door B." This is an organizational dysfunction, an imbalance between perceptions of leaders and constituents; it happens frequently in organizations. Since most leaders have no feedback communication system, they often make decisions based only on their own perceptions of the "facts." When this happens, there is often organizational turmoil, because that may not be the way their constituents see the problem at all. (It should be noted that often the "facts" as perceived by leaders are correct. Leaders usually have more reliable data on which to base a decision than others, since they occupy a "focal point of information" in the organization in which other people funnel them information.)

Most officials and leaders of organizations are responsible and are trying to do a good job as they see it. When leaders have an adequate feedback system, they perceive the dysfunction earlier and react naturally and spontaneously, by bringing their rationale to their colleagues or constituents. Why? Because from their point of view, their people are "misinformed" and "don't have the facts," so, being responsible leaders, they issue a press release, or a report, or they just go out and talk to their people. After a period of time, subsequent feedback will show one of two possibilities, for purposes of this explanation. First, it may show that the people want to go through "Door B," where the leaders wanted to go in the first place. That is, theoretically, the leaders conveyed their rationales to their people, and their people agreed. Under our representative form of government, which is pervasive in both the public and private sectors, the leader then grabs the tactical, short-range "legal" lever of power, which he or she controls as "representative," and turns it and both the leader and his or her people then go through "Door B," and everyone is happy. But notice if the same leader had tried to take the same people through the same doorway at a point in time earlier than their "consciousness" or "consensus" or "Zeitgeist" would have indicated was appropriate, there would have been hostility and tensions released into the group because the people were not ready for that action at that point in time.

Thus a leader can make the right decision, based on the right facts, but apply it at the wrong time, and fail as grandly as if he or she had made the wrong decision, based on the wrong facts. Timing is a necessary ingredient of decision making in all organizations, and timing depends on feedback. Leaders must not only ask, "Is this the right decision, based on the right facts?" They must also ask, "Is this the right time for this decision?"

On the other hand, subsequent feedback may show that the people are still determined to go through "Door A." At this point, another "natural dynamic" occurs (natural in the sense that no one has to tell the leader; the leader will tend to do it "naturally"). The leader asks the question: "Did the people hear me?" If the judgment is "No," he or she merely tries again. Why? Because from the leader's point of view the people are still "misinformed" and "they don't have the facts." But if the answer is "Yes," the people know the issue and the rationale, but they have concluded they must go through "Door A," then the leader, like Julius Caesar, faces the Rubicon and has to make an irreversible commitment and decision. He or she has the tactical, short range, "legal" power to take people through "door B" where they don't want to go. *However, any leader of any organization, big or small, who tries to take people where they don't want to go, is treading on thin ice.* If the leader takes them through "door B" *under those conditions of perception* (i.e., the leader knows they don't want to go there, and the people know the leader knows they don't want to go there) then we call this phenomenon an act of "statesmanship." Then, if the leader is successful and everything works out just the way he or she predicted, people say, "Mr. or Ms. Leader, you were right, we were wrong. We didn't understand then, but we understand now. We forgive you for doing that which we opposed; you are still our leader. In fact we will honor you with the title—statesman or stateswoman."

But if the leader fails under those conditions of perception, it is a mark against the leader's record. If the leader is an elected official, come election time, the people weigh the good marks against the bad. They either remove the leader from office, or allow the leader to remain, based on their perception of his or her overall performance. If the leader is not an elected official, such as might be the case with a bishop or minister appointed over a group or congregation by others, then the Theory of Authority comes into play which says, "Those who govern derive their power from the consent of the governed." The way it works is: the leader calls a meeting, and the people don't come; the leader asks for service, and the people don't provide it; the leader asks for money, and the people don't give it. That is the way people control leaders over whom they apparently have no control. They merely remove their consent to be governed in which case the leader may soon become extinct symbolically as a leader, because he or she will have no followers. If the ineffective leader cannot be removed by the people, then organizational resistance increases at ever-mounting economic and social costs to the organization and its constituents.

Learning is Expanded

When communication processes in organizations are developed which enable individuals to answer questions, contribute their opinions, and respond to the ideas of their officials, leaders, and others, those individuals participating are thrust into the dynamics of the Socratic Method. It is a primary source of individual creativity. Creativity is a process of bringing some new idea into an individual's mind that wasn't there before. It is "learning."

The steps of the Socratic method are awareness, frustration, insight, and verification. In the process of pondering questions, and making decisions, the individual achieves insights and grows in his or her abilities and capacities and learns. The fourth step, verification, is a group effort. The individual asks, "Do my ideas work? Are they practical? How do they stack up against the thinking of other people?" In the words of religious educators Howard Ellis and Ted McEachern:

What is occurring is a process—a doing, specifically a process interrelating a person and his world, bringing new meaning into the human situation.[54]

Learning through the Socratic Method begins to answer the identity questions which face everyone. "Who am I? What is my role in life? Where do I fit in?" Every human being needs answers to these questions. Every human being who is interested in doing so should be permitted and encouraged to contribute his or her most precious resource, his or her own thinking, to help fashion everyone's world of today and tomorrow in an ongoing process of organization and civilization building.

Peace is Enhanced and Tensions are Reduced

Finally, as essential as it is to develop programming to enable organizations and society to improve diagnosis and learning, *this third dynamic may be of greatest importance.* When people are provided viable opportunities to participate in the decisions that affect their lives and future, contribute their ideas and opinions, respond to the ideas and opinions of others, and respond to the queries of their leaders/representatives toward the solution of those problems which interest and concern them, the process is therapeutic. The process tends to lead toward peace. First, it tends to reduce stress and create peace of mind for those individuals participating. In the last analysis, peace of mind is the final sanctuary of every person. If an individual can capture a little peace of mind in his or her day-to-day routine, the world isn't all that hostile. As more and more people in an organization achieve peace of mind, this leads to organizational peace. When more and more organizations achieve peace, this leads to institutional peace. And when more and more institutions achieve peace, humanity will finally achieve the peace of civilization itself. Therefore, the *social processes and technology themselves* that enable people to participate meaningfully with their thinking may well be more important than the *actual data* which are tabulated and reported. That is, *the knowledge by people that they are enabled by their leaders to participate meaningfully in the decisions that affect their lives, public and private, is therapeutic, reduces tensions, and leads to peace.* This is independent of the responses of the participants that might reveal consensus or no consensus on an issue.

Peace then is a process that springs upward, spontaneously, from groups of people, large and small, and is not truly a process that can be controlled from the top down by force or coercion. We know this is true because as soon as the force is removed under those conditions, there is no more semblance of peace. What the world is trying to achieve is the *spontaneous collaboration* of people toward their organizational and societal objectives. This is best achieved in a free, open, and democratic culture of which we are a part and toward which the world itself is naturally aspiring and progressing as it learns new theories and administrative styles and as civilization matures.

Participative processes then, like voting, are therapeutic. Occasionally some persons say, "The issues of today are so complex that the average American citizen cannot even understand the issues, let alone make intelligent decisions at the polls. Only officials and experts trained in the area can make these kinds of decisions." It might then follow that we could do away with the voting process and save all that money. But if we hadn't had a viable voting process, it is not likely that our nation would have survived the first 200 years. The democratic process is therapeutic and tends to lead toward peace. People who lose or whose candidate did not win in an election can accept their failure to "get their way" because they had a viable, fair, and equal chance to participate just like everyone else.

When we develop programming in our organizations and society that reduces stress and leads toward peace among those individuals participating, we are really improving individual mental health. When we develop programming which tends to improve the mental health of many individuals participating, we are really improving community mental health, i.e., we are improving the happiness of people. And happiness is one of the fundamental reasons we form governments everywhere (public and private)—for "life, liberty, and *the pursuit of happiness*." [55]

Therefore, programs designed to help people feel better about themselves, their roles in their organizations and society, and their relationships with their leaders in public and private organizations in pursuit of their own agenda, may be just as important as physical programs, such as roads, schools, public utilities, police protection, military security, and economic prosperity. These physical programs are "life and liberty" issues. Governments and organizations at all levels have been nearly obsessed with these issues since the founding of the nation over 200 years ago and perhaps rightly so. Beginning now and increasingly in the future, however, our nation and its people, as well as the other nations in the world and their people, must devote more time, energy, and resources toward those human problems which directly involve the "happiness" of people—the pursuit of which is one of their "inalienable rights" as enumerated in The Declaration of Independence in 1776. Webster defines an inalienable right as one that is, "Incapable of being alienated, surrendered, or transferred. That is inalienable which one cannot give away or dispose of even if one wishes." This then, is not only a right of American citizens as they sweep past their 200th year anniversary under the United States Constitution begun in 1787. We believe it to be also a declaration of the right of every citizen in the world whatever their present state of suppressed political rights may be!

All nations in the world, as they mature and grow in their political and societal contexts, will move from the authoritarian (or totalitarian) administrative style, which has been the predominant organizing principle of the past and present, to the participative processes of a free and democratic society. These are cultural processes that can only be guided; they cannot be stopped—in the United States or elsewhere. These cultural processes are moving naturally and dynamically everywhere in the world today. They need not be exported or forced on nations whose governments are closed at present and have not yet become democratic, because the processes are evolving in the world—*naturally!* [56]

Conclusion to Administrative Theories

The Power of Values

We have surveyed our principal Administrative Theories. The 10 theories are like vertebrae in the spinal column of civilization.

Civilization builders are like all builders. They need building materials as well as builders. They need a building blueprint or plan. They need energies and fuel to inspire, direct, and complete the process of building. *Values* provide direction, energy and inspiration for civilization builders.

Civilization builders are also *clarifiers of values.* By their work of clarifying citizens' values, they release civic energies. They mobilize political power from the people, galvanize the political arts, and awaken civic inspiration and determination. Values are the energy focal points of civic ethics and morality. They are the lights that prevent culture from being degrading and destructive. They build social capital. Values are the moral core or spine of the prevailing beliefs and opinions of individuals, groups, nations, and of civilization itself. They are like switches on a railroad.

Organizations from families to nations often experience moral crises in their lives. They find that together they are approaching a decision-making junction. At that moment, the cumulative effect of all the information and values held becomes operative. The moral perceptions of individuals, the consciousness of groups, the paradigm, meta-perspective, or Zeitgeist of civilization *(which is their "prophecy")* will determine the choice made and direction taken at every junction.

An organization that is evolving is, at any moment, the sum of its previous value-laden ("moral") choices and decisions. The sequence of value choices made by the organization over time determines its future—for an individual, group, or society. For they tend to be self-fulfilling. As scientist Elton Byrd said, "People and their institutions, therefore, are more the creators of their own destiny than the victims of it."[57]

Values are also a moral force; they tell us right from wrong. They derive from our experiences and from the very depths of our God spirit. They set the ethos, direction, and mood within which we live and interact with others. And like the tide, they prevail—in the end.

Values are also the source of moral authority for the individual. This, in turn, is the only force capable of transcending or changing all legal authority. As we stated before, this is true whenever moral authority confronts legal authority, individually or corporately, publicly or privately. This covers the range from a parent-child relationship to the affairs of the state in its relationship with its citizens. People will make sacrifices and endure great hardships for their values. They will fight for them. They will even die for them. *So authority does not lie within some leader. It does not lie within some office, title, task, knowledge, or with property or things. Rather, it's in all of us.* "Authority always lies with him to whom it applies …. Authority is just another way of talking about the willingness of people to submit to collaborative systems."[58]

Values are directly related to the identity questions of this century. *Who am I? Where do I fit in? What is my role in life?* As humanity evolves to a planetary consciousness and participates in community and civilization building, individuals within it strive to fulfill their needs. These needs have been described as hierarchical: physical, security, social, ego fulfilling, and self-actualizing (Abraham Maslow's "Hierarchy of Needs"). Maslow later postulated *meta-actualizing* which approaches a spiritual effort to raise humanity and civilization itself to its highest potential. This can be done through the institutions of government, business, economics, civic, and religious organizations. These institutions, in turn, require organization, direction, and administration.

Historically, the basic organizing principle of the human race in the past and present has been and still is the "authoritarian hierarchy," i.e., (A>B>C>D>... etc.) *authoritarianism and dictatorships;* it provides no checks or balances in governance and minimum societal incentives. Our research indicates that the basic organizing principle of the human race in the future will be the "participative heterarchy," i.e., (A>B>C>A) *freedom and democracy,* i.e, (Administrators over Bureaucrats over Citizens over <u>A</u>dministrators); it provides checks and balances in governance and maximum societal incentives. The organizational question of the century may well be: *How* can we move from the closed, hierarchical, authoritarian administrative style of the past and present to the open, heterarchical, participative administrative style of the emerging future? Values are at the heart of that search! And every individual in civilization today must answer the implied question that has been posed to every citizen in every age: *"Am I going to be a part of the problem, or am I going to be a part of the solution to humanity's spiritual quest for a better future?"* This is effected by the individual's response to these questions: "What are my values today, and which civic, corporate, organizational, and societal choices will I make today for the future?" Civilization builders are those who have asked themselves searchingly, "What do I really think is 'the Good Society'? What would be the Ideal Society?" From this reflection comes the associated insight: "What would be the best imaginable citizen for the world today?" And, "Am I such a person? If not, why not?"

Most nations in the world today have discovered the truth of market forces. They have found that private property ownership inspires civic effort. We believe that the free enterprise system energizes social change and healing. Coupled with a viable democracy as its political base, free enterprise best provides the incentives to individuals to work and produce goods and services to share in their society. The centralism of communist totalitarian states has a critical, and, it turns out, fatal problem at the production end. It is unable to generate such incentives. It is unable to manage the complexity of production that a market economy can.

The way is dimly seen, but it seems to us that today the following areas in the Behavioral Sciences are of key interest to the solution of these problems:

Creativity

Leadership

Followership (followers *do* make constructive contributions to organizations)

Conflict Resolution

Fact Finding

Attitude/Opinion Formation

Individual Responsibility

Individual Growth and Development

Synergy

Teamwork

Empowerment

Organizational Effectiveness

Organization Development

Good Government

Civilization Building.

It is important to note that all of the above concepts rest on communication! And communication itself rests on *feedback systems and iterations of communication*. We think the required communication can be best achieved in the future through use of Many-To-Many Communication technology (how) in concert with new understandings of administrative theory (why) which are emerging in the world.

It all has something to do also, we believe, with a "meme." This is a new word coined by Richard Dawkins, in his books *The Selfish Gene* (1976) and *The Blind Watch Maker* (1986). A "meme" is a derivative of the two words "memory" and "gene." It denotes that culture, society, and civilizations have their counterpart to that nugget of coded information at the cellular level called a "gene." [59]

One major function of a gene is to transmit biological information from one organism to another. A second major function is to carry forward the work of evolution through mutation, i.e., by change. Mutation is the way growth, novelty, and change express themselves in the gene.

Similarly, social ideas and values are carried forward into the future of a culture, society, and civilization by memes and mutated socially as the process of civilization building continues.

Next, we explore dynamics related to administrative theory which we have come recently to believe are significantly different. We believe they can properly be named— *civilization theory*.

2

. . . .

General
Civilization
Theories

New Emerging Theories of Civilization Building

Civilization does not just happen! It is a high achievement by a society; it is the result of vision and inspiration. Its design and its building take great shared effort and the focusing of political will. A civilization is the crowning result of efforts by a people to create a just, beautiful polity where "the Good Life" can be lived by every citizen. A civilization is the fruit of the best political philosophy made real by the best political science, nourished by the finest political arts.

A civilization is the expression of society's deepest desire—to be a social place worthy of loyalty and love. Civilization building is the deliberate, but inspired construction of a society where *life together* is a glorious adventure. It is the building of a social family, a people in the truest sense, who join in pursuit of marvelous shared ideals and who delight in happy achievements.

The *study* of civilization building is the domain of civilization theory. This sounds formidable, but is really only a formulation of the values and nature of civilization as a people see it at a moment in time. Civilization theory is an instrument like a pair of spectacles, designed to help us see our subject more clearly—and to improve it.

"Theories are made to be destroyed. Theories give birth to new knowledge, which cannot be encompassed by the parents. New theories are then needed to give this knowledge form and meaning. A theory is useful to a researcher because it gives a benchmark from which to start, not a mooring against which to rest."[60] Thus, theories are helpful even if subsequently proven incorrect; they are useful until we get a better theory.

Kurt Lewin believed that, *"There is nothing so practical as a good theory."* This is the insight that the best science gives to social scientists. Theories are not "right or wrong," they are "fertile or sterile," said Claude Bernard. Theories grow by experimental investigation like a fire grows by burning, or as a child grows through eating nutritious food. Like a child, too, theories grow through stages. A later version of a theory outgrows an earlier one as an adolescent displaces a child in the growth of the person.

These are images that are helpful for understanding our next three "Theories," namely the Unified Social Field Theory, Social Quantum Mechanics, and A Theory of Civilization.

We have completed our presentation of the ten constituent theories of administrative theory. In this concluding section to Section One, we offer three theories for civilization building. Collectively, the Unified Social Field Theory, Social Quantum Mechanics, and Theory of Civilization comprise our first complete formulation of a *General Theory of Civilization*. Such "general theories" are part of a great tradition in social science and the humanities. Authors and scholars such as Stuart C. Dodd published a social cosmology; Talcott Parsons published a theory of society; John Maynard Keynes gave to the world the *General Theory of Money, Interest and Employment*.

There is also a "populist" approach to scientific method. Philosophers of science such as Nicholas Maxwell teach that "experimental science" is a radically human activity and must therefore be governed by compassion and conducted by the populace as a whole, not only "specialists." This viewpoint fits well with our Unified Social Field Theory, which implies that citizenship should include some participation in the social life of the society and its governance. In ancient Periclean Athens, the citizens were expected to delight in the planning and conduct of the life of the city—art, science, and politics.

Administrative theory contributes to a general theory of civilization. It is also a part of it. New Administrative Theory and the General Theory of Civilization are young theories. That is, they are in their early stages. Our book is offered so that citizens can contribute to the definition of the values and the hopes, the testing, and the improvement of these theories.

The Civilization of Tomorrow is a matter for the Citizens of Today. Civilization building is the way the Civilization of Tomorrow can be envisioned and made real. Civilization Theory involves a community of civilization builders—the Citizens of Tomorrow. We invite you to study the following theories, and by testing them, to advance and refine them. Together we will reformulate and improve Civilization Theory, for it's a public possession; it belongs to the people. It is a part of government "of the people, by the people, and for the people."[61]

Field theory has a profound contribution to make to civilization theory. This was well stated by Margaret J. Wheatley:

> *The invisible influences that field theory exposes can help us manage other*
> *amorphous aspects of organizational life. For example, vision—organi-*

zational clarity about purpose and direction—is a wonderful candidate for field theory. We would start by recognizing that in creating a vision, we are creating a power, not a place; an influence, not a destination. Now we need to imagine ourselves as beacon towers of information [individuals], standing tall in the integrity of what we say, pulsing out congruent messages everywhere. We need all of us out there, stating, clarifying, reflecting, modeling, filling all of space with the messages we care about. If we do that, a powerful field develops—and with it, the wondrous capacity to organize into coherent, capable form.[62]

We next present three Civilization Theories involving macro-cultural dynamics based on our studies to this date. We hope that you, the reader, will find these ideas helpful, and will do what you can, where you now are in the world, to help in their consideration and refinement.

The Unified
Social Field Theory

If a theory used at the micro-level (the relationship among individuals) is accurate for an individual or organization, then it is equally valid at the macro-level.

The Unified Social Field Theory concerns the functioning of society as a whole. It is a theory that asserts the fundamental unity of all the constituent parts and levels of society. Thus, it expresses an important idea about society: If a theory used at the micro-level (i.e., the relationship between an individual and someone else) is accurate and valid in an organization, then it is equally valid at the macro level.

For example, the social dynamics operative in simple groups and organizations could also be spoken of for institutions and nations. If these dynamics subsequently prove out at a lower level, then they should be applicable at a higher level. In other words, if it works at the micro level, it will work at the macro level. It is just harder to test at that level. Therefore, *if it works locally, it will work globally.*

The content of the Unified Social Field Theory is a new expression of an old idea that "life is one."

Medievals called this the Great Chain of Being, and this idea is fundamental to sociology as a whole. Indeed, the Unified Social Field Theory seems to reinforce the "Mass-Time Triangle" cosmological model of our late colleague, Dr. Stuart C. Dodd (see Appendix J).[63] In this remarkable study, Dr. Dodd looked at the march of civilization through a mathematical lens. At one place in his writing, I (RJS) noticed a curious reference to "one to the third power." Since the cube of one is still one, I asked him what it meant.

"*What it means is unity,*" Dr. Dodd said. "*Unity is what we in the human race are moving toward in the world.*"

This brings up an interesting conundrum: If $1=1$ and 1^n power also equals one, then perhaps we who are of this world—past, present, and future—are each now and always have been and always will be *simultaneously* an *individual and* a *corporate* (i.e., a "societal") *one!* I call this the "Royal One" or the "Royal^1" because it indicates that the real sovereignty—ranging from a small group or a large nation—is in the people and not the King or the dictator or the leader, i.e. "royalty."

Ms. Lyn Fleury Lambert writes:

[If] 1=1 (God = God); 1³ =1 (Father, Son and Holy Spirit = God); 1ⁿᵗʰ = 1 (All that is, immanent and transcendent = God), [then] we might imagine that all of God's children, united by the love that is God, fulfill 'God's image.' The Bible tells us that 'God created man in his own image' and I imagine that that means mankind or humankind all together, not any man individually. [64]

Perhaps this is an insight that should be considered when people think about our next theory, just being introduced here now in this book, which we call *Social Quantum Mechanics* (SQM), in the future study of administrative theory, social science and—spirituality.

Social Quantum Mechanics (SQM)

Physics and social-theory have much in common; both deal with the subtle organization of multitudinous elements. In the case of matter, it exists simultaneously as individual particles and as waves. In the case of people, they exist *simultaneously* as 1) individuals and 2) corporate (i.e., societal) entities.

Todd Stedl at the University of Washington writes,

"In 1690 Christian Huygens theorized that light was composed of waves, while in 1704 Isaac Newton explained that light was made of tiny particles. Experiments supported each of their theories. However, neither a completely-particle theory nor a completely-wave theory could explain all of the phenomena associated with light! So scientists began to think of light as both a particle and a wave."[65]

Stephen Hawking writes, *"One of the greatest discoveries of the 20th Century has been quantum mechanics. It is a very complex branch of physics, which rivals relativity theory for its opposition to common sense and for its use of super-advanced mathematics."*[66]

But like all science it offers powerful imagery and conceptual apparatus for social science.

Quantum Mechanics deals with the behavior of "quanta" (packets) of matter at the sub-atomic level. It deals with probabilities and uncertain outcomes, but as a whole its math works, and inventions such as transistors and integrated circuits depend on it. Daniel Liderbach explains:

"The quantum theory of the emission of atomized packets of energy explains that electrons and other particles of matter behave, not in accord with "classical physics," but more subtly. Matter is envisioned as particles that are 'granular' or discontinuous. All physical matter, according to the early quantum physicists, is a collection of 'grains' of energy that are discontinuous and discrete."[67]

Liderbach further explains,

"But quantum physics also reveals a universe, which is cooperative! Particles can be observed to behave in a manner which suggests that they have made decisions based on decisions made by other particles."[68]

Matter is a sub-atomic dance of collaboration. This is true even if the sub-atomic particles are far apart. There is, as physicist David Bohm says, an "implicate order."[69]

Old-style (classical) physics and old-style sociology postulated atoms, or social atoms (people), which were separate individuals, but "social quantum mechanics" can be seen to require a more subtle account of the elements of society and their ways of interacting. Margaret Wheatley in her book *Leadership and the New Science* has described some of her ideas in field theory, but here we generalize to a theory of society. In this way we follow in the footsteps of our mentor Stuart C. Dodd. Dr. Dodd, whose writings on "cosmic sociology" and "social cosmology" (from a collection of over 200 articles published in learned journals)[70] created a rich interaction of

Cosmology and Sociology. Thus, "social quantum mechanics" is a direct descendant of his work.

The subject of physics is immense and varied, including energy, matter and its elements (particles, waves, fields, quanta etc.), the power of these physical ingredients of nature, and their applicability in the service of humanity. The subject of social theory is society and *its* elements (individuals, groups, fields, organizations, societies) and social power, human thinking, behavior and energy, and their constituent elements. We believe it is not too much of a stretch to see that *if there is an "implicate order" in the structure of matter, there may also be one at work in human society.* Indeed, author A. Simmons writes:

"Dialogue is a process through which we shift our minds and thoughts from a particle state to a wave state. Just as light can be both particle and wave, so can our thoughts. As long as thoughts act like distinct particles, there is no flow. Our minds are separate and disconnected. Shifting to a wave state allows a group to find a frequency through which they can communicate. Getting on the same wavelength is the goal. Our words make implicit thoughts explicit."[71] (Communicating in this new "wave state" is described later in Section Two of this book about Zeitgeist Communication and in explaining our new terms of "Symbolic Dialogue" and "Social Audits.")

Indeed, according to our theory of Social Quantum Mechanics, humankind is *simultaneously* both separate and orchestrated; we literally "act in concert." We further believe that the *Zeitgeist* (the "Spirit-of-the-Time") is the *conductor* of this temporal orchestra; the *musicians* are both the elected and duly appointed leaders, i.e., the "chiefs of state" of society, public and private; and *those who listen,* i.e., the *audiences,* are the public, constituents, and members. Their *reactions,* at all organizational levels—small and large—further shape the *Zeitgeist* in a purposeful, harmonic, social melody in a "symphonic fusion and rhythmic orchestration"[72] of *civilization building* subsequently effected through the dynamics of the self-fulfilling prophecy.

The result of this societal metaphorical concert? A working democracy with improved organizational, community, and societal mental health, and an expansion of *"social capital"—all leading toward a sustainable world community that we call— CIVILIZATION!*[73]

For some, societal improvement is about improving the individual's performance in society—through improved education, more personal responsibility, a greater emphasis on individual morality and the like. By their philosophy, the real need is for greater cooperation and community building from *within* every person. The result— *better persons.*

For others, the real problem for societal improvement is organizational. We need better functioning organizations and institutions, both public and private. The result—*better organizations*. We believe the truth is—*we need both simultaneously!*

David Bohm, theoretical physicist, writes:

"I think, then, that there is the possibility of the transformation of consciousness, both individually and collectively. It's important that it happen together—it's got to be both. And therefore this whole question—of communication and the ability to dialogue, the ability to participate in communication—is crucial."[74]

Social quantum mechanics is the social theory appropriate to civilization building as we are defining it. As quantum mechanics led to the modern world of electronics and all its benefits, so "social quantum mechanics," we suggest, can lead to the building of brilliantly luminous civilizations of the near and far future.[75]

But, many ask, "How can I do it? I'm just one person. I'm not rich, powerful, or influential. It's just not possible in this big, impersonal world of insurmountable problems for me to count. I give up."

Perhaps some individuals will give up, but the human race in the world can not, should not, and we believe—will not give up on the social, technical, and economic problems of our day. *There is a way to be counted equally as individual "quanta" and simultaneously as participants in organizational and group relationship-webs. That way is to use Many-To-Many communication, the Fast Forum® Technique, and symbolic dialogue between leaders and people to create a vision of the future that* OUGHT TO BE, *i.e., "ethics."*

There is a name for the process—it is called "politics." But in this case the politicians and bureaucrats in our republic will have helped frame the larger social problems faced in common by all. Out of this routine interaction primarily by "chiefs of state" with their constituents in an on-going symbolic dialogue, a vision of the Zeitgeist, the "Spirit-of-the-Time" will emerge. Since the Zeitgeist is also the "Supreme Governor," political leaders and bureaucrats should tend naturally to develop regulations and laws consistent with the common vision; to do otherwise would entail political risk for them. If they feel the people "don't have the facts," (which is often the case) they will try to bring new information to the people. This kind of effort is a "natural factor" in action.

Yet our elected or appointed leaders will continue to make the legal and policy decisions as they now do because we live in a republic with representative government—not a pure democracy. Leaders everywhere, political and non-political, will have ample opportunity to exercise their statesmanship when they feel it is required.

It is just that they should now do it in open communication with their constituents. Better governing and "following" should result, with "authority" flowing strongly from the people in support of their political, economic, educational, religious, and cultural leaders, with a reduction of social and organizational tensions, greater social and economic efficiency, and an increase in happiness! So, again, we will then have come full circle, as *happiness* is one of the reasons we form *all* "governments," public and private—*for Life, Liberty, and the Pursuit of Happiness!*

Open Societies: A Strategy for Peace in the World

The best way for people to communicate with each other is face-to-face, eyeball-to-eyeball, which is merely the counseling relationship among human beings. Everyone participates in this process whenever he or she talks (and thus counsels) with another person. Far from being merely preparation for change, "it is dynamic change occurring itself," according to Howard Ellis and Ted McEachern. [76]

But we face a problem in logistics. No one individual has the time or the physical capability to talk with but a few of one's peers in any but the smallest group or organization. At this stage of mankind's technological development, the best answer seems to be to utilize new computer and scanning communication technology to "talk" to each other "symbolically" and on paper so that people in small groups of four to twelve, ideally without limitation as to numbers overall, can interact with each other. This will be an intellectual and rational experience in an on-going, problem-solving, creative-thinking, future-oriented, social-process approach. **This process will be humanizing and self-actualizing, even meta-actualizing, and an activity bringing dignity and relevancy to people presently lost anonymously in the vastness of large organizational, religious, and societal hinterlands.**

Similarly, George Soros, international financier and philanthropist, writes:

> *Collective decisions cannot be based on the dictates of reason; yet we cannot do without collective decisions. We need the rule of law exactly because we cannot be sure what is right and wrong. We need institutions that recognize their own fallibility and provide a mechanism for correcting their own mistakes .... Why should we accept open society as an ideal? The answer should be obvious by now. We cannot live as isolated individuals. As market participants, we serve our self-interest, but it does not serve our self-interest to be nothing but market participants. We need to be concerned with the society in which we live, and when it comes to*

collective decisions we ought to be guided by the interests of society as a whole rather than our narrow self-interest. The aggregation of narrow self-interests through the market mechanism brings unintended adverse consequences ... [p. 96].

Democracy is supposed to provide a mechanism for making collective decisions that serve the best interests of the community. It is meant to achieve the same objective for collective decision-making as the market mechanism does for individual decision-making ... [p. 200].

We need a worldwide alliance of democratic countries that cooperates in promoting the principles of open society. [p. 232][77]

We wholeheartedly agree.

As human beings exercise and use their greatest human capacity, their ability to think, against the foils of real organizational and societal problems by personally participating in the clarification of the Zeitgeist, they will learn. This is done through the dynamics of the Socratic Method, the Theory of Learning. At the same time in the process, persons participating in this counseling process become "new persons," psychologically speaking, and contribute to their own happiness, to improved morale, esprit de corps, individual and thus community mental health. In effect, the process is therapeutic and leads to peace—it leads to peace of mind for the individual participating, the final sanctuary for every person. If an individual can somehow capture a little peace of mind in his or her own daily routine, the world isn't all that hostile.

A Theory of Civilization

It is in the task of civilization building as a citizen that each person in the world finds his or her *true identity as a social being.* "Civilization is fundamentally spiritual, not material."[78] And the spiritual destiny of humankind is unity and love for each other!

When we talk of civilization building we mean *the dynamic, historical processes of human innovation and social evolution organized to improve the survivability of the human race and the success of the human species through its enlightened organizations and institutions.*

Author Jaideep Singh argues that: *"An enlightened organization is characterized by spiritual mission, unified intentionality, egalitarian hierarchy, situational leadership, harmonious teams, relational validation, self-determined self-actualization, entrepreneurial thrust, dynamic equilibrium, and symphonic fusion—the last attribute implying the rhythmic orchestration of all the above characteristics into the organizational way of life."*[79]

In our work-a-day world we are born, we are young, we are a student, we are a homemaker, we are employed or unemployed, or we are retired. Everyone participates and goes through these phases. But that constitutes our work-a-day world, which is a kind of "play" world in which we each play these roles. Before we enter that world, though, everyone is born into the "real" world as a citizen of the world, and has a task from birth until death. *That task is civilization building!*

We can be unemployed in the work-a-day world, but we can never be unemployed in our role as a citizen of the world. So, each of us—every last one of the now six billion people on this planet—is never truly unemployed or retired in the real sense of the word. Because from the day we are born to the day we die, we all have a singular, ongoing, inescapable responsibility: make civilization better!

Down through history, every individual has faced six questions:

"Who am I?"

"Where did I come from?"

"What is my role in life?"

"Where do I fit in?"

"Where am I going?"

"Where do I want to go?"

We believe that as humanity emerges from the Second Millennium, these six may turn out to have been the most important questions of the 20th Century. They are all spiritual questions. And of the six, the last—*Where do I want to go?*—implies the reciprocal question, *How can I get there?* which may turn out to be *the* organizational question of the Third Millennium for society itself in its quest for *civilization*.

So, according to our theory, it is in the task of civilization building as a citizen that each person in the world can find his or her true identity as a social being. This work, hopefully, will continue to take place within the theory of civilization that we are working to develop in the Forum Foundation and the Stuart C. Dodd Institute for Social Innovation here in Seattle and in Portland, Maine.[80] It is our hope that our readers will apply civilization theory imaginatively in their lives!

Zeitgeist Communication and Many-To-Many Communication technology (how to communicate) based on administrative and civilization theory from Section One (why we should communicate), will be the subject of Section Two, Technology Building, which follows.

II

Technology Building

3

. . . .

Many-To-Many Communication and Zeitgeist Communication

Section One of this book proposed a number of reasons why new and better social communication techniques are needed. Some of those reasons are:

Large meetings are costly, often frustrating, and require too much time, energy, and expense on the part of participants. We believe an alternative to many physical meetings is "symbolic dialogues" and "social audits" in which participants give their opinions and ideas through survey-like instruments.

Leaders of organizations need ways to tell their constituents what they, the leaders, are thinking and planning. Likewise, leaders need ways to hear what the constituents are thinking and wanting. Feedback systems that promote two-way communication between leaders and constituents can satisfy these one-to-many and many-to-one communication demands.

Since "the people" are the ultimate source of authority for government officials such as mayors, state governors, and statespersons, they, the people, need ways to communicate with their appointed and elected officials and vice versa. The wisdom of the people—individually as well as collectively—is a great wealth for society. But it is mostly neglected and wasted. We argued for periodic surveys of people's opinions and desires initiated by officials who would review and act upon the results when warranted. We proposed that people have a "right to be heard" by their elected and appointed leaders.

Responding to questions and problems requires thinking, which causes individuals to learn and grow. The more that people give their opinions and ideas, and respond to the opinions and ideas of others, the better. These Many-To-Many communication methods thrust large numbers of people into the Socratic Method of learning. This is one of history's proven learning techniques. We called for increased use of survey-like instruments on a wide variety of topics by a wide variety of audiences in order to benefit individuals and society alike.

We said that the "Zeitgeist" is the prevailing beliefs and opinions of a people at a point in time. It is the prevailing definition of "the truth" as they perceive it at a point in time. The Zeitgeist is also the source of moral authority, the bedrock upon which moral authority is derived. Finding ways to help people know the Zeitgeist and to understand its implications is a "good." We stated that there is a need for more people to contribute to defining the Zeitgeist so that a more accurate consensus of the truth can be built.

In this way the immediate ethical imperatives for a society are glimpsed. These imperatives give a vital direction to social evolution everywhere. They energize political change. They inspire leaders and cause ordinary people to become good, or even great, citizens.

In summary, we believe increased communication between and among people is good. The administrative theories introduced in Section One show the importance of communication processes for good governance, effective problem solving, conflict resolution, individual and community mental health, and civilization building.

Types of Communication Methods

So two questions need to be answered: What communication methods exist? What methods need further development? One way to think about the major types of communication methods is the following.

One-To-One Communication (Horizontal)

In this method, one individual communicates with another individual—face-to-face, by telephone, letter, e-mail, or whatever. Information and understanding are exchanged. The result of one-to-one communication is that each party gains a greater awareness of his or her own beliefs and opinions and the beliefs and opinions of the other party.

One-To-Many Communication (Downward)

In this method, one individual or organization communicates with many individuals—TV, face-to-face, by conference call, letters, e-mails or whatever. The result of one-to-many communication is that "the many" gain a greater awareness of the beliefs and opinions of "the one." Examples would be: a US President giving a "fireside chat," a press conference, or a State-of-the-Union Address to the nation on television; a company CEO making a video or audio tape for all the employees to view or hear; a politician giving a speech to an auditorium filled with voters, or a minister giving a sermon. This one-way communication can be effective for letting the many know what the one believes. Disadvantages are that the communicator does not know how the audience is reacting to his or her ideas, the audience may desire clarification on certain points but be unable to get it, and both parties may experience frustration due to the lack of a "response-ability" in this method, that is, lack of a feedback mechanism. Similarly and philosophically, other examples of "One-To-Many" communication are: newspapers, radio, television, magazines, books, lectures, speeches, sermons and the like which are all basically one-way, *downward*, communication *systems*.

Many-To-One Communication (Upward)

In this method, many individuals communicate with "the one," usually a "leader" — face-to-face, by petition, "walk-out," "sit-in," suggestion boxes, regular elections, or whatever. Many-to-one communications can reflect positive or negative sentiments. For example, a national hero gets a "ticker tape" parade, a factory manager experiences all employees walking off the job to protest perceived unsafe working conditions, or a recall petition is filed to remove a city's mayor. This one-way communication can be effective for letting "the one" know in general what "the many" believe. Disadvantages are that the method does not allow for nuances and subtleties of the sentiments to be well understood. There is limited ability for two-way interactive communication between the two parties.

Many-To-Many Communication (Horizontal and Upward)

In this method, many individuals communicate with many other individuals—face-to-face (in meetings or street confrontations), in "chat rooms," by surveys, opinion polls, boycotts, "bandwagons" (fads and fashions), or whatever. Many individuals are exchanging their opinions and ideas with many other individuals. This two-way communication method can effectively increase people's understanding of the prevailing views and opinions of a group or society (the Zeitgeist—"Spirit-of-the-Time"), increase individuals' perceptions that their ideas are being heard, increase leaders' understanding of what their constituents want, and raise society's awareness of desired future directions and goals. Disadvantages are that such communications can be costly in time and money, that good information gained through this method often goes unused, and that many cogent issues go unexplored. We have argued for the desirability of increasing Many-To-Many communication on topics of organizational functioning and citizen participation.

Improving Current Communication Methods

Our ideas about Many-To-Many communication and Zeitgeist Communication flow directly from the 10 administrative theories. If the theories are true, and we believe they are, they imply the need for improved communication processes and contexts and new techniques. Let's examine the "communication imperatives" inherent in the paraphrased administrative theories which follow.

The Basic Attitude in Civilization Building applies to all four basic communication methods—one-to-one, one-to-many, many-to-one, and many-to-many. Civility and civilization are built upon a foundation of respect and consideration for others' right to express their opinions and ideas in order to best protect one's own freedom to speak. The Basic Attitude must be present for effective communication to take place.

The Theory of Learning postulates that creativity and learning are enhanced when individuals respond to questions and problems posed to them. Participating in many-to-one and many-to-many communication opportunities increases learning, intelligence, creativity, and a sense of legitimate belonging in one's organizations and society.

The Theory of Leadership states that all people possess leadership qualities and the capacity for making greater contributions to organizations and institutions—if given the opportunity. The result will be greater organizational creativity and a tremendous increase in leadership capability. We believe these benefits result from increased many-to-one and many-to-many communication opportunities.

The Theory of Authority states that those who govern derive their power from the consent of the governed. Further, "the governed" can withhold their power if "the governor" violates their ideas of what is appropriate and right. To ensure that continued legitimate authority is exercised in organizations and societies, leaders should enable many-to-many communication between and among the constituents to gain clarity and consensus. Leaders should follow this up with many-to-one communication to the leader and one-to-many communication back from the leader.

The Theory of Politics states that all people are fundamentally equal, that progress comes through agreement, and that agreement can be best reached through compromise and collaboration. All four communications methods are involved in reaching agreements. As we said: "The principal way to reduce polarization in a political relationship is to increase interaction and improve communication between or among the participants and thus increase understanding." This will decrease conflict and misunderstanding while increasing wealth of many kinds.

The Self-Fulfilling Prophecy points to the important role of perceptions in determining the course of future actions. To obtain more accurate perceptions of reality and greater consensus on correct definitions of reality, increase one-to-many, many-to-one, and many-to-many communication in organizations and society.

The Administrative Process (a Definition) proposes that the steps in the administrative process are Diagnose, Theorize, Decide, Accomplish, and Review. When the people are allowed to make their opinions and ideas known through many-to-one communication and leaders make their plans and goals known through one-to-many communication, the administrative process becomes significantly more effective. We said: "Therefore, the discovery of new, vital, feedback communication techniques applicable in all human groups holds the key to the release of a fabulous amount of human creativity."

The Helping Professions (a Definition) emphasizes the importance of one-to-one communication in the helping/leading professions and shows the behaviors manifested by good helpers/leaders. This theory also contains implications for improved one-to-many communication.

The Zeitgeist Principle focuses on the importance of on-going communication feedback systems as a means to discover and communicate the prevailing beliefs and values of a human group to its leadership, i.e., the Zeitgeist—the supreme governor. Such feedback systems will typically include many-to-many, one-to-many, and many-to-one communication methods. We group all these feedback technologies under the label, Zeitgeist Communication, which is primarily concerned with communicating ideas and opinions about those ideas across and upward in organizations.

The Natural Factors theory states that when on-going feedback systems are operating well, good things happen: better decisions are made—naturally; learning, creativity, and leadership increase in organizations and institutions—naturally; legitimate authority flows to leaders—naturally; tensions and conflict are reduced while peace prospects are increased—naturally. These feedback systems rest primarily on many-to-many and many-to-one communication.

In summary, the Administrative Theories focus 1) on "the sovereignty" of individuals in a social context, 2) on the need to give all people a "voice" in contributing their thinking on matters of importance to them, and 3) a need to build better communication processes to allow the people's voices *to be heard* — all of which increases "social capital."[81] Administration is not about manipulating people, but about mining the intelligence, leadership, and wisdom of people by building "creative climates" and two-way feedback communication systems.

Zeitgeist Communication and the Fast Forum® Technique

An interest in testing and implementing the ten administrative theories led to the development of the concepts of Zeitgeist Communication and the Fast Forum® Technique.

Zeitgeist Communication is that field *primarily concerned* with communicating ideas, and opinions about those ideas, *across* and *upward* in organizations and society. This enables a process of *"symbolic dialogue"* between leaders/representatives and their constituents. It helps create the two-way feedback communication system that all organizations and institutions require to function properly. It brings "the people" into planning and decision-making processes. It gives "voice" to people's best thinking on matters that interest them.

The aim of Zeitgeist Communication is to build viable feedback processes in organizations and society so that people can understand the prevailing beliefs, values, and opinions of the time, the Zeitgeist. Knowing the Zeitgeist allows leaders to know what their constituents are thinking, allows constituents to know the degree of consensus on various topics, and informs everyone of the prevailing self-fulfilling prophesies held by the organization or society. Zeitgeist Communication is a form of Many-To-Many communication.

The Fast Forum® Technique is a technology based on an "approach" based on a conviction. The conviction is our belief that the world needs routine, two-way feedback systems to function better. The "approach" is based on: 1) participation theory (give people the opportunity but not the obligation to participate); 2) volunteerism (let people participate on matters of interest to them); and 3) symbolic dialogue (using iterations of survey-like instruments to discern people's opinions in related groups). The technology consists of a computer program to analyze survey results, a machine-scoreable response sheet or keying of data, a questionnaire format called an Opinionnaire®, and a computer generated database format utilizing computer profile reports which can be highlighted in a Viewspaper® if desired.

The Fast Forum® Technique is first and foremost a forum, that is, a marketplace where ideas are shared. We believe using the Fast Forum® Technique increases collective intelligence and awakens community synergy. Presenting one's opinions and ideas, and responding to others' opinions and ideas increases individual learning. Analyzing results of surveys increases one's understanding of the Zeitgeist. Analyzing responses of subgroups based on age, gender, ethnic group, and other demographics increases one's understanding of those groups, that is, it yields greater "Social Resolving Power." Communication between and among leaders and constituents creates a "symbolic dialogue." This in turn increases organizational commitment and clarifies organizational vision. This process assists in the formation of laws and regulations in the public sector and long-range planning in the private sector.

The Fast Forum® Technique involves a new groupware and socialware technology and methodology that in our organizations, institutions, and societies in the world can:

- Restore meaningful and constructive dialogue in organizations and society;
- Enable people to learn and grow in their abilities through the use of the Socratic Method;
- Allow all individuals who are interested to participate in the administrative process functions of Diagnose, Theorize, and Review;
- Project the ideas and opinions of individuals participating through feedback communications to their leaders and themselves;
- Produce printed attitudinal profile reports of participant opinions and attitudes for use in the public and private planning processes of governance;
- Reduce tensions, polarization, and destructive conflict among people by substituting human responsibility for futile strife and hatreds, thus moving toward peace among people in their roles as organizational members, constituents, and citizens.

Some special identifying features of the Fast Forum® Technique are: There are no Robert's Rules of Order, no motions, no amendments, no win-lose situations, no controversy, no arguments, no talking at the point of decision-making—thus there is no heat. Instead, there is just light, that is: swift, silent, rational, synaptic, mind-to-mind response to objective questions posed in writing—hence the name "Fast Forum."

In the next chapter, we present the foundations and mechanics of the Fast Forum® Technique in greater detail.

The Great Dilemma

Organizations that have large numbers of people, or are spread over large geographic areas, have a common problem. The problem is to balance the need to bring people together to discuss system problems as a whole, against the cost in time and money to do it. If people do not meet to discuss such system-wide issues and problems, they will not make the progress they should in their system as a whole. On the other hand, if people are continually uprooted and brought together for meetings, they may never be able to get their regular work done. This we have come to call "The Great Dilemma."

To a great extent, the use of internal organization computer networks to provide electronic mail and bulletin boards has helped the effort to think holistically. However, it has some problems, too. For one thing, people who are in the organization but outside the computer network cannot participate. Another and more potent problem, electronic mail and web sites are text-driven and as such it is easy to get "information overload." So much data and information becomes available that people, especially leaders who are usually at the focal point of information, often just cannot handle it all. While computers are high-tech, presently they are not always high-touch. Time will tell.

4

. . . .

The Fast Forum®
Technique
and How it Works

In *The Search for Enlightened Leadership, Applying New Administrative Theory*, (1996) Volume 1, the authors, Spady and Bell, stated that the need of people today everywhere in the world is to be able to make a positive and meaningful contribution to the decisions that affect their lives and futures, public and private. To do this, new organizational and societal contexts must be created to enable people to make such contributions. People must consider these contexts to be meaningful also in their "life work" of civilization building. Furthermore, new social measurement techniques must be created to serve in those contexts. These new techniques of organizational and societal processes must enable citizens (or organization members, constituents and the like) to participate meaningfully within their time and energy levels.

This has always been the goal toward which the Forum Foundation is working.

Further, we must discover new, vital feedback communication techniques that will facilitate this participation and release fabulous amounts of human creativity.

The Fast Forum® Technique was developed as a new, vital feedback communication technique. The Fast Forum® Technique (sometimes simply called Fast Forum) makes possible constructive, symbolic, connected, and collective dialogue, among public or private groups of any size, using optical scanning and computer technology.

From the beginning, it was the intention to design and make available a simple, inexpensive, grass-roots method of obtaining feedback by which governors, administrators, and other organizational planners could open up decision-making processes more to their colleagues and constituents. The goal of a feedback system of this kind is to create symbolic dialogues between and among leaders and members of organizations, institutions, and societies in order to make those institutions function better and to satisfy the needs of the people involved.

In this chapter, we describe the foundations of the Fast Forum® Technique and tell how it works.

Foundations

The Fast Forum® differs somewhat from other polling and survey methods. The differences are based on the theoretical and philosophical foundations that underlie the Fast Forum®. These foundations are: 1) Our Administrative Theories especially The Zeitgeist Principle and The Theory of Learning, 2) Participation Theory, 3) Mainstreaming, 4) Social Resolving Power, 5) Symbolic Dialogue, 6) The Polarization-Consensus Rating, and 7) Small Discussion Groups which include "Day-in-the-Sun" and "Future Molding Game" formats. A brief explanation of these foundations follows.

Administrative Theories

The Administrative Theories present a new paradigm for thinking about governance and authority in institutions. This new paradigm calls for significantly greater participation by members and citizens. Communication techniques designed to handle these increased participation requirements should be simple, systematic, inexpensive, and easy to use by grass-root organizations and citizen groups. It is all people can do everywhere to get a simple idea across and upward in organizations. What's lacking are communication tools that are for "the many" and not for "elites" only.

The Zeitgeist Principle argues for creating feedback systems so that governors and the governed can have "dialogues" on important issues. Again the need is for simple, inexpensive, "user friendly" tools that can be easily understood and implemented. For example, it is preferable to be able to develop useful, low key, routine surveys "in-house" without always requiring the use of outside experts who are frequently unavailable due to costs or time constraints. It's desirable to be able to present and analyze the results simply and informally so they can be easily understood by most people. It's desirable to be able to design valid surveys without the leader having to be an expert in random sampling and statistical analysis.

The Theory of Learning, based on the Socratic Method, proposes that people learn and grow when they make opinion choices and apply their own thinking to problems, questions, and ideas posed to them. In addition, they learn still more when they see feedback that shows how others think about the same issues. The needed communication tools would allow people to contribute their opinions and ideas as well as review the results in easy-to-understand formats.

Participation Theory

Participation Theory is our term for a combination of ideas underlying the Fast Forum®. The first idea relates to participation theory itself: The essence of participation theory is that "the right to participate viably is made available to everyone."[82] Not everyone will or must participate; but everyone must be enabled and has the right to do so if they wish. In a national presidential election, for example, not everyone will vote but all qualified persons who wish may do so. And the results are binding no matter what percentage of eligible voters actually voted. Extending the right to participate to all is an important foundation of the Fast Forum®.

A second idea related to participation theory is that the votes (and ideas) cast by the people who volunteer to participate *are important and count for something*. Specifically, there is *value* and *validity* in the opinions, ideas, and votes of those who offer their opinions, ideas and votes. In the election example, voters were the volunteers; they volunteered their time, energy, and votes for their candidates. Non-voters were non-volunteers; they declined the invitation to vote. The point here is that the opinions and ideas of those who volunteer (participate, contribute) their opinions and ideas constitute valuable information about what they think. Their social and political energies really matter.

Let us pause here for a brief comparison between participation theory and statistical theory.

There are different branches of statistics. Statistical *science* deals with the mathematical treatment of facts, usually facts summarized in numerical form. The point of such statistical summaries is to present a snapshot picture of activities in a group of items or people.

Statistical *theory* deals with the principles underlying the practice of statistical science. For example, statistical theorists make a clear distinction between *descriptive statistics* and *inferential statistics*. Descriptive statistics assembles mathematical facts about groups (sometimes called "populations" in a mathematical sense), and inferential statistics deals with analysis of the significance of the relationship between sets of data. These relationships might be difference, association, or correlation.

For example, one of the main goals of statistical science is to deduce, from the sample that we have, properties of the population from which the sample is drawn. If we have a million senior citizens in a small country, for example, we hope that by interviewing 100 of them we will learn something about the million. This hope rests on an assumption that is fundamental to statistical theory. This assumption is that broadly homogenous groups share many attributes.

So there is substantial overlap between participation theory and statistical theory. The participants in the Fast Forum provide information that is not only valuable, and valid for them, but is certain to have some significance as a representation of the large group to which they belong. The question of the exact "validity" in a mathematical sense of our data is not the central concern of participation theory; it is the task of the statistical theorists who work with the Fast Forum to gauge these fine points of statistical science. Participation Theory is concerned primarily to *activate* the participation of those who belong to a particular group, "population" or social category in which the Fast Forum® researchers are doing their work. Participation Theory is a theory of political energies and how to shift them from dormancy, apathy, repression, or suppression towards full expression.

This relates to a third idea underlying participation theory and the Fast Forum®: we are more interested in finding the thinking of the people who participated than we are in the thinking of "everyone" or "all people." We simply report the results of the participants as the thinking of the participants at that point in time. We (and they) make no claim that the resulting information represents anything other than what it is: their thought at that time. Is information from volunteers/participants valuable? Is it valid? We say definitely, "yes" to both questions.

People who volunteer and participate have something they want to say. These are the people who elect congresspersons every two years, a president every four years, and senators every six years in this country. These are the people who "vote with their pocketbooks" for Product A instead of Product B. These are the people who provide feedback to their governors about whether they are satisfied or dissatisfied with the way things are going and whether they will stay the course or vote with their feet and leave. Even though the information comes from participants/volunteers, we believe the information is valuable and valid. This belief is at the core of the Fast Forum® Technique.

At the same time, we certainly value and support efforts to discern the properties of statistical "universes" based on random sampling and statistical inference. These activities are important, valuable, valid. It's just that the Fast Forum® seeks to mine valuable information in accordance with the goals of participation theory rather than sampling theory.

Mainstreaming

Mainstreaming refers to activities that have "real-world" value and meaningfulness. The mainstreaming principle is: people willingly participate in activities that have mainstream value and avoid activities that have little or no mainstream value. If employees "perceive" and believe their political or organizational leaders really do not want their opinions, the employees may not give their opinions even if asked for them. If citizens believe an election is "rigged" they may refuse to vote. On the other hand, people willingly participate with their best thinking when they believe their efforts are *wanted by their leaders* and will be given real-world consideration to help in decision-making processes.

Social Resolving Power

Social Resolving Power refers to the fact that people's true beliefs about a topic become more clear as more and more individuals give their responses to a large number and variety of questions. It is similar to looking at the stars through a telescope that magnifies the field of study one thousand-fold, versus a pair of binoculars that magnifies the field of study one hundred-fold. Blurry, indistinguishable images are made clear; clarity and greater resolution result from using the more powerful lens. The Fast Forum® can analyze vast amounts of data and make the meaning of the data clearer. The Fast Forum® can analyze data from subgroups (e.g., males-females, old-young, ethnic family, geographic, political demographics, religious denominations, etc.) and make the meaning of the various subgroup data clearer. Furthermore, "compound searches" of data can be made, e.g., "How did teenagers in organization A in geographic district B in denomination C respond compared to everyone else?"

Symbolic Dialogue

"*Symbolic Dialogue*" refers to the fact that a "meeting of ideas" can take place through surveys and printed data feedback without the necessity of physical meetings. Symbolic Dialogue is one of our key terms. It has to be understood in easy stages:

- Symbolic Dialogue is *not* a physical dialogue of participants.
- Symbolic Dialogue does *not* mean dialogue about symbols!
- Symbolic Dialogue does *not* mean dialogue that symbolizes something else, except in this sense:
- Symbolic Dialogue *does* mean "dialogue" across a multitude of small groups, linked by a common theme or concern and a pooling of the total output of opinions and knowledge of the groups as a whole. Symbolic Dialogue occurs when printed reports are then returned showing total responses by gender, age, ethnic group and the like. It is like a multitude of separate but linked

conversations that are symbolic of a large meeting such as a Convention or a Town Meeting.

- Symbolic Dialogue *does* mean "dialogue" between a *governor*, e.g., a "Chief of State" (i.e., an elected *or* duly appointed public official or a corporate leader in the private sector), a parent, a teacher and the like, and the *governed*, e.g., citizens, children, students, organization members, and the like. This is so in two senses: 1) a number of Small Group discussions represent (symbolize) actual physical dialogue such as in old-style New England Town Hall Meetings, and 2) the Opinionnaire® and its resultant social data enact vital data exchange between the governor and the governed. The data exchange is in the form of first-order numerical counts, and second-order data such as percentages and the Polarization-Consensus Rating resulting in third-order analysis through "Social Resolving Power."

My (RJS) eldest son, John Spady, Director of Research for the Forum Foundation, just completed his Master of Science degree in Computer Science (Applied Information Management) and sums it up best:

It [symbolic dialogue] is the answers to the Opinionnaires®, from all multiple small group dialogues, analyzed by a computer program, reporting among others the Polarization-Consensus Rating and then returning a printed report to each small group participant, that constitutes the entire cycle of symbolic dialogue.[83]

John Spady's research documents that symbolic dialogues among large numbers of groups of people can impart as much understanding as physical, face-to-face dialogues among small groups.

The term "symbolic dialogue" is a creation of Spady and Bell (1998), and is defined by this researcher, and for this study, as a repeatable process where the values and opinions of numerous individuals from multiple small groups in independent dialogue are measured using an objective instrument such as an "Opinionnaire®" or a survey. Results of the measurement are analyzed by a computer program and represented for an observer as that of a single, and virtual, large group in dialogue. . . . This finding, which is graphically represented below, can be stated now as:

A small group in dialogue, and a (virtual) large group in symbolic dialogue, may share the same benefits of dialogue—while a large group [over 40], that is too large to dialogue as a single entity, may not.

In fact, we believe symbolic dialogues are preferable to physical meetings for a number of reasons.

The following table taken from John Spady's master's thesis lists the benefits of dialogue, according to the eight scholars studied, among three groups: "1) A small group in [physical dialogue], 2) a large group in [physical] dialogue [over 40 persons], and 3) a large group in symbolic dialogue [i.e., not meeting physically]."

Benefits of Dialogue Related to Three Categories of Interest

Benefits	Categories		
	1 A small group in dialogue	2 A large group in dialogue	3 A large group in symbolic dialogue
Develops coherence	√		√
A larger perspective	√		√
Sharing opinions without hostility	√		√
Sharing meaning among fundamentally different peoples	√		√
It works in the smallest of groups	√		√
Improved listening	√		√
The creation of a common reality	√		√
Its best use is its repeated use	√		√
Its meanings can be measured	√		√
Its ability to contain and flow meaning among people	√		√
Its explicit insight into collective tacit thoughts	√		√
Dangerous truths can be safely explored	√		√
The bigger it is, the better it is	√		√
It honors diversity	√		√

Thus, the Fast Forum® facilitates symbolic dialogues. It does so through the use of new social indicators which we have invented in the Forum Foundation and which are embedded in its proprietary computer program. These accurately measure opinions in easily understood profile reports. These can then be summarized and highlighted in a Viewspaper®, if desired, either simply or elaborately.

One of the earliest applications of "symbolic dialogue" was the Delphi Technique,[84] developed by Ted Gordon and Olaf Helmer and the Rand Corporation after World War II. The Delphi Technique was an exchange of ideas by having a panel of experts respond to their administrative leaders in three "waves" (or iterations) of survey questions. We have used some of its concepts in developing the Fast Forum® Technique.

Describing an early hypothetical Delphi project will clarify how the technique works. Government administrators needed to develop long range plans and budgets and make decisions for America's nuclear energy programs. But the administrators had minimal knowledge about the future of nuclear energy, its directions, and costs. Atomic scientists had the best knowledge, but they were scattered around the country, and sometimes they held widely differing opinions. Rather than call them to meet physically together, the administrators created a "meeting of the minds." A questionnaire was sent to the scientists/experts asking for their opinions on a variety of topics, such as how long they thought it would take to develop "technology X," or what facilities would be required to build "product Y." The Delphi administrator collated and summarized the responses and then prepared a second round of questions. Each expert then answered the second round of questions, which were collated and summarized by the Delphi administrator who then sent out a third round of questions. The scientists then responded to the third round of questions and their answers were collated and summarized by the Delphi administrator. At this point there was enough of a consensus on many questions. The administrators were able to draw up reliable future plans and effective budgets. The symbolic dialogue created by the Delphi Technique had produced satisfactory results at a fraction of the cost of holding physical meetings. The Delphi Technique has been applied successfully in the public and private sectors for many years.

We believe symbolic dialogue is a significant component of Many-To-Many Communication and Zeitgeist Communication, and we have made symbolic dialogue a key feature of the Fast Forum®.

The Polarization-Consensus Rating, (PC Rating™)

The Polarization-Consensus Rating was invented by Richard Spady in 1969 [85] and incorporated into the Fast Forum computer program in 1970. The PC Rating™ makes it easier to read and understand the results of large quantities of raw data.

The problem was that as the number of participants increased it became more difficult to interpret the meaning of their responses—the numbers were so vast one's mind could not easily comprehend them. We didn't want to use conventional statistical symbols such as standard deviation or variance because that would probably turn people off. The whole purpose of participation theory was to be able to communicate data back and forth between and among leaders and people. Everyone had to be able to understand the meaning of the data easily.

We reasoned that the most widely understood statistical symbol among non-technical people was the percentage; second to that was the arithmetic mean, the average. So we decided to report results using percentages, in addition to raw numbers. That way the size of the number of participants could vary widely, but the percentage of people answering Yes, No, or Abstain was always easy to calculate and report. In addition, we advanced the concept through the use of two percentages in juxtaposition to each other that was labeled the Polarization-Consensus Rating. [86]

The first number, the Polarization Rating, is a measure of the *weight* given a question by those participating in order to get a sense of the importance of the overall response to the question. It is the number of the people who were "polarized" and answered either Yes or No (excluding those who Abstained or Objected), divided by the total number of participants being tabulated, multiplied by 100. Thus a polarization rating of 100% means everyone participating answered Yes or No. A rating of 50% means half answered Yes or No. A rating of 0% means no one answered yes or no (which means everyone Abstained or Objected). The higher the percentage of polarization is, the more meaningful the answers will be.

The second number, the Consensus Rating, is the percent positive response of those who were polarized. It is a measure of the *agreement* for a given question or statement by those participating in order to get a quick sense of the overall consensus. It is the number of people who answered Yes, divided by the total number of participants who were polarized and answered Yes or No (excluding those who Abstained or Objected), multiplied by 100. Thus a consensus rating *above* 50% means the people answering favored the idea—up to 100% that means unanimously favorable. A rating *below* 50% means they were against the idea—down to zero that means they were unanimously against it. A rating of 50% means they were split, fifty-fifty. Thus, the Consensus Rating reflects the amount of agreement or consensus on a question and the amount of opposition—*simultaneously.*

For example, when 2000 people are asked if they agree or disagree with the value statement, "Seattle has a serious shortage of affordable housing," assume that 1500 choose "yes," 300 choose "no," and 200 choose to abstain. In percentages this would be 75% Yes, 15% No, and 10% Abstain.

The Polarization-Consensus Rating is calculated as follows. In this example 90% of the respondents were polarized (75% Yes, 15% No)—they took a stand on the item; and 10% (the Abstain votes) were not polarized. The Polarization Rating is thus 90%. In the example, 1800 people were polarized and 1500 of them voted Yes. Therefore the Consensus Rating is 83% [(1500/1800) x 100]. The Polarization-Consensus Rating is thus "90% — 83%" which by convention is reported as (90% — 83) and is read as: "90% had 83 consensus." This was done to reinforce the idea of the Consensus Rating as conveying two meanings simultaneously, i.e., "83 out of 100 answered yes," and thus "17 out of 100 answered no." The PC Rating enables people to quickly determine the importance (weight) of a question or statement (by experience we generally consider a Polarization Rating of 70% or higher as "good data"). The Consensus Rating encourages people to automatically think not only about the majority opinion but also simultaneously about the minority opinion. The Polarization-Consensus Rating neatly summarizes the most important information quickly, easily, and accurately.

From our experience the PC Rating provides more and better information compared to the use of percentages alone because the computer can rank all questions by polarization rating if desired. We consider those questions showing 70% or greater polarization to be "good data." In effect then, the four numbers (Yes, No, Abstain, and Object) are reduced to *one number*, the Consensus Rating, with a significant increase functionally in efficiency as a social indicator. If people feel they need all the information, it can be easily observed, but with experience one seldom looks beyond the PC Rating. The Consensus Rating is also a "fractal" as all the values of the raw data and percentages are contained in it as a single number.

It is for these reasons that we consider the Polarization-Consensus Rating one of the foundations of the Fast Forum® Technique.

Understanding the Polarization Rating, Consensus Rating, & PC Rating™

Polled Population = 100			
Yes		**No**	**Abstain +Object**
A		**B**	**C**
Results: 75		15	10

Polarization Rating $= \dfrac{A+B}{A+B+C} \times 100 = \dfrac{75+15}{75+15+10} \times 100 = 90\%$

Consensus Rating $= \dfrac{A}{A+B} \times 100 = \dfrac{75}{75+15} \times 100 = 83\%$ "yes"

                    (also 17% "no")

Polarization-Consensus Rating (PC Rating™) = (90% - 83)

           read as "90% had 83 consensus"

Small Group Discussions

Small group discussions are recommended as an integral part of the Fast Forum® process. While large meetings contain many liabilities and frustrations, small groups of four to twelve are ideal settings for discussing the content of an Opinionnaire® prior to completing the survey as individuals. In addition, small groups can meet anywhere and nearly anytime at the drop of a hat.

In a typical Fast Forum® program, a "convener" hosts (convenes) a small group of participants who are interested in the topic at hand. Some groups will meet on weekdays and some on weekends—whenever it is convenient for them during the window period designated. An audiotape (or video if preferred) from the "governor" presents the subject for discussion. Next, small groups discuss the issues then individuals complete an Opinionnaire®.

We have had great success with two small group discussion techniques—the "Day-in-the-Sun" and the "Future Molding Game."

Day-in-the-Sun

The Fast Forum® groupware technique, in most applications, uses small discussion groups that use "Day-in-the-Sun" to get discussion started in the small group.[87] Each person is invited to speak for up to two minutes as to his or her reaction to what has been presented in the tape. And the role of others in the group is to listen, not to find fault, not to criticize, not to comment, not to use body English, e.g., thumbs up or down showing approval or disapproval—but just to listen. The convener keeps time and limits speakers to two minutes each. The purpose is to keep things moving and give all an uninterrupted chance to present their ideas and opinions. After everyone, including the convener, has had an opportunity to have his or her "Day-in-the-Sun," an open discussion continues informally as the group considers questions about the ideas and reactions raised. The first administrative theory, The Basic Attitude, should always be observed. No one has to agree with anything said, but everyone should always respect another's right to say it.

The Future Molding Game

This configuration was invented by our late colleague Dr. Stuart C. Dodd, a professor emeritus of sociology at the University of Washington. It was demonstrated at the Evergreen Chapter of the World Future Society in Seattle in the early 1970s. Four persons lean forward in their chairs sitting almost kneecap to kneecap. Their heads are close together and they can talk—intimately. One could fill up a gymnasium with foursomes in this manner and it would still be quiet. But when larger numbers of people sit around tables, they usually have to raise their voices so that the person at the other end of the table can hear them. In a large room organized in this manner there can be a lot of noise that is distracting.

When two people talk to each other they are engaged in the "counseling relationship." It is not just preparation for change, *it is dynamic change occurring itself*.[88] They are what they were, psychologically speaking, plus their gain of new information that they receive in their dialogue together. They are new beings, psychologically speaking, after their dialogue.

Originally our experience and study suggested that 12 people was the upper limit of small discussion groups using "Day-in-the-Sun" to get started in dialogue. At first we felt the lower limit was eight, but then we decided that six was all right. Finally, we realized we were approaching Dodd's "Future Molding Game" of four persons, and that he was right. In fact *foursomes are imperative for adolescents* to effect Erik Erikson's theory of "Psycho-Social Moratoria."

These are the major foundations of the Fast Forum® Technique. Together they give the Fast Forum® its distinctive characteristics that set it apart from other polling/surveying techniques.

Components of the Fast Forum® Technique

Implementing the Fast Forum® is simple and straightforward. This section describes the components or elements of the technique. The next section describes a typical flow of events for Fast Forum® projects.

Recall that Zeitgeist Communication is primarily concerned with generating and communicating ideas, and opinions about those ideas across and upward in organizations and society. Such communication can create a symbolic dialogue between leaders/representatives and constituents when enabled by the leaders/representatives. The Fast Forum® Technique is designed to facilitate and enable such communication.

The following components of the technique will be examined next: 1) The computer program and machine-scannable response sheet, 2) The tabulation of data (general), 3) Keying of demographics and data, 4) Opinionnaire®, 5) Abstention and objection to the question, 6) Viewspaper®, 7) The formal clauses, 8) Response formats, 9) How to generate Opinionnaire® statements, and 10) Small group discussion methods.

Computer Program and Machine-Scannable Response Sheet

A computer program for analyzing data and reporting the results was developed in 1970 and modified a number of times since then. A machine-scannable response sheet also was developed. It costs only a few cents, but it allows a human being to interface directly with a machine—accurately, swiftly, and economically. With small groups using it in symbolic dialogue with political and organizational leaders, it's *low-tech but high-touch.*

Together these tools permit quick and efficient analysis of data, no matter how large the number of respondents. The response sheet, Form K, accommodates responses for up to 50 Opinionnaire® statements or questions and up to 15 demographic and psychographic variables. (Our most recent Form L sheet will accommodate up to 150 questions if needed using both sides of the response sheet. (See Appendix B.)

The computer program can perform simple and compound analyses based on demographic and psychographic variables of interest to the user. For example, "How did male and female participants respond who were, in their teens and 20's, living in King County in Washington state compare with those in other counties and with everyone else responding?" Literally there are millions of profile reports that could be generated from any specific data; as a practical matter only a few need be printed and distributed. Furthermore, the data generated can be posted on the Forum Foundation's website and any authorized person can massage the data and obtain their own profile reports for personal reference. For example, the annual conference directors or district superintendents of The United Methodist Church could generate reports comparing their conference or district or jurisdiction responses with others and the national total. The Forum Foundation is now designing this programming so it could be done automatically on line. The General Boards and agencies could do the same thing as could Bishops of the church. This kind of data and generated reports would empower parishioners and enable them to bring their theological relevancy to the level of the pew.

Tabulation of Data (General)

Participants in a Fast Forum® can record their responses in three ways. First, they can mark an Opinionnaire® directly which is then returned for key tabulation. Second, they can mark a Forum Foundation Reproducible Response Sheet (see example in Appendix C). This allows the response sheet to be returned for keying of the data and the participants to retain their Opinionnaires® for future reference. The convener of the group can make as many Reproducible Response Sheet copies as are needed for the group on short notice. Third, they can mark a Forum Foundation Machine-Scannable *Councilor*™ Response Sheet, which can be returned and scanned optically by machine by the Forum Foundation and the results tabulated by computer accurately, timely, and economically. Both the second and third ways listed allow the participants to keep a copy of the Opinionnaire® for personal reference to compare with overall results when returned, or they can allow the convener to display the questions from a transparency or to simply read an Opinionnaire® given to the group to reduce expenses if desired. The group's time, interest, and resources will determine the choice.

The machine-scannable forms are not reproducible on a copy machine, nor are they usually available from printers locally. Their timing marks and registers from the edge of the paper are critical and they require a special non-magnetic ink.[89] Data from reproducible response sheets are keyed either by the organization's communicator, e.g., in a church, or by the Forum Foundation for subsequent tabulation. Data from optically-scanned response sheets are scanned by the Forum Foundation.

Keying of Demographics and Data

User groups can tabulate their own response data using a computer. The data file is then transmitted to the Forum Foundation via E-mail on Internet or by diskette by U.S. mail for processing and return of profile reports generated. This process is the least expensive to the user groups and practical for normal purposes where fewer than 1,000 people are participating. (Students or communicators who wish to key data to be transmitted to the Forum Foundation, see Appendix F.)

Opinionnaire®

Today most people who look at a valid "Opinionnaire®" say, "Oh, that's a survey." Most people already think they know everything about surveys so they often drop the idea from their mind. But there are some significant differences between a "Questionnaire," which seldom allows abstentions to questions, and an Opinionnaire® which always allows abstentions and objections. Also, Fast Forum® reports always provide disclaimer, philosophy, and trailer clauses and report the polarization-consensus rating. These all are based on participation and administrative theory instead of statistical and mathematical theory which underlie objective, random-sample, and questionnaire survey instruments. There is a need to break through the stiffly resistant, stereotyped thinking of leaders and people to open up all to the new possibilities inherent in the new communication technology of Many-To-Many Communication which is emerging. One way to break through this resistance is to differentiate the processes, techniques, and theories in which questionnaires and Opinionnaires® differ from one another through their names.

The basic thrust of questions from a pollster using statistical theory is to question others about their opinions for his own or others' purposes. The basic thrust of questions from a leader using participation theory is to gain the opinions of constituents for better organizational or institutional decision-making while also building community, cooperation, "social capital," and improving community mental health within the constituency. Both approaches are valid and have their place.[90]

Instead of using random-sample objective questionnaires based on statistical and mathematical theory, The Fast Forum® groupware technique uses objective Opinionnaires® based on participation and administrative theory. Different rules apply as the Fast Forum® technique deals with the "statistical universe" and not a random sample. It is for this reason that the Forum Foundation has taken extra pains to differentiate between these two methods that equally provide valid social indicators.

The term, "Opinionnaire®" is a copyrighted and registered trademark of the Forum Foundation issued by the United States Patent Office. Trademarking is a very simple and effective method to let others know that these concepts are new, important, and different. The trademark "Opinionnaire®" can be used by others within the proper context of participation theory (but not statistical theory) with credit given to: "Forum Foundation, 4426 Second Ave. N.E., Seattle WA 98105-6191, www.ForumFoundation.org. Used by permission."[91]

Abstention and Objection to the Question

It is important that every objective question provide an opportunity for the individual responding to abstain if the person feels unable to respond because he or she is undecided, feels the need at that time for more information before deciding, or has another reason. An abstention is a valid response if it accurately records where that person is with that idea at that point in time. It is also a way for people to communicate to a leader posing the question that there might be a need for more information before making a decision, especially if the abstention rate is high. The effort is always to get as high a polarization rating as possible with the highest consensus rating before making decisions (normally a polarization rating of 70% or higher and a consensus rating above 66—2 out of 3 favoring). The leader who makes decisions where colleagues or constituents agree with a high consensus is on firm ground. As we said in the Theory of Leadership, the leader who makes decisions contrary to colleagues or constituent consensus is not on firm ground and is instead involved in acts of "statesmanship." This may or may not be appropriate in the long run; only time will tell.

In 1978, after eight years of research, a very slight technical change was made to the earlier Fast Forum® computer program and format of the profile reports. Again, while it was a very slight change to the computer program, it was a very great advancement in theory. The format of both the Opinionnaire® and the profile reports was changed to allow individuals participating to object to the wording of a question or statement if they felt that the wording was not clear or that a question or statement was misleading or inappropriately worded.

The problem stemmed from complaints by some persons who felt the questions were biased. They would say, "You can't use the data generated from that survey. The questions are loaded. They just beg the question. They are 'terrible,' and the like." Who was right? No one knew because it was a value judgment. The leader who prepares the questions and statements or collects them from others and places them before the total participants may think the questions or statements are highly appropriate. But if someone disagrees, who is right? It is a standoff, because it is a value judgment for both. It makes little difference if one has the expertise of a George Gallup and Louis Harris all rolled into one. The design of an objective instrument seldom evades some criticism like this; often, there is someone who complains.

Administrators and leaders are seldom trained in the preparation of objective surveys. They usually need help from an outside expert. The essential thing is that the leader (or staff in name of the leader), interact with his or her own constituents doing the best they can and not be reluctant to do so because he or she lacks the "expertise" to pose questions. The leader probably knows his or her own organizational problems and issues better than any outside expert would. To get around this problem, participants are permitted to object to any Opinionnaire® question posed to them. Now there is a difference.

If someone objects to the wording of a question, one can reply, "Well, let's see how the people who participated felt about that." If only four or five percent objected to the question challenged, one can place the criticism in its proper perspective, i.e., simply ignore it. But if one sees that a question has 20 or 25 percent of the participants objecting to it, one knows there is a problem. It is not necessary to be told. The response is not a random-sample based on statistical theory with a relationship between a pollster and people that is one-time and gone forever. Instead, usually the response is participatory and an ongoing feedback communication system. In the next iteration the defective question can be rephrased or additional questions submitted for further clarification. This can be continued until the administrator or leader reaches a point in his or her thinking and says, "There is no point in asking these people any more questions about this topic. We already know how they feel."

When that judgment is reached, then the objective of the program has been achieved because the Zeitgeist, the "Spirit-of-the-Time," has just been identified. It will not necessarily tell what is "right" or "wrong," but it will tell what those people participating *perceive* is right or wrong at that point in time. And the leader and group move forward to new areas of consideration.

Profile Reports and Viewspaper®

The Forum Foundation computer profile reports are designed to be complete reports showing titles, dates, organization, questions, data, legend, disclaimer, philosophy, and trailer clauses. Those profile reports selected can merely be reproduced, and distributed as might be appropriate. They are designed to stand-alone (see example in

REDMOND COMMUNITY FORUM   MAY 1992

VIEWSPAPER

TOPIC #4 YOUTH ISSUES

Letter from The Mayor

Dear Forum Participant,

I am very pleased to present to you the results of the Redmond Community Forum on Youth Issues. The large turnout of both adults and teens for this Forum demonstrates the importance we all attach to issues surrounding youth and their welfare.

At the City, we are renewing our efforts to find innovative and effective approaches to address the needs of our young citizens. An interdepartmental team has begun the task of developing a coordinated approach to issues affecting youth. The team is reviewing the results of this Forum, along with other sources of information to learn what issues Redmond citizens have identified as important.

I am proud of the level of commitment and involvement you have shown through your participation in this Forum, and I encourage you to maintain your interest in the affairs of our community. The next Forum will address "The Future of Redmond." I look forward to hearing from you through this and future Forums, and I hope you will invite your friends and neighbors to also join a Forum group. Working together, we will continue to make Redmond a community we can all feel proud of! Thank you for your help.

!YOUR VIEW COUNTS!

Rosemarie Ives

Rosemarie Ives, Mayor
City of Redmond

HIGHLIGHTS

*T*he Redmond Community Forum on Youth Issues was held from March 16 to April 3, 1992. 467 people participated and were surveyed through 34 community based groups and 7 high school classes. The following highlights were among the survey results:

◆ **Loosely structured activities** were favored by both youths and adults to address the recreational and leisure needs of teens. Youths felt "a place to hang out" would be the most important facility the City could provide. Dances, drop-in sports or other drop-in activities, and adventure trips (such as skiing or rafting) were seen as best addressing the needs of high school aged kids.

◆ **Business and community involvement** was endorsed by 97% of all participants. Personal involvement through mentoring programs and informal role model relationships was favored by many.

◆ **Teen center construction** was favored by three quarters of youth participants, and more than half of adult participants.

◆ **A City sponsored "Youth Commission"** was favored by nearly three quarters of youth and almost 90% of adult participants.

Complete analysis, a sample of the comments received, and a summary report of the answers to the Opinionnaire are included in this Viewspaper. A complete report, containing the answers to each question analyzed by each of the demographic variables, as well as copies of all written comments, has been presented to the Mayor, City Council members, and all Department heads, and is available for public inspection and copying at City Hall and the Library.

INSIDE:

Appendix D-3). They can also be summarized and highlighted in a Viewspaper if appropriate.

A newspaper is primarily a *feed-forward* communication instrument that reports news of events and the views and opinions of leaders, officials, etc. A "Viewspaper®" is just the reverse. It is a *feedback* communication instrument designed to report the views of people participating! A Viewspaper® is similar to an editorial statement by the people participating. A Viewspaper® can range from a one-sheet summary highlighting results of a forum to an elaborate stand-alone document for wide distribution and used over time as a reference. The previous page shows the cover sheet of a more elaborate stand-alone document completed by the City of Redmond in Washington State.

The concept of "Viewspaper®" is a social innovation in the field of journalism. I (RJS) coined the word "Viewspaper®" because of the need for a new term to describe a different kind of newspaper. I developed the Viewspaper® to emphasize that the results reflect the views and opinions of self-selected volunteers who wish to communicate with their fellow colleagues, citizens, organizational members, and the like.

The Viewspaper® is a vehicle for presenting results in a readable, interesting format. A Viewspaper® usually highlights important or surprising results, often contains a message from the initiator about next steps or future actions to be taken, and expresses the initiator's thanks to the participants.

See Appendix D-1 (also posted online at www.ForumFoundation.org/WUMBView9) for an example of a simple one-sheet, four-panel bulletin of a Viewspaper® completed in an evaluation of an early, experimental, nine-week national project involving a study of *The Book of Resolutions* of The United Methodist Church in 40 churches. The subjects studied included: Series Orientation, Authority in the Church, Families, Children, Aged, Health Care, Racism, Economic Justice, and Evaluation.

Significant learning and new insights occur when participants and others study profile reports and results highlighted in the Viewspaper®.

The Formal Clauses:

The Disclaimer Clause

Because we are involved in participation theory based on administrative theory and not in statistical theory based on mathematical theory, every profile report generated on the Fast Forum® computer program contains a disclaimer clause at the start that typically reads as follows:

The purpose of these informal reports is to communicate ideas, issues, and problems among people as a platform for future, meaningful discussions of concerns. Participants are assisted in becoming aware of their own beliefs as well as of those intellectual and moral beliefs of others—the Zeitgeist—"The Spirit-of-the-Time." The views and opinions expressed herein are those of the individuals who participated and do not necessarily represent the official views of the parent group or sponsoring organization. Nor will the views expressed necessarily represent those of the same participants at a later period of time; as humans we each have the ability to receive new information, consider it, and change.

The Forum Foundation

The Disclaimer Clause in effect frees people participating to speak because they speak only for themselves, which is every person's right. Thus, the data generated are 100% valid for those persons participating! The data generated are just as valid as letters sent to legislators and public officials. The data are just as valid as telephone messages, just as valid as personal meetings, and just as valid as information gathered in testimony at a public hearing, none of which is necessarily "statistically valid" and indicative of the values held by the public at large. It is also much easier to understand where people stand on issues of concern to them because the data can include demographics such as gender, age, ethnic families, geographic, legislative, and congressional districts, organizational departments, and the like which enable the "symbolic dialogue" to occur. As more and more people participate in the process, the data reports published just get better; they never get bigger. The process thus avoids the problem of "information overload" which is especially burdensome to leaders who must deal often with voluminous amounts of correspondence and thousands or more of constituents.

A Disclaimer Clause is always printed on every profile report generated by the Forum Foundation and released to users. Similarly, users should be careful, in turn, to disclaim the results to their colleagues or constituents to help avoid criticism by others who might be trying to find reasons to do so. Users should always print a Disclaimer Clause in any Viewspaper® they produce.

The use of the disclaimer clause is the key to being able to send the reports to others inside or outside the organization. For example, it permits reports to be used without the stilting, and perhaps even dehumanizing experience, of having to have the reports approved first by an administrative board, an executive committee, or anyone else. Such a requirement is an abridgment of the basic human rights of the people participating: freedom to assemble (symbolically), freedom of speech, freedom of the press, freedom to petition, and we believe, "*freedom to be heard.*" These are constitutional rights of every citizen; they apply in all contexts including government, business and industry, education, church, and community.

All such communication is *advisory only* to elected or appointed organizational and societal leaders i.e., "chiefs of state," who have the tactical, legal responsibility for decisions in our republic—a representative democracy. However, organizational and institutional members and citizens have an equally strategic moral responsibility as citizens to listen to their leaders and help their leaders and planners by participating with their thinking, e.g., their opinions, knowledge, and wisdom.

The Trailer Clause

The Fast Forum® computer program and profile reports always contain a trailer clause which provides an additional frame of reference for those participating and which typically reads as follows:

The Forum Foundation is a nonprofit educational-research corporation of Washington State. It conducts research in pure and applied social science—specifically in the field of Administrative Theory, which is a subset of Organization Development. The foundation is dedicated toward strengthening the democratic processes of our society through improved feedback communications from people. This Fast Forum® technique assists interested persons in our society and among its institutions and organizations to participate more meaningfully by expressing their individual opinions. Through written reports, as attached, these opinions assist those persons participating to illustrate to themselves, as well as to parent/ teacher/ school/ church/ business/ community, and government establishments, the values in which they believe. It is hoped that the overall communication process established will reduce apathy among people, improve community mental health, and assist in solving the human problems we face together in our society and world.

The Philosophy Clause

The Fast Forum® computer program and profile reports always contain a philosophy clause that provides an additional frame of reference for those participating and which typically reads as follows:

A creative organization or society is one that actively searches for solutions to its problems. The open exchange and discussion of ideas is the <u>mortar</u> that binds such a society together during this creative process. This exchange, in turn, leads naturally toward improved consensus, decision-making and spontaneous collaboration. Any group, organization, community, or society which inhibits the free movement of ideas of its members up, down, and across its organizational and societal structures (whether innocently or not) is *depriving itself of its greatest resource—human thought—and is in grave danger of being buried in history by an avalanche of the creativity of others.*

The Certification Clause

The Fast Forum® computer program and profile reports always contain a certification clause that provides an additional frame of reference for those participating and which typically reads as follows:

The data utilized in this report were submitted on individual Forum Foundation machine-scannable or other response sheets by the user organization and recorded by optical scanning or were keyed from Opinionnaires® provided by the Forum Foundation. The information tabulated by the Forum Foundation contained herein is certified correct barring unintentional errors.

The purpose of this clause is to acknowledge that the data are as accurate as possible under the processes being followed. The Forum Foundation tries its best to report accurate data, but cannot be responsible for inaccurate data supplied by others in the course of their participation in a project. Of course, keying data in itself, without verification, will have some errors; however, verification (like that required for bank transactions) is prohibitively expensive and, in this case, experience indicates that verification does not provide significant differences. The Fast Forum® computer program will abort if it detects keying errors over one half of one percent. The certification clause alerts all participants to accept the data within this context.

Response Formats

Several different response formats are available to users of Opinionnaires®. Depending on how your questions or statements are worded, one of the following formats should meet your needs nicely.

Yes/No/Abstain/Object

One good, simple, robust, understandable format uses the response categories Yes and No along with Abstain and Object. That looks like the following on the Opinionnaire® :

<u>Yes</u>   <u>No</u>   <u>Abstain</u>   <u>Object.</u>

A *Yes* means, "I agree completely with this statement or question." A *No* means, "I do not agree with this statement or question." An *Abstain* means, "I do not yet have an opinion on this statement," or, "I need more information," or, "I am not ready to answer at this time," etc. An *Object* means, "I object to this statement." Participants use the *Object* response when they dislike the wording, or the clarity, or the content or context of the statement or question.

Multiple-Choice

The standard multiple-choice question can also be used with two to five choices. This format looks like this on the Opinionnaire® : The following example has five choices.

Which is the best choice among the following proposals? 1) Proposal One, 2) Proposal Two, 3) Proposal Three, 4) Proposal Four, 5) Proposal Five. Abstain   Object.   Please select the one best choice.

End Anchors

A question can be posed with "End Anchors." For example, "How appropriate is this action to be taken now?" In this example "3" is the neutral position.

Not Appropriate   1   2   3   4   5   Highly Appropriate.   Abstain.   Object.

Likert Scale

The Likert Scale format is also clear, simple, and effective. This format looks like the following on an Opinionnaire®:

Strongly Agree   Agree   Undecided*   Disagree   Strongly Disagree   Abstain   Object

This format includes the Abstain and Object response choices and translates an Agree/Disagree choice into five options. The Likert format allows respondents to give more finely-grained answers and also conveys a clearer picture of how strongly people feel about an item. (*Or substitute Neutral if preferred.)

Converted Likert Scale

The final response format that can be presented in an Opinionnaire® is a special adaptation of the Likert Scale to use our Converted Polarization-Consensus Rating, (CPC Rating™). See Appendix E. This format looks like the following on the Opinionnaire®:

<u>Strongly Agree</u>   <u>Agree</u>   <u>Neutral</u>   <u>Disagree</u>   <u>Strongly Disagree</u>   <u>Abstain</u>   <u>Object</u>

How To Generate Opinionnaire Questions/Statements

Questions are formulated by leaders or staff and will end with a question mark. For example, "Do you favor adoption of this resolution?"

Statements on an Opinionnaire® are usually normative or declarative value sentences about an idea, policy, situation, event, or just about anything else. They state an opinion. Respondents are asked if they agree or disagree with the statements. They should be identified as coming from constituents or the leader. Here are some examples of opinion statements.

- I support the idea of building a third bridge across Seattle's Lake Washington.
- On balance, the annual Seafair Celebration is good for the City of Seattle.
- Seattle should not host more World Trade Organization conferences.
- I believe the City of X-Ville's Growth Management Plan is seriously flawed.
- I believe capital punishment is wrong.

It is important to make the questions and statements as clear, concise, and unbiased as possible. Good statements should be clear about what they are declaring. Good statements should refer to only one issue, not multiple issues in the same statement. Good statements should not be "loaded" either positively or negatively. Good statements avoid ambiguity, words with multiple meaning, jargon, and unfamiliar phrases.

Initiators of Opinionnaires® often have several topics on which they want information, such as (for a company): satisfaction with pay, satisfaction with benefits, evaluation of leadership, or understanding the company's strategic direction and the like. A good way to generate value statements for an Opinionnaire® is to have a small group "brainstorm" a large number of normative statements or questions about different facets of each broad topic. The leader and staff then choose the best items for each topic based on clarity, relevance, and understandability. These statements are arranged in logical order in the Opinionnaire®, i.e., they can be clustered into similar areas of concern, e.g., the nurturing community, the social community, the economic community, the political community, the ecumenical community and the like. It should be understood that the Fast Forum® is designed to be user-friendly. The leader does his or her best to articulate problems and suggest solutions, but if questions posed are not well done, participants can "object." And because everyone is involved with an ongoing feedback system (and not a one-time relationship as in random sampling), on the next iteration, poor questions can be rephrased until the leader gets it right. It works fine.

Small Group Discussions

As we said earlier, small group discussions related to Opinionnaire® statement topics are highly valued by participants, cause significant learning to occur, and energize the Fast Forum® process. We recommend including small group discussion opportunities whenever that is feasible. "The Future Molding Game" and the "Day-in-the-Sun®" have been shown to be effective in stimulating thoughtful discussions.

These are the main components of the Fast Forum® Technique. Over the years we have added and deleted components as we learned what worked and what didn't.

Flow of Events in the Fast Forum Technique

The Fast Forum® is used primarily to implement feedback systems in organizations, institutions, and societies. The Zeitgeist Principle introduced in Section 1 states:

To work most effectively, human organizations and institutions (from the smallest—the family, to the largest—civilization itself) require a functional feedback communication capability. Feedback systems are necessary in order to apprehend the Zeitgeist, the Spirit-of-the-Time. This is best accomplished in most organizations by a democratic, open, participative, reliable, viable, anonymous, routine, and objective feedback communication system. Few organizations, institutions, governments, and societies in the world today have such an envisioning system.

The Fast Forum® Technique represents our attempt to build a feedback communication system in the spirit of the Zeitgeist Principle. This section describes the flow of events of Fast Forum projects.

There are two starting points for the Fast Forum®, or ways that a Fast Forum® is initiated. These constitute the two basic contexts of the Fast Forum®. The first we call Top-Down; the second we call From-the-Ground-Up, i.e., "grassroots." An actual application might originate somewhere between these two extremes, or it might combine them.

In the Top-Down application a "governor" decides to investigate the people's (constituents or organization members) opinions on a subject. The governor wants—for whatever reason—to know the mind of the people on a topic. The governor wants a richer data set than might be achieved with a simple poll or survey, so uses the Fast Forum®. Whereas a plebiscite aims to know the mind of all the people on a vital subject, and a referendum polls them all in similar circumstances, the Fast Forum®

gets an in-depth reading of a set of all the people participating on whatever topics the governor chooses.

In the From-the-Ground-Up application of the Fast Forum®, an individual constituent (or small group of constituents) decides to ask the governor to investigate the people's (constituents or organization member) opinions on a subject. This "grass roots" application may occur when the constituents believe a governor does not know enough about the viewpoints held by the governor's constituents.

In both contexts the goal is to establish a feedback communication system between constituents and governors.

The generic model of the Top-Down application of the Fast Forum®, showing the "bare bones" structure of the process looks like the following.

Step 1. A Governor wants Information from Constituents and communicates that desire to Constituents.

Step 2. Governor produces an Opinionnaire®, gives to Constituents with supporting written and/or audio/visual documentation.

Step 3. Constituents meet in small groups of 4 to 12 persons, to listen to the tape, do Day-in-the-Sun, discuss the issues, answer Opinionnaire®, return Opinionnaires® to Governor.

Step 4. Governor tabulates Profile reports by various key categories showing percentage responses, analyzes data, prepares Viewspaper® if desired, and sends Profile Reports to Constituents in most cases.

Step 5. Governor studies Profile Reports for possible action. Constituents study Profile Reports as basis for gaining new knowledge of how others feel.

Step 6. The communication process continues routinely as might be required.

This is the basic structure of most Fast Forum® projects. Variations and embellishments are usually added, but the basic structure remains the same. In this model the Governor can be any leader/representative/planner—a plant manager, a governor, a county executive, a mayor, a school principal, a high school's student council, etc. The Information in this model can be on a variety of topics, sometimes topics of special interest to the governor and sometimes topics of special interest to the Constituents. The Constituents are always the constituents of the Governor, so that the process creates a communication link between governed and governor. The Opinionnaire® asks for Constituents' opinions on topics of interest. The Opinionnaire® is the vehicle for obtaining the desired Information.

The Profile Reports summarize the data and the major findings. The Profile Reports contain the Information the Governor wanted at the start of the process.

Here is an example of the actual flow of events from a Fast Forum® project with a city government that is reported in more detail in the next chapter. The Mayor and City Council of Redmond, Washington initiated a "Community Forum Program" to involve citizens in planning for the future of the city. Interested citizens were invited to participate through newspaper advertisements and public notices. The Mayor produced a video in which she thanked people for taking part in the project, and then introduced a narrator who conducted a guided tour of the city centered on the topic of "Growth Management." Assistance was provided by the locally licensed cable television company and others in the industry. Cassettes were distributed to people who volunteered to participate. The volunteers met in small groups in homes, libraries, public buildings, and workplaces. Each small group viewed the video tape, did Day-in-the-Sun, discussed the issues posed in the tape and supplementary materials, and then individuals completed their Opinionnaires®. The data were tabulated by the Forum Foundation. Profile reports were given to the Mayor's office. The Mayor's staff produced a Viewspaper® that was sent to each small group where its members met again to discuss the results.

Thirteen iterations of the Community Forum were conducted between 1990 and 1998 on topics related to the future of the city. Virtually everyone who participated strongly endorsed this simple, effective "Citizen Involvement" methodology.

In this example, the Mayor (Governor) wanted Information (citizen input on planning for the future) from Constituents (interested citizens) and obtained it through an Opinionnaire®. Additional features of this program included statements from the "Governor" (Mayor) on video introducing each topic, small group meetings of participants to discuss the topic before completing the Opinionnaire®, and group meetings to discuss the results. This is a very efficient and cost effective model for creating a symbolic dialogue between Governor and Constituents.

5

Examples
of Fast Forum
Projects

Selected Examples

I (RJS) developed the basic ideas and methodology for the Fast Forum Technique in 1969 during the Eastside Inter-Racial Clearing House project, described earlier in "My Personal Quest—Richard J. Spady's Story." Since that time we have conducted a number of Fast Forum projects and assisted others who wanted to use the method. Following are several examples illustrating how the Fast Forum works in actual practice.

Encouraging Dialogue and Reflection in a Church Denomination

During the American Bicentennial Celebration in 1976 one of the larger church denominations associated with the Church Council of Greater Seattle conducted a bicentennial program titled "Reaction, Reflection, and Response" to honor the nation's birthday. In my role as a member of the Church Council volunteer staff I (RJS) assisted them in the design of their program and generated their final Fast Forum profile reports.

The aim of the program was to get parishioners to reflect on various aspects of their faith such as education, worship, prayer, social concerns, ecumenical affairs, etc. and to engage in both a symbolic and actual dialogue with church leaders. Steps in the process were: 1) Parishioners completed an Opinionnaire®; 2) Volunteer parishioners met in discussion groups in their local churches to reflect on the results and develop recommendations for church leaders; 3) Parishioners met with church leaders in regional meetings to present their recommendations; and 4) Church leaders considered the feedback information and promised to respond to the ideas.

The process worked like this. A steering committee prepared an Opinionnaire®covering the topics of interest. The Opinionnaire® was administered at regular Sunday church services throughout western Washington State. In lieu of a sermon that Sunday, everyone "reacted" and read, considered, and responded to the items on the survey for the 15 to 20 minutes allowed. Over 50,000 people responded to the Opinionnaire®. This is the QUEST Forum™ format (QUICK ENVIRONMENTAL SCANNING TEST model described in Chapter 6).

After completing the survey, parishioners were asked if they would like to meet once a week for four weeks to "reflect" on the data. Thirty-five percent of the participants agreed to meet.

I tabulated the data and produced regional profile reports showing results from each church among ten churches in their region. Thus the volunteers at each church had data from their own church and nine other churches in their region. In addition I created a number of subgroup regional and combined profile reports using the categories they requested, e.g., gender, age, and region.

After a month-long "Reflection" period in local churches, regions then met with their Bishop and staff. Representatives from each church in the region reported to the total group by reading two statements prepared in response to each of the various issues considered—education, worship, prayer, etc. The idea was that the Bishop and diocese would have five years to "Respond."

It was a very innovative program. The diocese won national recognition for its bicentennial program. And I learned that our process could work with thousands of people—one way or another if the leadership were involved.

Using the Fast Forum for Long-Range Planning

I (RJS) have long believed that the Fast Forum® Technique is a useful tool for organizational planning. I had the opportunity to confirm that belief in a project with a national religious organization from 1978 to 1981.

The Forum Foundation was asked, through the Church Council of Greater Seattle, for assistance in futures research programming for a major denomination engaged in its own long-range planning. The national denomination had just been reorganized into geographic regions. The region containing the five northwestern states was trying to get its long-range planning efforts off the ground.

It was suggested they use the PLAN Forum® model (Planning Long-range Assessment Network Model described in the next chapter) as a way to avoid the problem of having big meetings at remote distances. They agreed. The denomination's Long-Range

Planning Committee used the model successfully for nearly four years. It involved several hundred people participating in local churches throughout the five-state region.

Audiotapes articulating issues were prepared by the committee and mailed with supporting papers, Opinionnaires® and response sheets to the conveners of committees in participating local churches. They would listen to the tapes, discuss the issues, respond individually on their own response sheets, and mail the responses back for tabulation and review by the Planning Committee. Subsequent reports from the committee to the Executive Committee were an ongoing process.

It was here in field test research with a religious denomination that it was learned that the small discussion group process — as advocated in the PLAN Forum® technique — worked over large geographic areas.

At the end of the third year, the process itself was evaluated by those participating. It had over an 80 per cent positive response and was another indication that the research was on the right track. The executive minister of the denomination was interviewed at the end of the project. He reported that the thing he liked most about it was that the process was able to generate data about controversial issues without itself exciting controversy.

That was a significant achievement for research at that time.

Citizen Participation in a Municipal Setting

The city of Redmond, Washington conducted a Community Forum Program that ran from 1990 to 1998. The program, originally sponsored by Mayor Doreen Marchione and later continued by Mayor Rosemarie Ives, used the Fast Forum Technique involving small groups in symbolic dialogue with the Mayor and city.

The city of Redmond stated their goals for the Community Forum Program to be:
- To make participation in Redmond government easier for citizens by allowing people to meet in small groups at time and places convenient to themselves.
- To give citizens a chance to meet, discuss, and learn more about issues that are important to the city.
- To go beyond open discussion and gather specific and objective opinions about the topic from every participant.
- To develop a process that is easily repeated at regular intervals throughout

the year.

By all accounts the Program was a great success. Let's look at what happened.

The City of Redmond used the Community Forums to gather citizen input on issues important to the city. There were 13 Community Forums from 1990 to 1998, each one addressing a topic important to the city of Redmond. Dates, topics, and number of participants for the Forums follow.

	Date	Topic	Total Participants
1.	1990-December	Growth Management	227
2.	1991-April	Downtown Redmond	313
3.	1991-November	Transportation	284
4.	1992-May	Youth Issues	467
5.	1992-October	The Future of Redmond	447
6.	1993-October	Regional Transit	641
7.	1994-July	Redmond's Economic Strategy	611
8.	1995-January	What About Water?	541
9.	1995-July	Rethinking Rubbish	425
10.	1996-February	Dealing with Disaster	1201
11.	1996-June	Taxes	186
12.	1997-October	Neighborhoods	383
13.	1998-October	Environment	360

The flow of events for the Forums was straightforward. Interested citizens were invited to phone and register with the city. From these volunteers, "conveners" were solicited to act as hosts for the small groups organized. The proposed forum was announced and advertised in the media, city newsletter, etc. Citizens and businesses were solicited for volunteers to participate in or organize a group meeting.

Conveners rounded up participants for their meeting (calling or sending invitations, and contacting neighbors or fellow employees). The conveners also attended a training session at City Hall to pick up the materials for the meeting and share information on how to conduct the meeting. In addition to volunteer citizen conveners, instructors at the local high schools also participated as conveners for their high school classes when students participated in the process.

Participants in the Redmond Community Forums typically met for about two hours in small groups of eight to twelve persons. Each group met at a time and place convenient to that group's participants, usually in the home of the convener, a school, or a place of business. The group meetings were held over a two to three week period.

During each group meeting, the participants watched a video prepared by the City for that Forum. After the video, each participant was allowed two minutes of non-interrupted time to express his or her views, i.e., Day-in-the-Sun. After an open discussion by the group, each participant responded to questions on the prepared Opinionnaire®.

The results were summarized and included in a newsletter called a Viewspaper® which was elaborate and several pages long. This newsletter was distributed to participants through their group convener and provided to all city employees.

Sometimes a follow-up workshop was held to review the results. The workshop was open to everyone and was attended by the Mayor and other city officials.

How was the Community Forum Program received by city staff and citizens? First, it is safe to say that a program containing 13 iterations spanning a nine-year period was probably viewed as quite valuable by the mayor, city staff, and citizen participants. Second, the number of people participating remained high throughout the program, suggesting a positive reaction to the overall process. Third, reactions by the citizens who participated were strongly positive, although a few negative comments were received. Typical comments by participants were:

- "The process worked."
- "The Forum was an outstanding idea and ours was very useful as an opportunity to discuss widely divergent views peacefully, respectfully, and insightfully."
- "This is a worthwhile process and if sustained, holds great promise of revitalizing the political process."
- "The idea of small group meetings is much more appealing than a larger, and often intimidating, community meeting."
- "I think this is a fantastic idea, and getting the citizens involved is the perfect thing to cure voter indifference."
- "[This was an] excellent way to communicate with others. Should be held every 3-5 months."
- "People are interested in government, but have no format other than elections to feel as though they are part of it. The Community Forum helps to provide this."
- "I think this is the best thing to happen to Redmond since the stop light at NE 85th and 161st Ave."

A large number of people simply wrote: "Thank you for this process."

In 1991 the Association of Washington Cities recognized the Redmond Community Forum Program with an Honorable Mention in their Municipal Achievement Competition. This award is designed to recognize innovative programs that benefit communities.

All in all, the Fast Forum Technique appears to be a robust tool for enhancing citizen participation.[92]

The Fast Forum Goes International and Multilingual

The United Nations Conference on Women (Beijing, China)

Dr. Jan Cate, a member of the Forum Foundation board, was a delegate to the United Nations Fourth World Conference on Women, held in Beijing, China in September, 1995. She administered an Opinionnaire® to some of the participants there to get opinions and ideas of women from different countries. Here are excerpts from her report, *Everywoman's Delegation and the Forum Foundation* Opinionnaire®.

Abstract: At the Beijing conference, the Everywoman's Delegation from Seattle, Washington developed an Opinionnaire® to demonstrate its potential in examining communality and differences in values among women participating worldwide through a democratic process.

There were three International Women's Conferences during the Women's Decade ending in 1985: the First World Conference in Mexico City 1975, Copenhagen, 1980 and Kenya, 1985. Ten years later another international conference was held in Beijing, China. As a result of these conferences women have continually monitored their concerns: poverty, education, health, violence against women, effects of armed conflict, economic structures and policies, inequality of men and women in decision-making, gender equality, women's human rights, media, environment and the girl-child. The statements and questions in the Opinionnaire® were based on these issues. A Platform for Action was the result of the Beijing Conference signed by 189 government delegates.

Out of 5,000 Opinionnaires® distributed 1,102 participants responded in four languages — English, 74%, French 4%, Spanish 12%, and Chinese 10%.

The Everywoman's Delegation was a volunteer group of women related to the non-profit organization, Global Security Studies. The delegation represented a diverse group of women ethnically, racially, vocationally, educationally and in age. As volunteers our access to translators and time was limited. This demonstrates what an interested and concerned group of women can accomplish. For the purposes here the most interesting responses are those sorted by language and the statements selected have become crucial for women since then. Examples would be women and violence, war, economic development, and world trade; and in health, HIV, plague, and the environment, including the growing scarcity of water.

The first 7 questions of the Opinionnaire® were demographic in nature. These were used to analyze the responses to the statements. With 1,102 respondents, 82% were female, 10% were male and 8% were not identified. The "typical" participant was 36-49 years old; the ethnic family — Caucasian, 31%; Asian, 27%; Latina, 13%; African, 9%. Those residing in North America were 37%; Asia, 23%; Europe, 14%; Africa, 6%; South America, 5%. Professionally, 26% were educators, 11% were administrators, 11% were students, 7% were in the medical field, 6% in the political field, and 5% were related to the media. Vocationally 19% were social workers. In response to education 46% had 17+ years of schooling; 27%, 13-16 years; 11%, 0-12 years with 16% not identified.

Partial summary of opinions:

Equality —"Women's health will improve if men assume greater responsibility for their sexual behavior." It was an overwhelming 84% that agreed with this statement. French-speaking rated 94% agreement.

In response to the statement, "Women's control over their reproductive choices should be viewed as a human right," 83 percent agreed with this statement and the French-speaking rated 98% in agreement.

"Both sexes receive equal access to educational and training resources in my community." 56% of the Spanish-speaking were neutral, disagreed, abstained or objected to this statement.

"There is discrimination and prejudice against women entering public life in my community." The majority of Chinese disagreed with this statement, 68%, as compared with the other language groups who agreed by approximately the same percentage.

"Discrimination against lesbians is a violation of human rights." 70% agreed with this statement, except for the 80% of the Chinese who disagreed, were neutral or abstained to the statement.

Economic Development — "Feminization of poverty exists because governments fail to respond to the human rights of women." While overwhelmingly the majority of respondents 80% to 90% agreed with the statement, only 27% of the Chinese speaking agreed with the statement.

Over 50% of the respondents agreed with the statement, "Childhood sex education and contraception would help to ensure young women academic success and economic security."

"Free Trade Zones expand employment opportunities for women." The results proved that responses to this statement expressed ambivalence.

"Establish an international tribunal where indigenous women may testify and present crimes against them and/or violation of collective rights." 87% of the Spanish speaking responded affirmatively to this statement and only 3% of the Chinese.

"The interest on international debts owed by economically poor countries should be forgiven if such debts exceed 10% of their gross national product." The French- and Spanish- speaking voted in the 80% bracket.

Peace — "Conclude by the end of the Year 2000 a negotiated binding schedule for the phased elimination of nuclear weapons within a time frame and with provisions for effective verification and enforcement." The total agreement average 84%

"The UN should establish a permanent war crimes tribunal to prosecute rape in war as a war crime. Government should be held responsible." Total agreement averaged 84%.

Trying to interpret a group of opinions is a challenge and if taken seriously can give some ideas of what grassroots people are thinking and this should guide those in leadership positions to accommodate the respondent and take very seriously the opinions expressed. This Opinionnaire® could be conducted over and over again. The Everywoman's Delegation actually conducted a similar one during the World Trade Organization conference in Seattle, Washington, November, 1999 under the auspices of Lelo, Northwest Labor and Employment Law Office.

—End of Report—

Soros Telecommunications Conference on Sexual Trafficking in Russia

Dr Tatyana Tsyrlina, Professor of Education
Kursk State Pedagogical University, Russia, 1998
Associate: Stuart C. Dodd Institute for Social Innovation (USA) and
Forum Foundation (USA)

Dr. Tsyrlina reports as follows:
As is now well-known, trafficking in women for the purpose of their sexual

exploitation is a very profitable shadow market. For years the main countries sending women were in Asia, mainly, Thailand and the Philippines. "The collapse of the Soviet Union opened up a pool of millions of women from which traffickers can recruit. Now, former Soviet republics, such as Ukraine, Belarus, Latvia and Russia, have become major sending countries for women trafficked into sex industries all over the world. In the sex industry markets today, the most popular and valuable women are from Ukraine and Russia (Hughes, D. "The 'Natasha Trade'—The Transnational Shadow Market of Trafficking in Women," *Journal of International Affairs,* Spring 2000). For a number of reasons those women were seldom heard by the state, and the population hardly knew anything about a problem which might have grown into a national disaster.

Luckily, the MiraMed Institute (Seattle, USA), which has an office in Moscow, raised the issue and joined the fighters for a world free of violence against women. One of the components of their fight was and is the fight against trafficking in women. Important facts and data were collected, and there came a moment when it became necessary to share the information and get an immediate response from large groups of people.

As a result of meeting in 1998 between John Spady, the Forum Foundation's director of research, and Mrs. Juliette Engel (President, MiraMed Institute)[93] , an Opinionnaire® on sexual trafficking was created for people all over the Russian Federation. After much debate, the two organizations assembled an Opinionnaire®. Being the representative of the *Stuart C. Dodd Institute for Social Innovation* and an associate of the *Forum Foundation* in Russia, I also participated in formulating some of the questions and in administering the process.

To work with an Opinionnaire® one needs to know a certain number of rules which are not complicated but critical to make the process effective and to get final reports. So to make it easy, we prepared a short video-film with all the necessary explanations and instructions. Copies of the film, together with the questions and computer-scannable sheets, were sent to all the Russian sites willing to participate. John Spady and I worked with a group of women in the Russian Volga city of Saratov. Around 50 women and men got together in the Saratov University Internet Center where they, first, watched the film from the UNO conference on violence against women (March 8th, 1999). Next, they discussed the problem in small groups, watched an Opinionnaire® orientation video, and finally worked at the Opinionnaire® itself.

The results, which required more than a month to collect, showed a growing interest in the trafficking problem. There was also a great deal of interest in the effectiveness of the Opinionnaire®. For example, judging by the replies, we realized that the problem was still new to large groups of the Russian population, and that it demanded a lot of legal regulations (like a law to deal with sexual trafficking) and many people's initiatives. On the basis of the results, MiraMed Institute conducted several Internet discussion groups, which brought together 153 sites from the Russian Federation and 52 International groups from England, Belgium, Germany, the Netherlands, and the USA. Final Fast Forum® reports became the basis of a new struggle against sexual trafficking in Russia.

To conclude, I can say that *Sexual Trafficking Opinionnaire* (March 1999) is a wonderful example of a symbolic dialogue held by 1,500 men and women all over the world, conducted by the Forum Foundation and MiraMed Institute. It's also a powerful example of the cooperation between two non-state, non-profit organizations, in their desire to solve critical problems of our today's life. Finally, it's an example of the raise of the people's interest towards a serious problem that was provoked by the mere fact that everyone's voice would be heard and considered important.

—End of Report—

In summary, the Fast Forum® Technique has been used successfully in a number of settings and for a number of different purposes. The technique appears to be flexible, simple to use, and both efficient and effective.

Lessons Learned

The SMILE Syndrome
(Scientific Method In Leadership-Expertise)

A Serious Social Malady that Alienates People from their
Organizational and Societal Leaders

The SMILE Syndrome identifies a major barrier to social progress.

The initial attempt to understand this phenomenon resulted in a paper written by Dick Spady in January, 1974, under the auspices of the Church Council of Greater Seattle. It was our first effort to explain the difference between "questionnaires" generating random sample reports based on statistical theory (which itself is based on mathematical theory) and reports based on participation theory (which is based on administrative theory). Different rules apply. Unfortunately, the differences are not well known. It was later that we adopted the word "Opinionnaire®" and registered the trademark to better lift up and alert people to these important differences.

The inappropriate reference and use of the "scientific method" by leaders/experts intent upon the rational defense of the exclusiveness of random-sampling survey techniques as the only valid social indicator—as against citizen-participation, social-feedback survey techniques of interested persons—is the root cause of the SMILE Syndrome which, in turn, is a wall across the pathway of social progress.

The SMILE Syndrome is a serious social malady that attacks society at all levels and is carried unwittingly for the most part, by organizational and societal leaders, academic humanists, and experts.

The late Dr. Arthur W. Combs, preeminent national educator and psychologist, gave an outstanding address on "Human Relationships" in Seattle at a meeting of the DAS Conference of the Washington Education Association in May, 1970. He asserted, "The Scientific Method is one of the sacred cows of our society. It works fine with things, but it doesn't work so well with people."

Specifically, while random-sample surveys are mathematically and statistically valid, the problem is that they fail to meet the *psychological and social needs of people* which Maslow and others have defined to include Ego-Fulfilling, Self-Actualizing needs, and Meta-Actualizing (i.e., civilization building) needs. The fact remains that the average person can go through an entire lifetime and never be asked for his/her opinion—at any time—on a specific issue of his or her concern from a random-sample survey. This situation does not meet the psychological needs of today's citizens who, compared with their historical counterparts, are much more highly educated and have available sophisticated TV, Internet, and electronic media together with a multitude of books, magazines, and references.[94]

George Gallup wrote,

In conducting thousands of surveys on almost every conceivable issue for nearly half a century, I have learned three significant things about our fellow citizens. One is that the judgment of the American people is extraordinarily sound. Another is that the public is nearly always ahead of its leaders. The third is that the electorate has become better educated and more sophisticated politically than ever before. [95]

It is important to realize that just because information or opinions are generated by "interested" or "self-selected" persons or groups does not mean that such information isn't useful. Such opinions are extremely useful in arriving at decisions in our society. Consider, for example, newspaper, TV, and radio editorials and interview programs. They do not necessarily represent the views of the people at large statistically, but they play a leadership role and tend to influence decision-making.

When a citizen (or 500 or 1,000 citizens) writes a letter to a public or organizational official, the views expressed are not necessarily "representative" of the views of the people at large. In addition, "public hearings" are used by "self-selected" people or organizations to lobby their views. Nevertheless, the public hearing is extremely important and generates much useful information for arriving at decisions. Like all citizen participation models, the public hearing plays a leadership role and tends to influence decision-making.

A start toward the solution of this important problem would be a two-track social information feedback system using a full spectrum of Zeitgeist Communication and routine, random-sample surveys for comparison when available. The purpose is to try to gain organizational and/or societal consensus. Social and organizational problems that are not solved by consensus have a way of cropping up again and again.

To accomplish this, leaders of governments, schools, churches, and community organizations must enable their constituents and stakeholders to participate. The people cannot do it alone; they need the help of their leaders to engage in a symbolic dialogue. *Someone has to talk, and someone has to listen.*

The Role of a Citizen — A Definition

Our research has defined the role of the citizen as:
1. To contribute his or her opinion.
2. To listen to the opinions of his or her peers.
3. To be enabled to respond to the queries of his/her leaders/representatives toward the solution of those problems that are of interest and concern.

These processes as a routine are hardly ever done today and our society and its public organizations are floundering because of it. It is an honor to be asked for one's opinion; governments and organizations everywhere need to honor their citizens and constituents.

Again, most of the knowledge in the world today is in books and computer data banks. But most of the wisdom in the world today is in the minds of people walking the earth. We have to learn how to reach it.

Furthermore, the overall process envisioned in Zeitgeist Communication is open to the regular news media at every point, but it is never dependent upon the media for its promotion or to maintain communication between people and their leaders. Perhaps it will help to think of the process not as a "survey" but rather as a way for "Chiefs of State" (i.e., *anyone either elected* or *duly appointed—public or private*) to "talk" with constituents or stakeholders *symbolically* and for them to be enabled to *"talk back."* All parties in a conversation are biased. But that is a moot point. What is important is the conversation, i.e., the *process* of communicating ideas among the participants. *The democratic process may be more important than the data derived from the questioning.* Marshall McCluhan's statement that, "The medium is the message" is true.[96]

Communicating opinions for the common good is essential to democracy.

The process of increased citizen participation, providing interested persons an opportunity to contribute their opinion on matters of the public and organizational good, is therapeutic—it reduces organizational and societal tensions and leads toward peace. First, peace of mind for those individuals participating, then organizational and societal peace, and then finally the peace of civilization itself.

Humanity's Greatest Resource

The exploration of ideas through symbolic dialogue is the *mortar that binds a creative organization or society*, i.e., an organization and society that is actively trying to solve its problems. That is, when dialogues are conducted rationally and courteously and people exchange ideas, the process (i.e., democratic) provides a "bonding"—and mortar—for the group searching. *Again, any organization, institution, community, society, nation, or civilization which inhibits, innocently or not, the free flow of ideas—and opinions about those ideas—down, across, and upward in its organizational and societal structures, is depriving itself of its greatest resource—<u>human thought</u>—and it is in grave danger of being buried in history by the avalanche of the creativity of others.*

The Social Conspiracy and Bureaucratic Inertia

In society, and in the world, there seems to be a natural dynamic that is counter-productive to the equally natural trend toward organization and civilization building.

We have called this dynamic "The Social Conspiracy." This dynamic is directly related to bureaucratic inertia.

"There are some things gravely wrong with our society as a problem-solving mechanism" said John W. Gardner, former Secretary of Health, Education and Welfare. "The machinery of the society is not working in a fashion that will permit us to solve any of our problems effectively. In the absence of healthy criticism, every organization tends to end up being managed for the benefit of the people who run it."[97]

Lewis Lepham states: "Something is evolving in this country away from democracy. There is a fear of democracy (among intelligentsia). Democracy is about confrontation, people disagreeing with each other." [98]

A Natural Selection Process May Be at Work in Society

People seem to gravitate to positions of leadership and management in both public and private organizations who are kind of "gutsy," take-charge, ordinal-type personalities used to working in hierarchical structures. They usually have strong egos and strong ego needs. They are often authoritarian. If their situations allow it, they resist naturally, but negatively, incursions of others into their "turf." It is probable that the popular stereotype of a leader contains these traits.

Most leaders of organizations and institutions in society are responsible and are trying to do a good job as they see it. There is no big plot to keep people down. However, there may be a natural selection process in society whereby persons gravitate toward positions of leadership who have personality traits similar to those who have gone before them and who, in many cases, probably had a hand in their selection.

The Forum Foundation first became aware of this negative dynamic of bureaucratic resistance to new ideas affecting organizational "turf" in 1974, when the "Citizen Counselor Proposal" — written by Stuart Dodd and Richard Spady, was published in *The Seattle Times* on Sunday November 10, 1974 as part of project IN-FORUM of the Church Council of Greater Seattle. The context of the article was: 1) a new idea was presented to improve the participation of citizens in the public planning processes of government, 2) this proposal came from a leading authority in social science research and opinion gathering, Dr. Stuart C. Dodd.

The project was co-sponsored by several responsible community groups, including Seattle's Department of Community Development. This was the first time that a scholarly paper had been presented at large in the Seattle community calling for small discussion groups of citizens to participate in interaction with public and community leaders in an ongoing planning process. This was the academic forerunner of today's "Citizen Councilor" models proposed later in this book.

Yet not one inquiry was received from any political leader. Not one inquiry was received from any community leader. Not one inquiry was received from any educator or university administrator. Not one inquiry was received from any church leader. No one inquired, "What do you mean?" No one said, "It won't work because . . . ."

In effect, *the silence was deafening*—and *attention-getting!*

Over the years we became sensitive to this phenomenon in the continuing research of the Forum Foundation. Thereafter (and even up to the present time), whenever we wrote or otherwise communicated to leaders, for example, political, educational, business, community, or church—whether they were mayors, city managers, councilpersons, bureaucrats, county executives, state legislators, governors, superintendents, university presidents, bishops, etc.—we not only noted their positive or negative response, we also noted their lack of response. Thus we began to recognize those nominal "leaders" of organizations and society who showed a lack of interest in expanding citizen or member participation as a concept. They were, in effect, exhibiting the characteristic of having controlling purposes instead of freeing purposes.

It did not take long to discover that the "not interested" list, which was the list indicating controlling purposes, was far larger than the interested list which had freeing purposes. This is especially important when compared against the research of Dr. Arthur Combs in his definition of the helping professions. He defines a characteristic of a poor helper/leader as one who has controlling purposes as against that of a good helper/leader who has freeing purposes.

Looking broadly at the characteristics of bureaucracies, which are one of the prevailing institutions in our world, one cannot help but note that they usually exhibit many of the characteristics of "poor helpers" (leaders) as defined by Combs. Bureaucracies certainly are usually highly involved in control through rules and regulations, in the necessity of order, in the insistence of the use of forms to complete their work properly. And they usually have narrow purposes.

However, in defense of bureaucracies, one would be hard pressed to organize them otherwise.

It is only through a division of labor that a complex task can be broken down into manageable parts in organizations and society. The point is, however, that bureaucracies are created to manage a particular environment by some leader above them and are not created to take the place of the leader. The leader in this case is interested in control and so tends to select naturally those persons who can do that job best. Therefore, it appears that there is a self-perpetuating natural selection process in which managers are chosen with some negative traits of leadership.

Since even a casual observance of life in the world indicates that the predominant organizing principle of the present and past is the authoritarian hierarchy, (A>B>C>D>...), many of the managers, perhaps even most, in organizations and society, appear to have controlling purposes. Since bureaucracies are the prevailing organizations in both our public and private sectors, managers with these personality traits are numerous. Subordinates who emulate them are even more numerous because pay increases for most come from being selected as managers.

But what of society as a whole?

Most people probably do not have these traits. Many people are more passive, contemplative persons who seldom seek the limelight, who may be reluctant to speak in large groups, but who provide the dedicated, hard-working, capable, intelligent service that has characterized the American citizen and worker through the dynamic growth of the nation. These same people are the ones we trust to sit on our juries and decide the guilt or innocence, often life or death, of citizens charged by the state.

We do not allow state bureaucrats to both make the charge and decide on the guilt or innocence of a citizen. Only a jury of peers does this. Are such citizens characterized by a "lack of leadership" ability? We think not. It is just that up to this time the social invention of bureaucracies and management have not been able to encompass a process that could utilize their leadership contribution adequately.

What are the Implications?

This phenomenon of the social conspiracy and bureaucratic inertia seems more pervasive to us all the time. It seems that people may be gravitating naturally to positions of leadership in organizations and society who exhibit in themselves many characteristics of being a poor leader. That is a paradox. They seem to have a natural "Theory X-type" resistance to sharing their leadership function. Such sharing probably feels like diluting their power. It may appear to them to be a threat to their control, in the management of their sphere of organizational or societal responsibility. For example, many public officials and legislators often give the impression that the last thing they want to see is another interested citizen. The prevalent attitude of most public officials still seems to be that "the average American citizen is uninformed and not capable of making a positive contribution to the solution of my problems."[99]

How important will these dynamics be in impeding the growth of citizen participation in organizations and society in the future? It seems exceedingly important as a negative dynamic. It suggests that many political, organizational, and bureaucratic leaders and others will not share their perceived prerogatives of leadership without a struggle. If people are unable to establish participation models through legislative processes, they will naturally do so themselves, probably through the initiative process. This should be no problem to the people once they understand what is at stake. They have the power in their *Zeitgeist*, the supreme governor, and in the reality of the Theory of Authority.

Up to now, Government itself has seemed unable to discuss the merits of citizen participation in the public planning processes of government in a substantive manner. The effort should be to move beyond "public relations," "citizenship education," and even "citizen participation," and to move resolutely to "*democratize planning and civilization building.*" These barriers to social progress and participation by citizens everywhere debilitate and devitalize our organizations, institutions, and nations and are a direct threat to civilization itself.

It is possible, however, to remedy this problem in an organization, institution, or society as a whole by clarifying that *moral authority* stems from the people. Moral authority then begins to influence and direct the legal authority of institutions and their bureaucracies—*naturally*. It is our belief that Zeitgeist Communication and the Fast Forum® technique can help accomplish this.

The next chapter describes several different ideal models or applications for the Fast Forum®. As you will see, the technique can be easily adapted for a variety of uses.

6

. . . .

Potential
Applications of the
Fast Forum Technique

Uses of the Fast Forum: Suggested Models

Through the past 30 years of research in social science to enhance citizenship, we have learned a lot of things that *do not work*. Research in social science is a very slow, almost at times a glacial process. It may take one, two, or more years to duplicate the setting, make a change, and try again. However slow, progress has been and is being made. What follows in this chapter is our best thinking at this time as to next steps that could and should be taken at state, county, city, municipal, school, church, and organizational levels to utilize the Fast Forum® technique to achieve symbolic dialogue in an overall process of civilization building. These models are: The Citizen Councilor Network Forum for state governments, The Citizen Councilor Network Forum for city/county governments, The Spiritual Councilor Network Forum for religious organizations, Psycho-Social Education for schools, PLAN Forum® (Planning Long-range Assessment Network) for organizations and QUEST Forum[a] (QUick Environmental Scanning Test) for organizations.

The effort here is timely because the "United Nations Year of Dialogue among Civilizations" is the year 2001.[100] Hopefully, the suggested models which follow will help initiate that dialogue in the next millennium.

The Citizen Councilor Network Forum
For State Governments

Washington State Citizen Councilor Bill

In the last year we have come to recognize a State Auditor as the natural administrator for Zeitgeist Communication programming in state governments. Professionally, state auditing has moved from fiscal audits (primarily to prevent fraud) to compliance audits (compliance to higher authority and laws) and performance audits (compliance with a municipality's or agency's own laws or regulations). These reports that are generated by a State Auditor are helpful to administrators being audited.

The auditor, an elected public official, is administratively neutral, but performs an essential outsider function that, however, is based on *constitutional authority* (at least in Washington State). It is natural for the auditor to ask citizens to help do the job of auditing state government and all other governments and agencies dispensing public funds within the state. We believe the concept of a "social audit" using the Fast Forum® technique can be developed over the years ahead as another major professional tool to audit "intangible" assets. This can be used by auditors *everywhere*. In the public application what will be created *is basically a feedback communication system owned by the people but provided for the benefit of all governments—state, county, city, and regional. The same is true of universities as well as economic and cultural institutions, e.g., trade associations, Chambers of Commerce, and community and church organizations.*

People are not anti-government, they are not anti-business, they are not anti-schools, they are not anti-religious. These are all vital organizations in the survival of our society and civilization and what people want is for them to *succeed.* Mistakes will be made, that is sure, but we will learn! Hopefully, all governments, through the cooperation of officials and administrators, together with the news media will help in the task ahead of civilization building. It is a noble goal.

We hope you find the letters and legislative bills which follow of interest and use.

Forum Foundation

Enhancing Communication in Organizations and Society

Symbolic Dialogue, Opinionnaire®, Viewspaper®, and Fast Forum® Services

Founded in 1970
Non-Profit

MEMO: October 1, 2000

To: Senators and Representatives
       57th Legislature, 2001 Session
       State of Washington

From: Dick Spady, President

I have been involved in research in social science in the field of administrative theory nearly full time since our founding in 1970 when I was a graduate student in the School of Business at the University of Washington. I was also a member of the Evergreen Chapter of the World Future Society (WFS) in Seattle which first proposed, with Dr. Stuart Dodd, Dr. Ed Lindaman, and Tom Sine, a "futures study" for the state. Its proposal was accepted by Gov. Dan Evans and effected in the two-year statewide program "Alternatives for Washington" in the early 1970's. This program is still considered as a "classic" in futures research.

Dr. Stuart C. Dodd, professor-emeritus of sociology at the University of Washington wrote in an article titled "Citizen Counselor Proposal" in the November 10, 1974 Sunday issue of <u>The Seattle Times</u>: *As human systems and organizations grow ever larger, more complex, and more impersonal—in our schools, in our communities, in our churches, in our governments, and in our industries and commerce—the individual shrinks toward facelessness, hopelessness, powerlessness, and frustration."*

At the time, there was no reaction to the article from the leaders of either church and state or from business and education except our research did continue in the religious community through the years following. Unfortunately, this assessment of Dr. Dodd (and Lou Harris later in 1976) continues today that "people are alienated and feel they are not adequately involved in the decisions that affect their lives—public and private."

Enclosed is a "Citizen Councilor Bill," Flow Chart, and Frontispiece that are another step on our quest toward civilization building. Our country is on the verge of major discoveries in social science and some of the key discoveries are occurring right here in our own back yard in Seattle and Washington state in the emerging field of "symbolic dialogue." If you will phone before December 1st and let us know that you are willing to sign on this bill next January, I will confirm with you and include your name on a copy of the bill to be included in our new book to be released January 2001. It will be titled *The Leadership of Civilization Building (Administrative and Civilization Theory, Symbolic Dialogue, and Citizen Skills for the 21st Century).* I urge you to sign on and be a part of "the rest of the story;" we are making progress. If you need more information, please call me. Thank you.

Cc: Governor Gary Locke; John Carlson; The Seattle Times; The Seattle P-I; WFS; FF Directors

Seattle Office
4426 Second Avenue N. E. ● Seattle, WA 98105-6191 ● Fax (206) 633-3561 ● Phone: (206) 634-0420
www.ForumFoundation.org

Founded in 1970
Non-Profit

Forum Foundation
Enhancing Communication in Organizations and Society

April 29, 2000

The Honorable Brian Sonntag, State Auditor
Legislative Building
P.O. Box 40021
Olympia, WA 98504-0021

Dear Mr. Sonntag:

As you know, I was the author of the original Citizen Councilor Bill submitted by Representative Paul Sanders in 1980. Through the years as I lobbied the bill, I continually made changes trying to meet the concerns of legislators, the governor, and the Dept. of Community, Trade, and Economic Development.

Enclosed is a draft revision of SB 6698, Citizen Councilor Bill, that was submitted to the 56th Legislature at their 2000 regular session. As you will note, I have determined that the State Auditor is the elected public official that could most naturally administer this program to citizens through the present constitutional mandate to monitor state government. I hope you will agree.

Please study the draft and make any recommended changes you feel appropriate. I will be flying to Moscow, Russia on May 7th returning May 14th to attend a conference, "Planning for Education in the New Millennium" co-sponsored by the University of the Russian Academy of Education and Seattle Pacific University, International Center for Curriculum Studies. I will present a paper on "New Administrative Theories and Psycho-Social Education, Community Education for the Next Millennium." On my return I would like to meet with you and others as appropriate to discuss this proposal further. Please let me know.

As a researcher in social science, I will include this proposal in my new book, *Leadership and Civilization Building,* to be published next fall. Hopefully, the 2001 legislature will pass this proposal, it will be approved by the Governor, and implemented by you. In any event, from the book, it will be available to others as they might see fit. Thank you for your past interest and support. We are making progress.

Sincerely,

Richard J. Spady, President

Cc: Directors, Forum Foundation

Seattle Office
4426 Second Avenue N.E. • Seattle, WA 98105-6191 • Fax (206) 633-3561 • Phone (206) 634-0420
http://weber.u.washington.edu/~forum

"Citizen Councilor" Bill (Flow Chart) 10-1-00
2001 Washington State Legislature

[If legislators wish to sign on this bill or wish more information, please contact Dick Spady, president, Forum Foundation, at (425) 747-8373. For further information see: Senate Resolution 1993-8636 or www.ForumFoundation.org.]

Abstract: • This bill constructively addresses the implications of Initiative 695 and has no fiscal impact. A self-funded, citizenship program, to better enable all citizens, young and old, to exercise their constitutional rights of freedom of speech, the press, assembly, petition, *and to be heard* in *symbolic dialogues* with the Governor, Legislature, and others evolving from new administrative theories in order to celebrate, evaluate, and enhance the political, educational, and economic climates and the *social capital* and *community mental health* of Washington State through the routine publication of *social audits* of its intangible assets.

• A community development, volunteer, citizen participation, and psycho-social education program in Zeitgeist ("Spirit-of-the-time") Communication using Fast Forum® "socialware" computer programming first developed at the University of Washington in 1970 and partnering with school, university, business, civic, and cultural organizations.

1.<<< GOVERNMENT

• Suggests Issues: Governor, Officials and Planners, Legislature, Citizen Councilors, Public.

("When leaders honor us with opportunities to know the truth of what is occurring and support us to explore the deeper meaning of events, we instinctively reach out to them." Margaret J. Wheatley, *Leadership and the New Science,* 1999.)

2.<<< STATE AUDITOR

• To organize, State Auditor appoints a volunteer Citizen Councilor Coordinator and Deputy.**
• Selects priority of issues suggested for public discussion and submits to Steering Committee for consideration. Steering Committee is composed of representatives without vote from: (a) the governors office, (b) one member of the minority and majority party of both houses of the legislature, (c) State Supt. of Public Instruction, (d) the Citizen Councilor Coordinator and Deputy, (e) any organization with over 50 groups statewide of 8-12 Citizen Councilors, (f) others invited by the State Auditor.
• Assigns issues reviewed by the Steering Committee to the Citizen Councilor Coordinator and Deputy who assign official "Value Reporters" to prepare materials. (Value Reporters represent "the people's right to know.")
• After review by the Steering Committee, authorizes distribution of materials prepared by the Citizen Councilor Coordinator to the Citizen Councilor Conveners.

3.<<< CITIZEN COUNCILOR COORDINATOR AND DEPUTY COORDINATOR

[Are volunteers selected by and amenable to the State Auditor.]

• Solicits Citizen Councilor groups and volunteers from community service, educational, civic, business, unions, religions, and other organ-izations.
• Assigns "value reporters" to interview scholars, experts, officials and planners, leaders, and others concerning issues.
• Produces cassette tapes and printed materials evenhandedly as possible on public issues for the State Auditor.
• Mails approved materials to Citizen Councilor Conveners and/or to participating school districts involved in student citizenship, psycho-social education, and critical-thinking programs with citizen and parents using state materials.
• Provides mailing labels and Citizen Councilor response sheets and materials at regular costs to a participating organization, county, municipality, or school district if a private iteration of their own Councilor or youth groups is desired at their own expense or schools participate in the "State-of-the-Union and the Youth of America" national project.

4.<<< CITIZEN COUNCILOR CONVENER

• Convenes and hosts group meeting of 8-12 Councilors in homes or workplaces on thirty-day notice by the Citizen Councilor Coordinator.

** When $10,000 has been received in donations, a 1-800 number is established and ads placed. The Coordinator acknowledges subscriptions and asks for volunteer Citizen Councilor Conveners to act as hosts for meetings in homes or workplaces. When a total of $40,000 has been received in donations or subscriptions (estimated at $15-$20 per year), the State Auditor calls in the subscriptions, establishes fees and services, and initiates the program.]

5.<<< CITIZEN COUNCILOR

(Councilor: "One elected or appointed to advise a sovereign or chief magistrate." Webster)

• Meets in own small group of 4 (youth) or 8-12 persons (adult) on call of the Convener, listens to audio cassette tape, studies materials received from the Citizen Councilor Coordinator as approved by the State Auditor, and states own position to others in a two-minute "Day-in-the-Sun" period, and then participates in open discussion on issues raised with other Councilors.

6.<<< CITIZEN COUNCILOR

• Responds individually to objective questions posed on an Opinionnaire® (yes, no, abstain, object; multiple-choice; Likert or "end anchor" value scales etc.) using mark-sense, machine-scannable, Forum Foundation Citizen Councilor® response sheets.

7.<<< CITIZEN COUNCILOR CONVENER

• After meeting, mails completed citizen response sheets and tape (for reuse) to the State Auditor for tabulation by the Citizen Councilor Coordinator and completes meeting evaluation questions.

8.<<< CITIZEN COUNCILOR COORDINATOR AND DEPUTY COORDINATOR

• Scans and tabulates response sheets using the Fast Forum® computer program that is available without cost to this state project as in-kind services by the Forum Foundation, 4426 Second Ave. N.E., Seattle, WA 98105-6191. Tel. 206-634-0420; Fax 206-633-3561. [The Forum Foundation was organized in 1970 as a Washington State, non-profit, research corporation in the field of education to enhance communication in organizations and society. (See Washington Senate Resolution 1993-8636. Richard J. Spady is president, a volunteer, and authored this bill.) see *The Search for Enlightened Leadership, Volume 2: Many-To-Many Communication, A Breakthrough in Social Science* (Spady and Bell), 1998—page 45 "The Community Forum," and page 57 "Psycho-Social Education," and page 75 "How to Make Ideas Count." Copies are available in the State, King County, Seattle, and University of Washington libraries and from the University Bookstore in Seattle at 1-800-335-READ.

9. <<< STATE AUDITOR

• Oversees tabulation and summarization by the Coordinator. Returns a Viewspaper® summary and a profile report to officials and libraries and to participating Citizen Councilor groups. Maintains profile reports generated by the Citizen Councilor Coordinator and Deputy for reference by the media and the public. Provides data that legislators and others may analyze electronically.

10.<<< GOVERNMENT AND SCHOOLS

• Officials: Review public advisory "social audit" data and information generated to assist in public policy and planning processes.

• Schools: Students participating engage in a "symbolic dialogue" with the President of the United States, their parents, and adults nationwide using the "State of the Union" curriculum materials available. ("The medium is the message." Marshall McLuhan, *Understanding Media*, 1964.)

[www.ForumFoundation.org]

Note: [Forum Foundation is a Washington state non-profit. educational research corporation that was organized in 1970 to do research in the field of administrative theory while Dick Spady was a student in the Graduate School of Business at the University of Washington. The following trademarks of the Foundation are registered, United States Patent Office: "Fast Forum," "Opinionnaire," "Viewspaper," "PLAN Forum," "Citizen Councilor," "Fraternity Councilor," and "An Inspirational City in Pursuit of Happiness!" "Quest Forum™," "PC Rating™," and "CPC Rating™" trademarks are pending. The Forum Foundation permits use of its trademarks, where appropriate, when credit and reference (www.ForumFoundation.org) is given to the foundation. See The *Leadership of Civilization Building (Administrative and Civilization Theory, Symbolic Dialogue, and Citizen Skills for the 21st Century.)* (Richard J. Spady and Richard S. Kirby with collaboration by Cecil H. Bell, Jr.). Estimated publication date, January 2001. The Forum Foundation Fast Forum® computer program was first developed at the University of Washington Academic Computer Center in 1970. The proprietory computer program of the Forum Foundation is copyrighted 1970-2000.]

```
 1    _____
 2                        "CITIZEN COUNCELOR" BILL
 3                    LEGISLATIVE  REQUEST January, 2001
 4        [Draft Revisions 10-1-00 by Dick Spady, President, Forum Foundation, bill author,  of
 5     SENATE BILL 6698 and HOUSE BILL 3049, State of Washington, 56th Legislature, 2000 Regular
 6            Session. Legislators: To sign on, please call 425-747-8373 to confirm. Thank you.]
 7    _____
 8
```

9   WHEREAS: the passage of Initiative 695 in 1999 is a social indicator that governments, business, media,
10   and community organizations need improved listening skills which can involve citizens responsibly in
11   the political process. And
12
13   WHEREAS: The Governor has a constitutional responsibility to administer state affairs and the Legislature
14   has a constitutional responsibility to enact legislation in the state, and citizens have a political right to be
15   heard and enabled to participate viably in their organizations, institutions, and governments in the state
16   *in a process of building "social capital," * And
17
18   WHEREAS: The Washington State Auditor has a constitutional responsibility and independently serves
19   the citizens of Washington by promoting accountability, fiscal integrity and openness in state and local
20   government and the approach of an auditor's work is constantly professionally evolving through new
21   administrative theories involving the use of "symbolic dialogues" and "social audits" *of intangible assets*
22   along with regular financial, compliance, and performance audits in Washington and other states and
23   furthermore, in working with these governments in partnerships, the auditor strives to ensure the proper
24   use of public resources to enable its citizens to more clearly envision their future in the theme, "Washington,
25   an Inspirational State in Pursuit of Happiness!" And
26
27   WHEREAS: More than 2,400 local governments of 33 different types and 168 state agencies, colleges,
28   and universities, board and commissions are administered and audited for fiscal accountability of roughly
29    $40 billion annually. Furthermore, as relationships are in partnerships with governments, and State Auditor
30   reports are constructive management tools for them to use. And
31
32   WHEREAS: Accountability is a goal both of administration and auditing but accountability is fundamental
33   to the work of the state auditor as audits touch heavily on legal compliance with state laws and regulations
34   and governmental entities' own policies and ordinances. And
35
36   WHEREAS: Similar experiences in other states including Texas, Colorado, Oregon, and Utah have been
37   positive to create a public forum to restore citizen's trust in their governments, expand social capital, and
38   improve community mental health. And
39
40   WHEREAS: Washington has long been recognized as a precursor state in social and economic innovation.
41   It was the only state that emerged from the national bicentennial celebration in 1976 utilizing the last of
42   its resources from royalties to fund ongoing programs in "citizen participation." Washington was able to
43   discern that it was not quite "volunteerism" they were after (i.e., give me your body, your hands, your
44   time). Rather Washington was more interested in "give me your mind"—which was significantly different.
45   Furthermore, our nation is now on the verge of major discoveries in social science and some of the major
46   discoveries have been occurring here in Washington State and the greater Seattle area by the Forum
47   Foundation and was recognized as such in Washington State Senate Resolution 1993-8636. And
48
49   WHEREAS: It is natural in our democratic republic that the citizens of Washington State be invited to
50   participate in its governing processes in the exercise of their political rights whenever possible and within
51   their time and energy levels and help the Governor, Legislature, and the State Auditor in their constitutional
52   responsibilities to administer, legislate, and monitor all governments and public entities and public funds.

BE IT THEREFORE RESOLVED THAT THE FOLLOWING BE IMPLEMENTED:

S-0836.1 _____

SENATE BILL 5651
_____

State of Washington   **57th Legislature**   **2001 Regular Session**

By Senators Jacobsen, McDonald, Haugen, Horn, Kohl-Welles, Rasmussen, McAuliffe, Winsley, Costa and Thibaudeau

Read first time 01/30/2001. Referred to Committee on State & Local Government.

H-0771.1 _____

HOUSE BILL 1570
_____

State of Washington   **57th Legislature**   **2001 Regular Session**

By Representatives Dunshee, Esser, Miloscia, Santos, D. Schmidt, Veloria, Romero, Barlean, Ericksen, Tokuda and Kenney

Read first time 01/30/2001. Referred to Committee on State Government.

1   AN ACT Relating to creating the citizen councilor network; and
2 adding new sections to chapter 43.09 RCW.

3 BE IT ENACTED BY THE LEGISLATURE OF THE STATE OF WASHINGTON:

4   NEW SECTION. **Sec. 1.** The legislature finds that:
5   (1) The passage of Initiative Measure No. 695 in 1999 is a social
6 indicator that governments, business, media, and community
7 organizations need improved listening skills which can involve citizens
8 responsibly in the political process.
9   (2) The governor has a constitutional responsibility to administer
10 state affairs, the legislature has a constitutional responsibility to
11 enact legislation in the state, and citizens have a political right to
12 be enabled to participate viably in their organizations, institutions,
13 and governments in the state in a process of building "social capital"
14 and improving community mental health.
15   (3) The Washington state auditor has a constitutional
16 responsibility and independently serves the citizens of Washington by
17 promoting accountability, fiscal integrity, and openness in state and
18 local government, and the approach of an auditor's work is constantly
19 professionally evolving through new administrative theories involving

1 the use of "symbolic dialogues" and "social audits" of intangible
2 assets along with regular financial, compliance, and performance audits
3 in Washington and other states. Furthermore, in working with these
4 governments in partnerships, the auditor strives to ensure the proper
5 use of public resources to enable its citizens to more clearly envision
6 their future in the theme, "Washington, an inspirational state in
7 pursuit of happiness!"

8   (4) More than two thousand four hundred local governments of
9 thirty-three different types and one hundred sixty-eight state
10 agencies, colleges, universities, boards, and commissions are
11 administered and audited for fiscal accountability of roughly forty
12 billion dollars annually. Furthermore, as relationships are in
13 partnerships with governments, and state auditor reports are
14 constructive management tools for them to use.

15   (5) Accountability is a goal both of administration and auditing,
16 but accountability is fundamental to the work of the state auditor as
17 audits touch heavily on legal compliance with state laws and
18 regulations and governmental entities' own policies and ordinances.

19   (6) Similar experiences in other states including Texas, Colorado,
20 Oregon, and Utah have been positive to create a public forum to restore
21 citizens' trust in their governments, expand social capital, and
22 improve community mental health.

23   (7) Washington has long been recognized as a precursor state in
24 social and economic innovation. It was the only state that emerged
25 from the national bicentennial celebration in 1976 utilizing the last
26 of its resources from royalties to fund ongoing programs in "citizen
27 participation." Washington was able to discern that it was not quite
28 "volunteerism" they were after: "Give me your body, your hands, your
29 time." Rather Washington was more interested in "give me your mind,"
30 which was significantly different. Furthermore, our nation is now on
31 the verge of major discoveries in social science and some of the major
32 discoveries have been occurring here in Washington state and the
33 greater Seattle area by the Forum Foundation and was recognized as such
34 in Washington State Senate Resolution No. 1993-8636.

35   (8) It is natural in our democratic republic that the citizens of
36 Washington state be invited to participate in its governing processes
37 in the exercise of their political rights whenever possible and within
38 their time and energy levels and help the governor, legislature, and
39 the state auditor in their constitutional responsibilities to

1 administer, legislate, and monitor all governments and public entities
2 and public funds.

3   NEW SECTION. **Sec. 2.** The legislature recognizes that some
4 citizens have difficulty accessing political processes that rely on
5 public hearings held at locations that are often distant or held at
6 inappropriate times from their residence or workplace. To increase
7 public participation in the political process, the legislature intends
8 to establish and support a self-funding pilot process in cooperation
9 with the state auditor by which citizens can receive information about
10 public issues and provide feedback to elected officials in a
11 convenient, timely manner and local setting.

12   NEW SECTION. **Sec. 3.** (1) The office of citizen councilor is
13 created in accordance with section 11 of this act. According to
14 Webster's Dictionary, "councilor" means an official advisor to a
15 sovereign or chief magistrate. Any citizen registered to vote, or who
16 lives or works in Washington but is not a registered voter, who
17 volunteers to act as an official government advisor may become a
18 citizen councilor on request by sending a letter to the state auditor
19 or by calling a special toll-free number and subscribing to a nominal
20 fee as set by the state auditor to recover substantially the direct
21 costs from citizen participation in the program. The indirect costs of
22 public officials and government employee participation to provide
23 information to citizen councilors in their discussions shall be borne
24 by the government entity participating. Citizen councilors shall act
25 collectively as official advisors or a sounding board for the governor,
26 the legislature, the state auditor, or other public officials and
27 agencies such as the department of community, trade, and economic
28 development on issues of public interest or concern.   Conveners of
29 citizen councilor groups shall be those designated by the citizen
30 councilor coordinator or deputy citizen councilor coordinator under
31 section 5 of this act from among citizen councilors who volunteer to
32 host a group. Every effort shall be made to assign citizen councilors
33 to a group that meets at a convenient time and place for those
34 participating. Meetings will usually be in small groups meeting in
35 similar resident or work area zip codes.
36   (2) Citizen councilors may participate:

1   (a) In a citizen councilor group of approximately eight to twelve
2   persons organized by residence or work area zip code with the
3   assistance of the citizen councilor coordinator;
4   (b) In a citizen councilor organizational group under section 8 of
5   this act; or
6   (c) As an individual if the individual is unable to attend meetings
7   in groups due to age, disability, remote location, or personality
8   conflict.
9   (3) Citizen councilors will be reassigned a group on request to
10   assure that their group meeting place, time, and makeup is convenient
11   and compatible, or the citizen councilor coordinator may make
12   individual assignments of a councilor when deemed necessary.

13   NEW SECTION.   Sec. 4.   (1) The state auditor shall determine
14   suggested issues for public discussion approximately quarterly but not
15   more than monthly from suggestions received from the governor, the
16   legislature, public officials, agencies, and individual citizen
17   councilors and recommend an appropriate issue or issues for
18   consideration by citizen councilors to a steering committee in rotation
19   and in accord with subsection (2) of this section.   An advisory
20   steering committee shall be composed of the following nonvoting
21   members: (a) A representative from the governor's office, (b)
22   legislative members: One member of the minority and one member of the
23   majority party from each house of the legislature, (c) a representative
24   from the superintendent of public instruction, (d) a representative
25   from each county, (e) a representative from each regional government,
26   (f) a representative of higher education, (g) a representative from the
27   association of Washington cities, (h) a representative from any
28   organization participating with over fifty groups of eight to twelve
29   persons under section 6(7) of this act, (i) the citizen councilor
30   coordinator and deputy citizen councilor coordinator selected as
31   provided in section 5 of this act, and (j) others invited by the state
32   auditor.
33   (2) After consideration by the members of the steering committee,
34   the state auditor shall determine and assign the issue or issues
35   approved for discussion to the volunteer citizen councilor coordinator
36   for preparation and implementation by value reporters and others,
37   except that the first meeting of a group will be an orientation meeting
38   prepared by the state auditor. Thereafter issues will be determined in

1   rotation first by the governor, second by the legislature, and then by
2   the state auditor. If the governor or legislature at its turn fails to
3   determine an issue for discussion within ten days of its consideration
4   and adjournment by the steering committee, the determination will be
5   made by the state auditor.   Value reporters assigned to gather
6   information on issues shall be careful to present all issues as
7   evenhandedly as possible, taking care to present the generally
8   prevailing viewpoints surrounding an issue or issues from experts,
9   officials, scholars, and others in an effort to provide the public with
10 information needed for discussion. Value reporters shall represent the
11 "people's right to know" and conduct interviews of experts, officials,
12 scholars, and others to solicit their various viewpoints and record
13 such interviews on audio or video tape for later reproduction and
14 distribution to citizen councilor groups.   Before any materials are
15 released to citizen councilor groups, however, persons interviewed and
16 taped shall approve their taped interview for release or complete
17 another interview to their satisfaction, otherwise their statement
18 shall not be included in materials sent to citizens.
19   (3) The state auditor shall refer the public information material
20 prepared by the citizen councilor coordinator, deputy citizen councilor
21 coordinator, and staffs to the steering committee for its review and
22 recommendations. The governor, legislative committee assigned, or the
23 state auditor, whichever determined the issue, shall then make the
24 final determination of any materials distributed to citizen councilors,
25 except if the governor or legislative committee assigned fails to make
26 a final determination within ten days of adjournment of the steering
27 committee giving its recommendations, then the state auditor shall make
28 the final determination and distribute the materials to the citizen
29 councilor network.

30   NEW SECTION. Sec. 5. The offices of citizen councilor coordinator
31 and deputy citizen councilor coordinator are created within the office
32 of state auditor.   The state auditor shall appoint the citizen
33 councilor coordinator and deputy citizen councilor coordinator with the
34 advice of the steering committee.   The citizen councilor coordinator
35 and deputy citizen councilor coordinator shall serve at the pleasure of
36 the state auditor, until terminated with the approval of the steering
37 committee, and shall be citizen volunteers and serve without
38 compensation, but shall be reimbursed for actual expenses incurred in

1   carrying out their duties under sections 1 through 11 of this act as
2   funds for subscriptions and donations are available.

3   <u>NEW SECTION.</u> **Sec. 6.** The citizen councilor coordinator and deputy
4   citizen councilor coordinator shall:
5   (1) Promote to the citizens of the state the citizen councilor
6   program and its contribution to public and private planning processes;
7   (2) Oversee preparation, tabulation, summarization, and
8   dissemination of data and information by the government and volunteer
9   staff;
10   (3) Receive, on behalf of the citizen councilor revolving fund,
11 gifts and donations of real or personal property, including cash and
12 in-kind services;
13   (4) Hire a value reporter and other paid staff to assist the
14 volunteer staff if funds are available;
15   (5) Contract for any services including without limitation a toll-
16 free telephone number and answering service, keying, optical scanning,
17 computer tabulation, recording, reporting, research, consulting,
18 printing, and mailing to carry out sections 1 through 11 of this act;
19   (6) Solicit volunteers to assist in administering the program from
20 community service, educational, civic, business, religious, and other
21 organizations;
22   (7) Solicit citizen councilor groups from existing organizations;
23   (8) Solicit individual citizen councilors to participate in local
24 groups organized by mutual convenience usually within the same
25 residence or work zip code area;
26   (9) Assign value reporters to interview scholars, experts, public
27 officials, planners, leaders, and others on tape concerning topics of
28 discussion assigned by the state auditor;
29   (10) Produce audio or video cassette tapes, or both, and printed
30 materials as evenhandedly as possible;
31   (11) Mail public information materials to citizen councilor
32 conveners or individual citizen councilors, or both, after final
33 approval by the state auditor;
34   (12) Provide, at cost, group mailing labels of its own conveners on
35 request of an organization participating or to a county, regional
36 government, municipality, or school district if a private iteration of
37 their own constituents is desired at their own time and expense;

1   (13) Machine-scan or key, or both, citizen councilor response
2 sheets and tabulate data;
3   (14) Mail organizational, community, school, business, or church
4 profiles to the leaders of such participating organizations for their
5 information and without cost when they have over fifty groups
6 responding statewide. Such information shall be filed for public
7 review;
8   (15) Prepare summary reports of data generated and press releases;
9   (16) Mail summary reports and other information to all citizen
10 councilor conveners for their groups and to participating
11 organizations, and to those public officials who have indicated to the
12 citizen councilor coordinator that they are interested; and
13   (17) Maintain data generated for public and media reference in the
14 state auditor's office.

15   NEW SECTION. Sec. 7.   The citizen councilor coordinator shall
16 actively encourage citizen councilor groups to form throughout the
17 state. Citizen councilor groups shall usually consist of a minimum of
18 eight and a maximum of twelve regularly assigned members and meet on
19 call of their convener at times and places they deem most appropriate
20 during a thirty-day or other designated time period. Citizen councilor
21 groups might normally meet approximately two or three times per year on
22 state issues, one or two times on county or municipal issues, and one
23 time on federal issues in response to the president of the United
24 States through the state-of-the-union address.   They shall have the
25 opportunity to listen to audio or video tapes articulating an issue of
26 public interest or concern and study other materials prepared or
27 authorized as described in section 4 of this act. Citizen councilors
28 shall have the opportunity to respond anonymously making their opinions
29 known on individual mark-sense response sheets for return to the
30 citizen councilor coordinator for keying or optical scanning,
31 tabulation, and analysis.

32   NEW SECTION.   Sec. 8.   Eight through twelve citizens from
33 organizations such as, but not limited to, community service, civic
34 associations, cooperatives, unions, religious, business, or school
35 district groups may enroll as an organizational group with their own
36 convener designated.   An organizational profile report shall be
37 provided the leaders of organizations with fifty or more groups without

1   cost to inform them of how their members responded to public issues
2   posed or approved by the state auditor and shall be open to public
3   inspection in the office of the state auditor. If additional profiles
4   or services are requested by an organization of its own constituents,
5   the policy, rules, and fees to cover such costs shall be paid
6   separately. Organizations with fifty or more groups may purchase
7   mailing labels of their group conveners from the state auditor and
8   prepare and mail their own group materials for tabulation at their own
9   effort and expense. These data shall not be tabulated by the citizen
10 councilor coordinator and shall not be combined with the public data
11 nor available for public inspection at the office of the state auditor.

12   NEW SECTION. Sec. 9.   Each citizen councilor shall be asked to
13 make donations from time to time to help cover the costs of the citizen
14 councilor program estimated at fifteen to twenty dollars per person per
15 year at present costs. It is also the intention of the state auditor
16 that donations and gifts be solicited from public-spirited individuals,
17 businesses, and foundations for the purpose of assisting in the funding
18 of the program and the providing of scholarships to unemployed or low-
19 income citizens. However, since all direct costs of this program are
20 provided by donations and subscriptions with no funds from public
21 sources, the citizen councilor coordinator shall use his or her
22 discretion in determining the scale and the scope of the program so
23 that expenses do not exceed available funds.

24   NEW SECTION. Sec. 10.   A citizen councilor revolving fund is
25 created and shall consist of donations and subscriptions collected
26 under sections 1 through 11 of this act and any moneys appropriated to
27 it by law for specific purposes.   The state treasurer shall be
28 custodian of the revolving fund. Disbursements from the revolving fund
29 shall be on authorization of the citizen councilor coordinator.   In
30 order to maintain an effective expenditure and revenue control, the
31 citizen councilor revolving fund shall be subject in all respects to
32 chapter 43.88 RCW, but no appropriation is required to permit
33 expenditures and payment of obligations from the fund.

34   NEW SECTION. Sec. 11.   (1) The state auditor may provide the
35 citizen councilor coordinator and his or her volunteer staff with space
36 in existing offices and with clerical services from existing staff to

1   assist in establishing and conducting the citizen councilor program.
2   Appropriations are not required, but the state auditor may consider the
3   services provided under this section in submitting the department's
4   budget.
5   (2) The citizen councilor coordinator shall seek to obtain
6   donations from citizen councilor organizational groups, citizen
7   councilors, and public-spirited individuals, community service
8   organizations, businesses, and foundations to help cover the costs of
9   the program.   When ten thousand dollars in donations have been
10 received, the state auditor shall authorize the citizen councilor
11 coordinator to establish a toll-free telephone number and answering
12 service and to develop a list of the names, addresses, and telephone
13 numbers of persons and groups interested in serving as citizen
14 councilors, citizen councilor conveners, or in citizen councilor
15 organizational groups, or in making donations. Whenever possible, the
16 names, addresses, and legislative districts of registered voters
17 maintained by the secretary of state shall be copied to reduce costs of
18 the state auditor while increasing accuracy of the citizen councilor
19 records. When forty thousand dollars in donations have been received,
20 the citizen councilor coordinator may initiate the new communication
21 process contemplated in sections 1 through 11 of this act and continue
22 it at a scope and scale that is supportable by the resources available.
23   (3) In the event the program under sections 1 through 11 of this
24 act fails to support its direct costs and is necessary to be terminated
25 by the state auditor, funds remaining after payment of all outstanding
26 expenses and disposal of equipment and supplies owned shall be
27 deposited in the general fund.

28   NEW SECTION. Sec. 12. Sections 1 through 11 of this act are each
29 added to chapter 43.09 RCW.

--- END ---

The Citizen Councilor Network Forum
For City/County Governments

This model is derived from the state model but instead of a state law to administer it, the city or county has to pass an ordinance. It is important to do so because of the concept of "mainstreaming." People must believe that what they are being asked to do is "mainstream" and a part of the decision-making processes of their governments, or they won't get too excited. *They must believe that someone is listening.* The effort must be perceived as something more than "citizenship education" (providing information to citizens of what they need to know) or "Citizen Participation" (providing citizens an opportunity locally for input to meet the standards of some higher political body, e.g., federal). The passage of the ordinance sounds a clear bell that government officials and bureaucracies truly want to "talk" (symbolically) to their constituents. That message is not clear at this time. In general, our present cultural reliance on big public meetings do not allow conversations but only confrontations—officials see citizens who are upset rather than at their best (as in juries). But symbolic dialogue of small groups connected by the Fast Forum® Technique to each other and their leaders retains all the attributes of small group, eyeball-to-eyeball, communication yet allows thousands of people to interact with each other. We hope that you will find these ideas of interest and use.

Key Points of the Model

1. The program is open to any citizen who volunteers to meet on call in small groups of 8 to 12 persons approximately quarterly but not more than monthly during a 30-45 day window period. People meet usually in their own homes or workplaces; these are places where people already are. They do not have to go to a big meeting at an often-remote distance to participate. Their role is as a councilor—"one appointed or elected to advise a sovereign or chief magistrate."[101] An ordinance should be passed establishing the program and appointment of any citizen who volunteers to become a "Citizen Councilor." With one simple stroke of the pen, this law will create the three essential conditions for the successful functioning of the future of society postulated by Peter Drucker:

"No society can function as a society unless it gives the individual member <u>social status</u> and <u>function</u>, and unless the decisive social power is <u>legitimate</u> <u>power</u>. Status, function, legitimacy: [are] the essentials of the new order (emphasis added by Tarrant).[102]

It will also meet the essential condition postulated by Alvin Toffler.

"I would urge all of us as futurists to devote some of our energies to finding new ways to destandardize, deconcentrate, descale, delimit, and <u>democratize</u> planning. (emphasis added)." [103]

It also meets the criteria of John Gardner:

"If we are to solve the problems of the cities we must greatly strengthen local government. And given our tradition of private-sector independence, we must invent ways in which local leaders in and out of government can work together to formulate community policies and purposes." [104]

2. Program is usually funded by the government entity organizing the network. Grants can be limited to the first one, five, or ten thousand citizens who apply to enroll in the network. Above that initial number set, any citizen can participate who contributes to cover the variable direct costs of the program estimated to be between $15-$20/year currently. Alternatively, the entire program can probably be self-funded by nominal annual fees of $25-30/year if desired; it need not require tax funds to implement. In effect, a communication network could be established owned by the people but available for use by government officials and planners at the state, county, and municipal levels when citizen participation is desired or required. Provisions can be made for scholarships to assist citizens who are unemployed or handicapped.

3. Citizens (and school youth too when desired) can interact symbolically with the Mayor, County Executive, Governor, President (i.e., "chiefs of state"), planners, or other officials. A network established and maintained by a municipality can be utilized on occasion by the county, region, or state with approval by the municipality. Citizens will then learn of a variety of topics at all governmental levels and will become increasingly better informed and able, over time, to contribute positively as a citizen to their public planning processes of civilization building "in pursuit of happiness."

Washington State was identified as one of five precursor states in social innovation by author John Naisbitt in the best seller *Megatrends*.[105] It is true. For example, Washington was the only state that emerged from the United State's bicentennial celebration in 1976 with a recommendation and funding by its commission for ongoing programming to try to enable its citizens to participate better in the public planning processes of government. Several states established ongoing programs in volunteerism, while most just turned the key, locked the door, and walked away from their celebration of two hundred years of democracy. Washington, however, was the only state able to discern that where citizenship was concerned, it was not quite volunteerism they were after, i.e., the idea of "give me your time, give me your body, give me your hands." Washington was more interested in "give me your mind"! That is significantly different!

The Citizen Councilor concept is *symbolically* interactive. People meet on call through mailed notices to their group conveners who each arrange for their own small group to meet at times and places convenient to themselves, usually in homes or the workplace where they already are. Citizens then listen to an audiotape (or watch a video) and study printed materials prepared by government officials and planners concerning the issue being discussed. After discussion, including a two-minute Day-in-the-Sun, each participant responds individually to an enclosed Opinionnaire®. These can contain demographics of sex, age, county, city, neighborhood, legislative district, congressional district, census tract, ZIP code, etc. They also can contain up to 50 objective questions (yes/no/abstain, multiple-choice questions with up to 5 choices, or value scale questions, e.g., strongly agree, agree, neutral, disagree, strongly disagree, or abstain) or those using "end anchors", e.g., "Not Appropriate 1 2 3 4 5 Highly Appropriate" and the like. The Citizen Councilor bill is an adaptation of the PLAN Forum® model; both use the Day-in-the-Sun group process.

The Citizen Councilor model was designed originally to operate at the level of the state with provisions for utilization at the county and municipal levels. That is still the ideal public arena. It is being adapted here, however, to begin at the municipal level with provisions for later compatibility with systems initiated at the higher county and state levels. The reason is that there are more opportunities to start at the municipal level and gain experience rather than start at the state level. The model provides an informal public information system to citizens to allow them to learn about a public issue and respond with their opinions about it *before laws are passed*. This is in contradistinction to a formal public information system as is the case with the Washington Voter's Pamphlet that is typical in many states. In the voter's pamphlet all citizens face a choice—vote for the law proposed as it is with all of its complexities or vote against it. There is no middle ground.

Value Reporter

In the process proposed in this model "value reporters" are assigned by public officials or a steering committee to prepare the audiocassette or videotapes and develop materials for the citizen councilors network to assist in their discussions. This is a person trained in searching out the facts of an issue much like a reporter, an attorney, or one trained in debate. A value reporter differs in two significant ways from an investigative reporter. First, a value reporter tries to present all sides of a controversial issue fairly and in an unbiased manner to help groups focus their discussion. *The Value Reporter represents the people's "right to know."* The research is not meant to be nor could it ever be exhaustive. It is meant to help stimulate people in their discussion and dialogue processes. The value reporter always returns to the experts and officials interviewed and has them inspect prepared tapes and materials meant for distribution to small groups participating. If a person interviewed is not satisfied with his or her previously recorded statement, the interview is simply done again until the person literally signs off that the statement given fairly represents his or her views. If one misspeaks during an interview, the danger of improper utilization and embarrassment is avoided which might be the case with investigative reporters who often have different agendas. The second difference, as mentioned, is that a value reporter researches only those issues assigned by the government official or steering committee and is representing the people's right to know. An investigative reporter, on the other hand, is usually not so circumscribed and often reports on the sensational. While the role of the value reporter, as we see it, is more deliberate and circumscribed than that of an investigative reporter, both are important.

Convener/Host

Each group has a convener. Usually this is someone who agrees beforehand to act as host or hostess and to convene the group, which is organized earlier, usually to meet within a 30-45 day window period. This allows each small discussion group to arrange their own meeting at a time and place convenient for themselves rather than be asked to attend a big meeting at a remote distance that is the cultural norm. Since there are only about two to six couples in the group, it is not a big task for a convener to get the group together. At their meeting, the person designated as convener helps lead the group through its discussion first by playing a cassette tape. This is usually a 20 to 30 minute audiotape prepared earlier by the organization leader or by his or her staff or "value reporter" with an introduction by the leader followed by a presentation of the issues by others. After listening or viewing the audio or videotape, the convener invites each person in turn to have his or her two-minute "Day-in-the-Sun," if the person wishes to do so. An open discussion follows.

At least fifteen minutes before the group is scheduled to leave, each person is given a copy of an objective Opinionnaire® covering the issues under discussion. Each person then individually completes the demographics and answers the questions posed on the optical scanning response sheet provided (or on the Reproducible Response Sheet if used instead).

The machine-scannable response sheet does the same thing as a computer terminal. It allows a human being to interface directly with a machine accurately, swiftly, and economically. Though low tech, it is high touch. This application, in conjunction with Zeitgeist Communication and the Fast Forum technique, is a breakthrough in social science!

Response sheets (and tapes for reuse) are returned by mail for optical scanning of responses. A Viewspaper® with highlights of results can be returned to each participant by mail and one or more detailed computer profile reports are also returned to each convener for study by participant groups as desired. Results are distributed to public officials and planners as advisory data only. Thus, people act as *official advisors* and a sounding board to assist in the public planning process. All reports are properly disclaimed as described under "The Formal Clauses." (See Chapter 4.)

If organizational and political leaders want organizational and political stability, they should not be up in the crow's nest just giving orders (authoritarianism) and swaying to each pitch and yaw of the organizational ship of state. Instead, they should be as close as possible to the center of organizational stability, near the keel, where the people are. The closer a leader stays in touch with his or her colleagues and constituents, the more stable the organizational and political relationship is between and among them all. This is why authoritarianism, centralism, and dictatorships are all doomed ultimately to fail; they simply cannot compete with the openness and dynamics of a fully functioning democracy. The Community Forum model has great potential. We commend it to organizational, societal, and political leaders everywhere.

Hopefully, political, civic , and cultural leaders will respond. History waits.

The Spiritual Councilor Network Forum for Religious Organizations

Lay Councilor Network Proposal

A religious denomination should use its good offices to take the lead to organize a grassroots discussion of its own theological policies and publications or, as a starting point, of *The Book of Resolutions* of The United Methodist Church.[106]

I (RJS) have been a certified or local church lay speaker[107] of The United Methodist Church annually since 1967 in my research in communication and social science. After the Bible and the hymnal, I consider the *Social Principles* and *The Book of Resolutions* to be the greatest written treasures of our church. The 1996 edition has 294 resolutions of policy statements concerning moral issues faced by an individual, the church, and the society itself within which the church functions. They are carefully considered and well crafted. Forty-three percent were new—just passed by the General Conference, the highest governing body of the church, in 1996. The new 2000 edition is now available from Cokesbury Bookstore and has 338 resolutions; 55% were passed or amended and readopted in 2000.

When I read the *Social Principles* and *The Book of Resolutions*, I am highly influenced. I know it is my corporate church trying to give me, as an individual member, and the church, and the society of which we are a part, a moral sense of direction. However, we are Protestants, and as such, we do not believe in the infallibility of the church. Thus, I am free, as every member of the church is free, to disagree with any part of the theology and policies recommended without being ostracized from the church. Why? Because it is not the corporate church that has the primary responsibility—*it is the individual disciple!* That is a very powerful theology that can bring spiritual relevancy and empowerment to the level of the pew in our churches. Accordingly, our task as laity in the church is to *talk symbolically* together through our study of the *Social Principles* and *The Book of Resolutions* of The United Methodist Church, or similar publications from religious leaders in other denominations, as we build civilization together.

We conducted a nine-week research program from January 16 to March 13, 1994. About 400 parishioners in The United Methodist Church throughout the country in nearly 40 churches participated in a study of issues considered by *The Book of Resolutions*. The nine weeks included Program Orientation, Authority in the Church, The Family, Children, Aging, Health Care, Racism, Economic Justice, and Program Evaluation (see the Viewspaper® summary in Appendix D-1. The research was well received and approved by the participants and proved to be a robust feedback communication technique. We learned—and made progress.

Leadership in the Faith-Forming Community

Dan Dick and Evelyn Burry, authors of *Quest, A Journey Toward a New Kind of Church*, write:

> *Leadership in the faith-forming community paradigm will create an environment where every person can find a place for learning, growth, formation, and meaningful service.*
>
> *To accomplish this shift into the new paradigm, leaders of The United Methodist Church — at all levels — will need to focus attention in four areas: 1) to accurately identify the current reality of the church [e.g., **study the 'current reality' of its theology as contained in the <u>Social Principles</u> and <u>The Book of Resolutions</u>, which are updated every four years by the General Conference**], 2) to articulate the desired reality of the people [e.g., **enable parishioners to meet as 'Lay Councilors' in groups of 4 to 12 to discuss issues in the <u>Social Principles</u> and <u>The Book of Resolutions</u> using the Fast Forum® technique**], 3) to design appropriate systems to move the church from its current reality to its desired reality [e.g., **conduct 'symbolic dialogue' between 'Lay Councilor' parishioners and some or all of the following: general boards, agencies, and the general conference. This symbolic dialogue can be done through use of the Fast Forum® technique. For ease of analysis, the data can be posted on a website. The Polarization-Consensus Ratings can also be published in subsequent issues of the <u>Social Principles</u> and <u>The Book of Resolutions</u>. The ratings will show the degree of personal ratification of resolutions discussed**], and 4) to adopt a "balcony perspective" to observe and improve the entire process [e.g., **by studying the profile reports of Lay Councilor responses at the national, jurisdictional, conference and district levels by gender, age, ethnic family etc., on a website and publish Viewspaper® summaries when appropriate.**]"[108] (The bold-faced bracketed passages in the above quotation were inserted by the present writers.)*

While The United Methodist Church at the present time considers *The Book of Resolutions* to be a reference document, *it has the capacity to be a truly great **dynamic** document. This can be achieved through symbolic dialogue and Zeitgeist Communication to help clarify the overall theology of all religions to their ministry of civilization building to the world.* The process can equally help society at large which can participate too; the computer can keep track of all responses and groups and make reports accurately, swiftly, and economically.

All meetings would be held in small groups in local churches or in homes weekly, bi-monthly, or monthly and be open to all members who are interested in participating (including the public as the computer can keep track easily). Here is how we see it working. Small packets can be sent to local churches participating containing:

1. An instruction and assignment sheet patterned after the experimental research done in 1974.

2. An Opinionnaire® listing questions for each subject studied using multiple-choice or value scale "end anchors" questions, e.g., a) *How appropriate is this resolution?* Participants can respond: Not Appropriate 1 2 3 4 5 Highly Appropriate; b) *All things considered and as now written, can you personally ratify this resolution?* Participants can respond Yes, No, or Abstain (similar to the options provided citizens when they vote in elections on laws pages long).

3. A Fast Forum® machine-scannable response sheet on which individuals can record answers (no "punching" of ballots or generation of "chad" that were often used in the 2000 Presidential elections of Governor Bush and Vice President Gore which proved so controversial).

4. Completed "Reproducible" response sheets, if used, can be returned by the deadline date at the end of each assignment and tabulated by: a) a local church "communicator," if available, who keys participant responses into a computer for transmission to the Forum Foundation by e-mail or mailed diskette for tabulation of profile reports without cost, b) by expressing the completed response sheets with identifying church letterhead together with a check for 50 cents for each sheet to be keyed by the Forum Foundation, or c) by replacing reproducible response sheets in advance with machine-scannable response sheets from the Forum Foundation at 25 cents per sheet in packets of 100 sheets which includes scanning services. (Note: all costs are nominal, but all prices are subject to change without notice.) At present the Forum Foundation plans to advertise this research project to a random selection of the 36,000 local churches in the United States in 2001 to get started.

If you would like your church to participate in the Spiritual Councilor Network Forum using the Fast Forum technique, fax (206-633-3561) or write to the Forum Foundation, 4426 Second Ave. N.E., Seattle, WA, 98105-6191 and request a copy of the Spiritual Councilor Forum Monograph containing the Lay Councilor Network program information. Any religious groups can participate and modify their own materials if required as long as they follow along in the basic format of the program.

5. Results will be optically scanned and tabulated by the Forum Foundation using the Fast Forum® computer "socialware." The computer program is now being updated for the seventh time. Profile reports showing symbolic responses by Gender, Age, Geographic, and Ethnic Family can be provided to denominations for return to participating churches. A simple, single sheet, folded Viewspaper® of summary highlights can be prepared for return to local churches for reference by the study groups participating and/or inserted in their Sunday Bulletins as ongoing information for all members of the local congregation if they desire. Religious leaders also will be able soon to access their national, jurisdictional, or district database to produce specific profile reports eventually of member attitudes and opinions in an ongoing symbolic dialogue of civilization building. (After December, 2001, see www.ForumFoundation.org/UMissues2001 for the first year's postings. We are continuing to learn.)

Other Favorable Factors

- Inasmuch as the 1996 *Book of Resolutions* adopted a new resolution titled "Realizing Unity Between Lutherans and United Methodists" (page 713), the Evangelical Lutheran Church in America could easily be included in the project if desired.

- Inasmuch as the UMC 1996 *The Book of Resolutions* adopted a new resolution titled "Make Evangelism the Number One Priority for the Next Quadrennium," (page 695) the project could be easily expanded to invite citizens from local church communities as "Citizen Councilors." Anytime anyone from outside the church comes to a local church for any activity—that is evangelism. The problems and issues under discussion are not just "church" issues, they are personal, family, national, and international issues in which all citizens are interested. The computer can easily keep track of the different responses and a church, through its organizing efforts, can contribute to civilization building.

- Inasmuch as the UMC 1996 *The Book of Resolutions* readopted a resolution titled "Enlist and Involve Youth in the Life of the Church" (page 735), as a program emphasis for the 1997-2000 Quadrennium, this project could easily be expanded in the years ahead to fulfill that objective with important overtones for the youth and citizens of the society at large. In addition, church youth can participate in Psycho-Social Education and the "State-of-the-Union Address" which follows next. (See www.ForumFoundation.org for more and current information.)

Conclusion

As reports are generated, responses will be returned routinely to the appropriate denominational boards and agencies for their reflection. The responses should help them in their continual task of perfecting the statements and resolutions in the new *Book of Resolutions* or other religious documents being prepared. Presently, each resolution listed in *The Book of Resolutions* ends with the word "Adopted" on a line showing the year of adoption or readoption noted. The overall responses of United Methodist "Councilors," for example, to their study and discussion of resolutions considered, could be reported on this same line in the next publication of the book (every four years). This would complete the feedback loop for everyone's information and benefit and without adding one line more to the book. In this manner The United Methodist Church, or other participating denomination, will have created a national feedback system in which religious leaders of the church and the laity of the church at large can "talk" symbolically to each other and create a balcony perspective as their Zeitgeist becomes visible.

What is the critical "action" that every individual must take in this process of civilization building? It is to think—what is best for the common good and express it in *symbolic dialogue*.

This will meet the criteria of administrative theory number nine, "The Zeitgeist Principle," stated in Section One of this book.

> *To work most effectively, human organizations and institutions (from the smallest—a husband and wife, up to civilization itself—the largest) re-*

quire a functional feedback communication capability. This is best ac-
complished in most organizations by a democratic, open, participative,
reliable, viable, anonymous, routine, and objective feedback communi-
cation system. Most organizations, institutions, and governments in the
world today have no such system.

If this experimental research project is successful, it will be a significant contribution to the successful functioning of society at large by participating religious organizations. It will be a significant contribution to the noblest experiment in governance in the history of humanity—democracy!

"What is occurring is a process — a doing, specifically a process of interrelating the person and his or her world, bringing new meaning into the human situation," *(Reflections on Youth Evangelism,* 1959, by Howard Ellis and Ted McEachern, The Methodist Church, authors).

Psycho-Social Education For Students and Parents

The Need: A New Type of Social Knowledge

Psycho-social education is profoundly concerned with communication and collaboration. It can lead to important new knowledge.

> *As human systems and organizations grow ever larger, more complex, and*
> *more impersonal—in our schools, in our communities, in our churches,*
> *in our governments, and in our industries and commerce—the individual*
> *shrinks toward facelessness, hopelessness, powerlessness, and frustration.*
> — Dr. Stuart C. Dodd, University of Washington professor emeritus
> of Sociology and Richard J. Spady, in their article, "Citizen Counse-
> lor Proposal," *The Seattle Times,* November 10, 1974.

Harvard Professor Elton Mayo, sometimes called the "father of the human relations movement," wrote in the preface of the classic *Management and the Worker* by Roethlisberger and Dickson published in 1939:

The art of human collaboration seems to have disappeared during two centuries of quite remarkable material progress. The various nations seem to have lost all capacity for international cooperation in the necessary tasks of civilization. The internal condition of the nation is not greatly better; it seems that only a threat from without, an unmistakable emergency, can momentarily quiet the struggle of rival groups .... How can humanity's capacity of spontaneous co-operation be restored? It is in this area that leadership is most required, a leadership that has nothing to do with political 'isms' or eloquent speeches. What is wanted is knowledge, a type of knowledge that has escaped us in two hundred years of prosperous development. How to substitute human responsibility for futile strife and hatreds.

Again, notice that it wasn't just more "knowledge" per se for which Mayo was searching, but rather a "type" of knowledge that somehow we have missed. It is our thesis that the new type of knowledge and leadership, for which Mayo was searching, has been found in Zeitgeist Communication and the Fast Forum® Technique using symbolic dialogue!

This new kind of knowledge appears when the Fast Forum® Technique is used to enhance democracy.

The Solution: Enhancing Democracy (A>B>C>A ...)

It's as simple and profound as ABC—**A**dministrators over **B**ureaucrats over **C**itizens over **A**dministrators—Democracy! Our national and global institutions of state, economic, religious, and social enterprises require organization, direction, and administration. *But how and where do these democratic solutions all start?*

In the Schools: Psycho-Social Moratorium

This idea deals with the theory of the late Erik H. Erikson, a preeminent national and international school psychologist, advocating the need for "Psycho-Social Moratoria" for youth. Robert Pranger, a political scientist at the University of Washington in Seattle, wrote a small book in 1968 titled *The Eclipse of Citizenship.* In it he stated, "This need of the adolescent for Psycho-Social Moratoria, as defined by Erikson, is so important, it is of equal importance to the need of a small child for maternal care." This section explains how to conduct such a program in schools using new "socialware" and "symbolic dialogue" communication technology.

The Curriculum: Intellectual Gaming

A child is told by his or her parents, teacher, and culture, "*this* is a fact." But when the child reaches adolescence, the youth begins to realize that there is ambiguity; there are differences of opinion—everything is not clear-cut. We all must realize that teenage youth exist at a *crucible-forming time* in the development of the human personality between childhood and adulthood. And if parents and society "don't get it right then"—

they may never get it right. During this special formative time and place, this period and place of *psycho-social moratoria*, there are no "right" or "wrong" answers by young people as they reflect on the "facts" they have learned in a search together for "meaning." What they need is an educational arena in which to do it. *It is the responsibility of adults organizationally, locally, regionally, nationally, and internationally to provide this neutral, mentoring, supportive, loving, and caring community.* Moreover, these basic processes of democratization are therapeutic, they reduce organizational and societal tensions among people, that is, they lead to peace!

The process proposed here is a kind of *intellectual gaming* in schools and for exactly the same reason that we have physical gaming. As the children exercise their bodies, they get stronger physically. Similarly, as youth exercise their reasoning abilities with ideas posed about real problems in life and their future, and they share their opinions with each other, their parents and others—they grow stronger intellectually, i.e., they *learn* through the dynamics of the Socratic Method! Socrates didn't "tell" his students as much as he "asked them questions." In the process they achieved their own "insight" that up-welled from within themselves. "Ah-ha, that's the answer to my problem," or "Ah-ha, that's the answer to the question—it's "yes" or it's "no!" *And it makes no difference which is chosen at that time; it has nothing to do with what is "right" or "wrong."* What does occur, however, is that the youth's mind becomes "psychologically benchmarked" with the problem or the question and his or her own creative response to it, and the youth *learns!* And when an individual learns "X" amount, the organization and the society of which he or she is a part learns exactly the same amount and all move toward being able to solve problems better in the future.

The moral to the story is that if leaders and educators in society are really interested in improving the abilities and capacities of their citizens and of their children and youth, then *they must enable them* to make lots of decisions about lots of real problems in life! Through the dynamics of the Socratic Method—they will learn! The first three steps in the Socratic Method (awareness, frustration, and insight) are personal—just the individual and his or her world; no one else is involved. But there is a fourth step, and it is a group effort. It is called "verification." The individual needs to know, "Are my ideas practical? Will they work? How do they stack up against the thinking of other people?" Thus, intellectual gaming requires a systematic feedback component.

Printed or computer reports generated in the process are all disclaimed and do not purport to represent the views of the parent or sponsoring organizations or others not participating. This allows people to speak; they speak only for themselves which is every person's right. The results are, however, 100 per cent valid for the students, parents and citizens participating. In the final analysis, it allows the parents to say, "Look, son or daughter, even though all other students say this or all other parents say that, I want to call your attention to this 'additional fact.'" They then can present their own value judgments to their own child as is the parental prerogative, and the process ends right there with remaining questions still unanswered, just as in the story of "The Lady and the Tiger." While the adults participating as mentors search for their own "right" answers to the questions posed, the youth participating are not told by anyone ahead of time which is the "right" answer to the ideas and questions posed. They need to seek their own solutions. Educational leaders will ask, "But how can you assure that young people will have the "knowledge" and "right" information to make such choices?"

The Moral Stance: No Right, No Wrong

There are no "right or wrong" answers for children and youth in their *search for meaning* as they grow to maturity at this point in their lives between childhood and adulthood. They will begin to discern the morality, the diversity, and the insights of their peers, parents, and other citizens as they learn from the process itself using the dynamics of the Socratic Method to gain insights and mature their critical thinking and civil discourse skills.

The process will build in students the essential citizenship and democratic skills of listening respectfully, stating one's own opinion, and interacting respectfully in civil discourse with public officials, planners, and other citizens in their own "pursuit of happiness" with others for a better future. *Governments are not charged with providing their citizens with all the amenities of life they feel they need to make them happy, but all governments are charged with enabling their citizens to pursue their own happiness!*

The Methodology: How It Would Work

Traditionally, in schools, democratic institutions are mimicked by students electing their own officers and representatives. The expectation then is that the officers and representatives will determine school policy and administer projects and that thus this process "teaches the principles of democracy." That is wrong. While this is a valuable and positive learning experience for those few students elected, it is a negative democratic learning experience for those defeated or not even running for office. The democratic and educational philosophy that is really being communicated to our children and youth by this methodology is, "If you are not elected or duly appointed in organizations or society, you don't count." That philosophy is anti-democratic—it strikes at the very foundations of a democratic society. Further, that flawed administrative process produces apathetic citizens instead of interested and informed citizens actively striving to improve the quality of life for themselves, their community, and the society of which they are a part.

What should be done differently in the initial step?

1. After the officers and representatives are elected, they should determine the *subject* for class or school discussion. Usually at the start of the school year the subject is "What should our class or school do this year?"

2. All students should be invited to print, legibly, on one side of a 3 X 5 inch card an idea or proposal concerning the subject under discussion.

3. The officers and representatives should read all cards and select, edit, and rephrase, if required, up to 50 key, representative, "value questions or statements" (the new Form L response sheet will allow up to 150 questions if needed). Note: It is all right if statements are similar—even differing by just one word. The important thing is that the statements are typical, from the students, and help illustrate different choices.

4. The officers and representatives should prepare and administer an "Opinionnaire®" listing the selected ideas and providing demographics of gender and class such as freshman, sophomore, junior, or senior. In this case participants will respond: *Strongly Agree, Agree, Neutral, Disagree, Strongly Disagree, Abstain,* or *Object.* To most people, this will look like a typical "Questionnaire" random-sample "survey" using objective yes/no, multiple-choice, and value-scale questions. But a Questionnaire is based on statistical theory that in turn, is based on mathematical theory. An Opinionnaire®, however, is based on participation theory that, in turn, is based on administrative theory. There are essential differences in some small but critical, theoretical, and practical ways, e.g., an Opinionnaire® *always* allows students to *abstain* or *object* to any question. Different rules apply!

5. Let all students respond to the Opinionnaire® by circling their responses on the Opinionnaire® for keying into the computer or marking their response sheet. Response sheets are either machine-scannable or reproducible, in which case the data are keyed into the computer. When appropriate, ask parents to respond, too.

6. The officers and representatives should organize and oversee the hand or computer tabulation of the data and the preparation of printed profile reports

using the Fast Forum® technique showing responses to each question or state-ment by gender and again by grades. It is essential that each report show the Disclaimer Clause that follows.

Disclaimer Clause

"The purpose of this informal report is to communicate ideas, issues, and problems among people as a platform for future, meaningful dis-cussions of concerns. Participants are assisted in becoming aware of their own beliefs as well as of those intellectual and moral beliefs of others at a point in time—"the Spirit-of-the-Time." The views and opinions expressed herein are those of the individuals who partici-pated and do not necessarily represent the official views of the parent group or sponsoring organization. Nor will the views expressed nec-essarily represent those of the same participants at a later period of time; as humans we each have the ability to receive new information, consider it, and change."

The Disclaimer Clause actually frees all participants to contribute their opinions because everyone knows the societal context in which their opinion is being given. They speak only for themselves which is every person's right. It allows each individual to contribute his or her greatest gift—human thought. Furthermore, the model deals with the statistical "universe" and not just a random sample.

7. A "Viewspaper®" should be prepared, posted, and distributed which is a short summary report of response highlights that also must contain the Disclaimer Clause.

What is the second step?

1. The officers and representatives should study the detailed reports and prepare a second Opinionnaire® iteration listing the representative's opinions of the prevailing consensus of the students. For example, "The elected representa-tives of (school) have studied the reports generated and discussed the results and the following value statements appear to be the prevailing consensus among the student body. Do you agree?" The Opinionnaire® could list up to 50 (or 150) statements or questions with the demographics of gender, class, ethnic family, role (e.g., student, parent) and/or other demographics felt appropriate.

2. The officers should then administer and tabulate the second Opinionnaire®.

What is the third and final step?

1. The officers and representatives should organize and oversee the hand or com-

puter tabulation of the data and the preparation of the printed profile reports and the Viewspaper® using the Fast Forum® technique.

At this point, after this third step, the forum would normally end. However if the elected officers and representatives feel there is still no general consensus or if there are other specific areas that need to be explored, they could continue the iterations. Otherwise it is at this point that the officers and representatives would begin their in-depth discussion of the information, make policy decisions, and administer the programs desired.

Notice that in this process, the elected officers and representatives still retain all their prerogatives to make the final decisions, but they just go through the preliminary democratic process first in order to enable their constituents to participate. What is the main thing to be gained by this approach? Authority will begin to flow from the students to their elected officers and representatives making ultimate decisions by the representatives easier and more acceptable to the student body as they "pursue their own happiness."[109]

This model using Psycho-Social Education and Intellectual Gaming in schools holds great promise. It is a model that can be tabulated by hand using arithmetic if a computer is not available in a classroom or school. This itself is an exercise for students that can build skills and learning (and reduce expenses). Opinionnaires® can be administered verbally to students with their responses made on reproducible sheets. Alternately, responses can be made onto machine-scannable "Forum Foundation *Councilor*™ Response Sheets (Councilor: "One appointed or elected to advise a sovereign or chief magistrate.")[110] The machine-scannable response sheet does the same thing that a computer does but at a fraction of the cost—it allows a human being to interface directly with a machine, accurately, swiftly, and economically.

Further QUEST Forums™ or PLAN Forums® (described later in this chapter) can be held approximately quarterly to expand the psycho-social education curriculum as determined and administered by the officers with topics selected by the representatives. Typical questions which might be considered and from which questions and value statements are derived are:

- How can we tell when a person is "grown up?"
- What makes "growing up" most difficult?
- What "concerns" you about growing up?
- What do you believe is the most difficult part of being a parent?
- How might one become a "successful parent?"
- How might we change the "family" to make it a better place to grow up?[111]

The Summary: Psycho-Social Education!

The Forum Foundation started a research project in 1999 with a new psycho-social education model involving a symbolic dialogue between the President of the United States and the youth of America based on the State-of-the-Union or inaugural address. Any teacher may enroll a class for a one-hour "State-of-the-Union" session. An enrolled class can hold its session at any time between March 1st and November 1st. Teachers and students will engage in the following activities: 1) listen to about 20 minutes of excerpts of the address (to stimulate discussion), have "Day-in-the-Sun" and discussions in foursomes in "Future Molding Game" groups, 3) respond to an Opinionnaire® on either machine-scannable response sheets (or by e-mail if the class key their own data responses), 4) the teacher mails in scanning sheets (or e-mails data) to the Forum Foundation, 5) gender and role profile reports (students/parents/other adults) are returned by mail or e-mail showing responses for the class, 6) the teacher and class discuss responses and compare their own responses to those of their parents (if participating). In December, a report and Viewspaper® of totals from all sources including other students and other adults, is sent to the President and to each teacher participating. A final class discussion of these materials takes place thereafter.

PLAN Forum®
(Planning Long-range Assessment Network)

Leaders of society itself and organizations that have either many employees/constituents and/or are spread over large geographic areas have a common problem. We call it the "Great Dilemma." *It is the continual need of leaders to bring people together to talk about their system problems against the cost in time and money to do it.* If all people do is have meetings, they can never get any of their own work done. On the other hand if they don't get together for meetings, they can't solve their system problems.

The PLAN® Forum using symbolic dialogue can solve this apparent dilemma because it can eliminate many big meetings at often remote distances for people by organizing them into: 1) small-groups of four to twelve people with a "convener" for discussions, 2) meeting during a 15-to-45-day window period convenient for themselves, 3) listening to a 20-30 minute audio or video tape of the leader describing problems and perhaps suggesting solutions, 4) giving each person in turn a two minute "Day-in-the-Sun" to be heard, 5) engaging in open discussion in the small group about the issues, 6) responding to an Opinionnaire® prepared by the leader by marking Fast Forum® Councilor™ Response Sheets which provide opportunities to "abstain" or "object" to questions, 7) receiving Fast Forum® feedback reports and/or a Viewspaper® from the leader with data open to all (i.e., a "leadership" forum) or with the prior understanding that no data will be returned to participants (i.e., a "management" forum) such as is typical of most random-sample surveys.

The Plan Forum® should be a tool in the quiver of all government, corporate, school, and religious human resource personnel and organization development practitioners. See Appendix H, Forum Foundation Fact Sheet and website — www.ForumFoundation.org — for further information about the availability of various Fast Forum® monographs for specific applications as they are developed.

QUEST Forum™
(QUick Environmental Scanning Test)[112]

Key Point of the Model

The QUEST Forum™ (QUick Environmental Scanning Test) model is designed to get quick survey-type information from constituents without their meeting with others.

The idea of the QUEST Forum™ is to send out an Opinionnaire® to a closed, organizational constituency quickly by mail without the need for small discussion groups or any other supporting information. It is a quick, simple, uncomplicated way to scan and test a specific constituency individually about current issues without using discussion groups. It can be either a management forum where the data returned are kept private and confidential or a leadership forum where the data are public and open to all.

For example, a QUEST Opinionnaire® sheet could be sent by mail directly to local church pastors nationally, regionally, or in a smaller conference or district that are members of a denomination. They could be asked to make copies of the Opinionnaire® for each ministerial associate and for four key laity in leadership positions. This permits tabulation to compare results of pastors, associates, and key lay persons. The data should be interesting and credible to church leaders. Completed responses using Forum Foundation optical scanning sheets could be used and returned in a church envelope with a secretary's signature authenticating the data as long as participants remain anonymous by categories. In this manner, the denomination can best assure the validity of the data returned if required.

This model has never been used as designed to date of this writing, but the format is a viable research proposal. The model has great flexibility in program design and should be of immense use to improve communication in appropriate situations in organizations.

A REVIEW OF POTENTIAL APPLICATIONS
OF THE FAST FORUM® TECHNIQUE

User	Model	Need	{See Pages}
Teacher	State-of-the-Union Address	Teach Citizenship Skills	{255}
	Psycho-Social Education	Emotional Maturity	{210}
Students	State-of-the-Union Address	Learn Dialogue and Listening Skills	{255}
	Psycho-Social Education	Gain Emotional Maturity	{210}
Parent	State-of-the-Union Address	Teach Citizenship Skills	{255}
	Psycho-Social Education	Emotional Maturity	{210}
Governors/	State-of-the-Union Address	Governing and Social Capital	{255}
Legislators	Citizen Councilor Network	Governing and Social Capital	{184}
Public Officials/	State-of-the-Union Address	Governing and Social Capital	{255}
Local	Citizen Councilor Network	Governing and Social Capital	{200}
Minister/Priest	* PLAN Forum®	Small Group Dynamics and Long-range Planning	{217}
	** QUEST Forum™	Quick Survey (Public or Private)	{218}
	Time and Talent (Form L)	Inventory Interests and Skills	{260}
Administrator/Org.	* PLAN Forum®	Long-range Planning	{217}
	** QUEST Forum™	Quick Survey (Public or Private)	{218}

*Planning Long-range Assessment Network

**QUick Environmental Scanning Test

7

....

Citizens,
Communication, and
Civilization Building

A Practical Handbook for Civilization Building

This chapter represents an epitome of the whole book, and could be used as the beginning of a course based on the book. It could be used for one module or a day (or a week) of classes or sessions designed to introduce the major themes of the book. A teacher's/leaders's guide for this book will be published soon.

Our *purpose in this text* has been to offer a manual, a practical handbook for civilization building in the 21st Century.

Because we aim that this should be a complete textbook, we have covered the elements of both *the theory and the practice* of civilization and civilization building. Theory and practice are not rigorously separated, but are creatively intermingled throughout our work. We offer both social science and social theory. We have presented a philosophy of society and a theory of society. We have presented social change and social innovation as natural to a growing, healthy, inspirational society. And we see all communities, right up to the level of complexity of world civilization, as societies (groups, organizations).

Our hope is to provide both *inspiration* and *direction* for the builders of the civilization of the near and far future. We have presented the materials for a comprehensive set of citizenship skills.

Our readers, we have assumed, are people interested in the theory and practice of *civilization building*. There are many groups who fit this description. We pick out and offer the following categories or social groupings from a larger set: political and civic leaders, managers, parents, teachers and students—and those who are administrators, professors, analysts, and observers of education—journalists and media analysts, futurists, business owners and analysts, and leaders of culture, statesmen and stateswomen, clergy and religious leaders, city managers and analysts, administrators of schools and industries, government agency staff, banking professionals, financial specialists, investment fund managers, financial journalists and commentators, international aid staff; workers in international global government and world politics, civic activists, ecologists and environmentalists, animal rights advocates—and of course *citizens* everywhere. Civilization building, we believe, is accomplished by "administration." "Administration" cuts across nearly all fields of human endeavor.

Our audience is multi-national. Although many of our examples, and much of our thinking, is American in origin, we believe the problems of civilization are universal. Therefore, it is our expectation that our text and ideas, which have already been presented to audiences in North America, Russia, Europe and Africa, will be used by teachers and learners and practitioners of civilization building in many lands. For civilization building is a global issue, an international concern, and a world-citizen's skill set.

Values, the prevailing beliefs and opinions of individuals, groups, nations, and of civilization itself, are like switches on a railroad. As a decision-making junction is approached, the cumulative effect of all the values held at that point in time become imperative. The perceptions of individuals, the consciousness of groups, the paradigm, meta-perspective, or Zeitgeist of civilization (which is their "*prophecy*") will determine the choice made and direction taken at every junction. Sequential value choices over time, in turn, determine the future for an individual, group, or society for they tend to be self-fulfilling. The result? Again, *people and their institutions, therefore, are more the creators of their own destiny than the victims of it.*

Three Main Themes

Our purpose in this volume has been to offer a practical textbook. We have had three main themes.

1. The presentation of a new approach to *Administrative Theory*. We call this, appropriately enough, New Administrative Theory. This "theory" is presented as a set of 10 theories, or master principles for management with the deepest moral basis. New Administrative Theory is a general theory for the presentation of a set of principles with one overriding goal: to carry forward any organization, group, community or society towards the achievement of its own goals, objectives or purposes. It is a formula for successful social management and leadership.

2. The second theme is the existence of *new social technologies*. In particular, we

present the fruits of 35 years experience developing the Fast Forum® technologies. Our research had shown us some of the major impediments to the appearance in society of a more vital, more informed, more intelligent democracy than has previously existed. We identified the problems of big meetings, and the difficulties that citizens have in making their views heard there. *Civic or political dialogue,* according to our analysis, requires social innovation to accommodate the views and wisdom of the many as opposed to the few. We have presented *symbolic dialogue, social audits* and in particular the *Fast Forum® Technique* as a way to solve the problems of multiple simultaneous dialogue.

The benefits of dialogue are many in the building of civilization. John Spady, director of research in the Forum Foundation, and eldest son of this book's co-author, completed his Master of Science degree (Applied Information Management) at the University of Oregon in August, 2000. His thesis titled "A Selected Study of the Benefits of Dialogue in Small Groups and Implications for Symbolic Dialogue in Larger Groups," was a study of eight authors writing in the field of Dialogue, including Bohm, Senge, Isaacs, Ellinor and Gerard, Simmons, and Spady and Bell. His Abstract ended, "Conclusions [of his study] list the benefits of dialogue attributed to small groups and relate ways to scale them to larger groups using the technique of symbolic dialogue as defined by Spady and Bell (1998)." His findings were significant. He found that these benefits could be created in larger groups using the technique of symbolic dialogue as defined by Spady and Bell (1998). He reports, "The term 'symbolic dialogue' is a creation of Spady and Bell (1998)"[113]. *We believe our new terms of "symbolic dialogue" and "social audits" are pathfinders to the future in civilization building.*

3. The third theme is the task of *civilization building.* We approach this through a philosophy or theory of civilization and its advancement, and through an analysis of the nature and opportunities of citizenship. This means that our objectives include the presentation of a set of skills for effective citizenship. These citizen skills are a vital part of contemporary culture and the building of world civilization. We believe this civilization exists in two ways, in two contexts: planetary and local. Civilization, and its problems and opportunities, exists therefore as a global or collective—a human—phenomenon; and within each nation or land.

A Breakthrough in Social Science

These three themes could be depicted as linked vehicles on a shared journey to a better future for humankind. We can imagine them as railway cars. Our three themes are like vehicles composing a train on a set of curving tracks, curving towards the high purposes of civilization building. But the track itself is a new one in social and political science.

We claim that this track represents a breakthrough in social science. That is a bold claim. But it is not an unreasonable one. Historians of science have shown that science is not a continuous sequence of unbroken discoveries. It is an alternation of "normal science" and periods of revolutionary change. These are called "paradigm shifts" (cf. Kuhn,[114] 1970, Lakatos and Musgrave).[115] Breakthrough science certainly requires a large measure of imagination, faith and intellectual daring. "Every genuinely revolutionary work," writes David Wick in his history of quantum physics, requires a "leap beyond logic."[116] Werner Heisenberg, who was born in 1901, writing his first paper, peppered it with "…startling leaps in logic, baffling appeals to analogies between classical and quantum, and bizarre mathematical objects casually mixed with familiar formulas." (Wick, p.18). Our faith is that we can see, coming in the 21st Century, breakthroughs in social science comparable to those that marked the appearance of quantum physics in the 20th Century.

We believe that the breakthrough in social science that we claim to see happening is part of the revolutionary impact of quantum thinking on social science. So we have described our theory of civilization change, in part, as *Social Quantum Mechanics* (SQM). It is a theory of dynamic social change. It travels on wings of innovation, and innovation is ingredient to its content and its form. Social innovation is its currency and its result.

Social Quantum Mechanics is a young theory, being crafted and tested by many experimental and theoretical hands and minds; but we believe it will have far-reaching consequences for the vivification of cities and citizens. In other words, we envision a true revolution of the best kind in the enhancement of democracy.

This is due partly, but not wholly, to the development of new communication techniques. We have described our approach as centering upon symbolic dialogue within multiple simultaneous communication and many-to-many or many-to-one communication. We have developed the computer and information technology to go with this.

But our concern has not just been a breakthrough in social science or mathematical sociology; we also see a breakthrough in human affairs, in citizen empowerment, in the life of the body politic. For Social Quantum Mechanics is a philosophy and theory, a model or picture of society as a whole. It is an implicit political science deriving from a new approach to sociology based on the activation of the energies of the citizens.

We see this breakthrough as a kind of political counterpart of the Reformation (16th Century). Just as Martin Luther and his collaborators in the Reformation decentralized authority and spoke of the *priesthood of all believers*, so we see the power of political change becoming more and more universal among citizens everywhere. But for this, citizens need citizenship skills as well as a vision of a better society.

Citizenship Skills for a World of Citizens

Our three theories of civilization are the starter-kit for a set of world-citizenship skills for a world of citizens.

Our purpose, however, is not primarily to train up "citizens of the world" and in this way to sabotage or dilute feelings of patriotism and nationalism. Our reasoning is more subtle. We understand the power of self-esteem, and anchoring of personal development that comes from identification with a particular nation or fatherland/motherland—that is, a sense of citizenship. World citizenship is a more abstract concept that comes at a later stage of moral development. Thus our first intention is to equip citizens for effective insight and action in their own hometown, their region, and their nation.

Nevertheless, citizenship is a set of human or personal roles or identities. We can picture them as a series of concentric circles. The innermost circle is that of the family. Next is the workplace. Following that is the local community: the person is a citizen of a town or district. The next circle, going outward from the center, is the citizen of a city or metropolis or megalopolis or nation; then there is the circle representing the citizen of a region such as an association of countries or a hemisphere; finally there is the idea of the citizen of the whole inhabited world. This is the circle, or level, or global (world) of planetary citizenship. Astronomers, astronauts and cosmically minded folks such as science fiction writers can also postulate a layer of identity that they might term cosmic citizenship. These citizens of the cosmos are citizens of worlds.

These concentric circles are a way of picturing our multiple citizenship roles, our layers of citizenship identity. They help us understand that "symbolic dialogue," while enabling the individual citizen to contribute an opinion, *simultaneously* helps communication among all of these disparate groups of the values in which they believe. But our book aims to equip the reader—and those who will be educated by the reader—with citizenship skills.

In offering this concluding summary, we want to distinguish three elements of the set of citizenship skills. The first is the citizen's grasp, moving towards mastery, of the *theory (or theories) of citizenship*. The second is skill in the *practice* of citizenship. The third is the skills associated with networking, or *collective citizenship action*. We are going to say a few concluding words about each of these.

1. The first is the citizen's grasp, moving towards mastery, of the *theory or theories of citizenship*. A citizen highly skilled in this component of citizen skills is able to give a coherent and progressive, usable account of his or her privileges and rights, duties, responsibilities and opportunities as a citizen. This includes the right to refine the theory of citizenship itself. It also includes the citizen's right and duty to discern and communicate his or her vision of the common good.

   A subsidiary skill is actually a set of skills: the skills of self-knowledge. The skilled citizens grow in their understanding of themselves and their own moral vision. They advance cumulatively in their capacity to identify and overcome their resistances or blocks to their own civic involvement. Growing skill in the ability to overcome their resistances will allow citizens to envision the Good Community and Society, the Beautiful, the Ideal City, and to contribute to its realization on earth. Citizens skilled as visionaries will be growing in the arts of the inspiration of citizens and society (political arts). They will be able to make a significant difference towards the building of their own and other cities in "*An Inspirational City in Pursuit of Happiness!®*"

2. The second component of citizen skills is skill in the *practice* of citizenship. Communication is a key element here. In particular, we offer our readers ways to set up effective channels of communication between governors and their constituents. The citizen skilled in the practice of citizenship will be skilled in communicating to those near and far, to those low and high, their ethical vision for the communities of which they are a part: in other words, their concerns and plans for the common good.

Action is also required of every citizen: action on behalf of the common welfare. The highly skilled citizens will grow in the ability to move into action: to place their talents in the service of the community and its growing culture and civilization. The citizen will grow in the ability to understand scientific method. They will learn how to do an experiment in civic science, and how to build their own knowledge relevant to citizenship, and how to access and mobilize their own civic wisdom, hope, and energy. The citizen will be continually growing in effectiveness as a "Citizen Councilor," and as a builder of civilization. Individual citizens are learning *how and when and where and why and with whom to act*, to get going, accomplishing significant actions on behalf of the Good Society.

But what is the "action" required of every citizen? It is to think about problems posed by their leaders, talk with their peers, and then make choices that are felt best for the common good. In the process of symbolic dialogue with their "chiefs of state" (i.e., the president, governors, county executives, mayors, and leaders of big organizations, public and private), they will help all to build a vision of "what ought to be." As symbolic dialogic matures and the visions of the future become more real, the vision itself (which is a "field") begins to be effected "naturally" into society through the dynamics of the self-fulfilling prophecy. Humanity, thus, is more the creator of its own destiny rather than the victim of it.

The people and their leaders will thus provide the "steering mechanism" for society while the "propulsion" is provided primarily by the institutions of government and business with the assistance of schools, universities, and religions. Governors will grow in their ability, through symbolic dialogue, to ascertain the vision of their constituents. They will grow, like top pilots, in their ability to fly with maximum information on the information panel; they will gradually reduce their habit of flying blind. Zeitgeist Communication offers a set of such skills to governors and governed alike.

3. The third component of citizen skills is skill in the activities associated with networking, or collective citizenship action. The highly skilled citizens will grow in the ability to build community. They will be increasingly mastering our ideal models. They will grow in their ability to employ social and political experimental method and so to develop the power of communities of citizens across many regions, and for many significant purposes.

Civilization Building: An Art and a Science

Civilization Building is not an exact science; it is an art, and a work of art. Indeed, in one sense all civilization is the sum of a series of works of art. What kind of art? Many kinds—political and architectural, civic and cultural arts; and moral arts too. For a civilization is a synthesis of ethical arts: it is a moral masterpiece, and therefore a high achievement and art form in social ethics.

But the fact that Civilization Building's "science" cannot be ultimately, and permanently, codified (i.e. as an exact science) does not mean it is not science at all. It is simply a social science, inspired by political art, an exercise in both the *soluble* (science—see Medawar[117]) and the *possible* (politics).

Our book is, among other things, a charter for particular experiments in civilization building. Our ideal "models" such as symbolic dialogue, social audits, citizen and spiritual councilors, and PLAN and QUEST Forums™ are offered as frameworks. They are the setting, and sometimes the actual structure, within which to conduct these experiments in the advancement of civilization.

The models themselves are not final statements; they are invitations to get down to cases, to practice civilization building by trial and error in particular times and places, with particular people. The important thing, as with all experimental science, is to do those experiments! One can be a theorist of civilization building from an armchair. But one can be a builder of civilization only on Main Street or its equivalent . . . by "getting among the people"; by doing experiments in real or symbolic space, with real people— children and adults!

In the days of the Internet and its successors in a cyber-world, silicon-based civilization and civilization building is certainly possible. Even robots, androids and perhaps aliens too can vary in their level of civilization and their contribution to it. Computers and their technologies are a major part of the armamentarium of SQM and civilization building.

But we remember that it is all for "the people." In the final analysis, our book and our theory are instruments for the accomplishment of the purposes of society so memorably stated by Abraham Lincoln that government should be "of the people, by the people, and for the people." [118] Our aim is to equip multitudes of governors—ordinary people—with the citizenship skills needed to build a greater civilization than history has yet recorded. This is the highest vision of the Leadership of Civilization Building. *The mortar that binds a creative organization or society—that is, one that is actively searching for solutions to its problems—is Dialogue—respectfully given and received!*

Thank you for reading this book. We hope you found the ideas in it of interest and use and that it will help you enable Symbolic Dialogue and Civilization Building imaginatively in your life. *YOU ARE THE LEADERSHIP OF CIVILIZATION BUILDING!*

Richard J. Spady and Richard S. Kirby

Epilogue—by H.G. Wells

"Reach Out Their Hands Amidst the Stars"

"The greatest futurist of the 20th Century, perhaps of any century, was Herbert G. Wells," according to Edward Cornish, President, World Future Society. For that reason, we can think of no better ending for our book than to quote key extracts from Wells' address given in 1902 to the Royal Institute of Great Britain.[119]

" . . . And now, if it has been possible for men by picking out a number of suggestive and significant looking things in the present, by comparing them, criticizing them, and discussing them, with a perpetual insistence upon why? without any guiding tradition, and indeed in the teeth of established beliefs, to construct this amazing searchlight of inference into the remoter past, is it really, after all, such an extravagant and hopeless thing to suggest that, by seeking for operating causes instead of for fossils, and by criticizing them as persistently and thoroughly as the geological record has been criticized, it may be possible to throw a searchlight of inference forward instead of backward, and to attain to a knowledge of coming things as clear, as universally convincing, and infinitely more important to mankind than the clear vision of the past that geology has opened to us during the nineteenth century?

I must confess that I believe quite firmly that an inductive knowledge of a great number of things in the future is becoming a human possibility. I believe that the time is drawing near when it will be possible to suggest a systematic exploration of the future. And you must not judge the practicability of this enterprise by the failures of the past. So far nothing has been attempted, so far no first-class mind has ever focused itself upon these issues; but suppose the laws of social and political development, for example were given as many brains, were given as much attention, criticism and discussion as we have given to the laws of chemical combination during the last 50 years, what might we not expect?

To the popular mind of today there is something very difficult in such a suggestion, soberly made. But here, in this Institution which has watched for a whole century over the splendid adolescence of science, and where the spirit of science is surely understood, you will know that as a matter of fact prophecy has always been inseparably associated with the idea of scientific research. The popular idea of scientific investigation is a vehement, aimless collection of little facts, collected as the bowerbird collects shells and pebbles, in methodical little rows, and out of this process, in some manner unknown to the popular mind, certain conjuring tricks—the celebrated wonders of science—in a sort of accidental way emerge. The popular conception of all discovery is accident. But you well know that the essential thing in the scientific process is not a marketable conjuring trick, but prophecy.

And if I am right in saying that science aims at prophecy, and if the specialist in each science is in fact doing his best now to prophesy within the limits of his field, what is there to stand in the way of our building up this growing body of forecast into an ordered picture of the future that will be just as certain, just as strictly science, and perhaps just as detailed as the picture that has been built up within the last hundred years to make the geological past?

In reply to which I would advance the suggestion that an increase in the number of human beings considered may positively simplify the case instead of complicating it; that as the individuals increase in number they begin to average out.

Let me illustrate this point by a comparison. Angular pit sand has grains of the most varied shapes. Examined microscopically, you will find all sorts of angles and outlines and variations. Before you look you can say of no particular grain what its outline will be. And if you shoot a load of such sand from a cart you cannot foretell with any certainty where any particular grain will be in the heap that you make; but you can tell—you can tell pretty definitely—the form of the heap as a whole. And further, if you pass that sand through a series of shoots and finally drop it some distance to the ground, you will be able to foretell that grains of a certain sort of form and size will for the most part be found in one part of the heap and grains of another sort of form and size will be found in another part of the heap. In such a case, you see, the thing as a whole may be simpler than its component parts, and this I submit is also the case in many human affairs. So that because the individual future eludes us completely, that is no reason why we should not aspire to, and discover and use, safe and serviceable generalizations upon countless important issues in the human destiny.

Such, then, is the sort of knowledge of the future that I believe is attainable and worth attaining. I believe that the deliberate and courageous reference to the future, in moral and religious discussion, would be enormously stimulating and enormously profitable to our intellectual life.

It is possible to believe that all past is but the beginning of a beginning, and that all that is and has been is but the twilight of the dawn. It is possible to believe that all that the human mind has ever accomplished is but the dream before the awakening. We cannot see, there is no need for us to see, what this world will be like when the day has fully come. We are creatures of the twilight. But it is out of our race and lineage that minds will spring, that will reach back to us in our littleness to know us better than we know ourselves, and that will reach forward fearlessly to comprehend this future that defeats our eyes. All this world is heavy with the promise of greater things, and a day will come, one day in the unending succession of days, when beings who are now latent in our thoughts and hidden in our loins, shall laugh and REACH OUT THEIR HANDS AMIDST THE STARS."

In closing, we believe Wells is describing some of the principles of our new theory of Social Quantum Mechanics.

We are also struck by the similarity between administrative theory and theology. Theology is the application of one's religious beliefs in the world; it is where "the rubber meets the road." Similarly, administrative theory is the application of one's social, organizational, philosophical, and administrative beliefs in the world. *Perhaps administrative theory, as a pathway to civilization building, is just a secular version of theology and another continuing chapter in "His story" together with that of other religions in the world!*

Appendices

Appendix A

An Essay and Case Study
By Richard J. Spady

The Legitimacy of Public Corporate Power

My colleagues, Richard Kirby and Cecil Bell, have asked me to place this essay here because the case study presented does not fit readily elsewhere with the other themes in the book. It is however, directly related, in my opinion, to administrative and civilization theories and stems from my belief in the viability of capitalism and its genius concept of the entrepreneur. I feel it is my responsibility, as a student and practitioner of administrative and civilization theory, to write of a fundamental question that has sprung from my studies and research concerning "authority" and use of "legitimate power" in the free enterprise system.

I hope that others, with more perspective than I, will consider the problem and propose and apply solutions.

A Problem: Public Corporations and Economic Power that are "Not Legitimate."

Let us reflect again on the thinking of Peter Drucker. In the book, *Drucker: The Man Who Invented the Corporate Society*, author John J. Tarrant writes of the philosophy and writings of this towering and original business thinker, who is perhaps the most prolific and influential writer in the field of business in our time. Tarrant states that a Drucker theme is:

"The corporation is not just an economic entity. It is social and political. Its purpose is the creation of legitimate power." Drucker is right. Tarrant explains Drucker further:

> *Once, the corporation had been truly responsive to its shareholders. The power of the managers of the corporation grew out of the property rights of the individual. Thus, this power was legitimate power. But not any more. Now the vast majorities of shareholders did nothing but sign proxies. They had no say in management. The stockholder had not been deprived*

of his rights; had abdicated them because he could not be bothered to do otherwise. But no matter how the situation had come about, the management of the corporation was no longer responsible to the ownership. It ruled independently, controlled by no one and responsible to no one. By definition then, corporate power was illegitimate power. The rule of the managers must be made legitimate.[120]

Drucker has diagnosed correctly the problem facing society and large, modern-day public corporations. The management of the public corporation is no longer responsible to the ownership through the common practice and use of the proxy device. Drucker points out that it is not so much that today's corporate managers are exercising illegitimate power, it is just that their power is not legitimate. That is, corporate managers did not wrest their power illegitimately from owners, it is just that most owners, as mere investors, defaulted their overseeing responsibilities and could not be bothered with managing. The result is that the power of the managers of perhaps most of today's large publicly-held modern corporations are not exercising legitimate economic power. This weakens the corporations and the free enterprise system as a whole in the eyes of society itself whose members fear and often observe economic excesses such as the savings and loan scandals and what appears to be excessive pay for some CEOs of public corporations.

The Importance of Legitimate Authority and Economic Power

Capitalism and the free enterprise system have a critical problem that must be solved.

While the free enterprise system provides maximum incentives to individuals in a democratic society, the managers of its publicly-owned corporate, economic, and business institutions are critically hampered in their economic "rule" by not being able to exercise legitimate economic power. Again, they are not exercising illegitimate power; it is just that their power is "not legitimate."

Ian Wilson, author of *The New Rules of Corporate Conduct*, is reviewed in *The Futurist* (November, 1999). Cynthia Wagner, editor, writes:

> "One of the most controversial economic trends of the last two decades has been the soaring increases in pay for top business executives … . The problem isn't just that chief executives officers are paid a lot; so are basketball players and movie stars. The problem is that they get paid well even if their companies lose money, and they get paid far more than the lowest-paid workers in the company.
>
> "The globalization of the economy is one factor that has driven

up the prices of CEOs. It isn't just salaries either; there are also perks and stock options. In sum, the average CEO's total pay in 1997 was 325 times that of the average factory worker. Plato reasoned that the "right ratio" between the top and bottom is five to one; contemporary business guru Peter Drucker put it at 20:1. The norm in Europe and Japan is a multiple of between 15 and 20."[121]

The managers of large public corporations often manage by default, through their usual control of proxy votes. Their power is not legitimate power because they are not owners taking entrepreneurial risks. *It seems to me that employees of publicly owned corporations can be considered economic bureaucrats of the state in the same way that government employees are civic bureaucrats of the state.*

The purpose of economic managers and workers, however, is to produce and distribute goods and services to the public. But the purpose of government and the free enterprise system as a whole is to meet the overall needs of its citizens to enjoy life, liberty, and to pursue their own happiness. Because both private property and the free enterprise system are so dynamic, they can result in the rapid dislocation of people from eliminated jobs. Many social and personal hardships are a consequence of such dynamics. These include retraining, relocation, joblessness, and homelessness. These results cannot be borne by just those firms having to make decisions to close or reorganize. There have to be safety nets for people from the free enterprise system and society as a whole as transition occurs. This must come from government that has responsibility to oversee the successful functioning of the free enterprise system and society. *But governments can do this only with the full participation and support of its citizens who must provide the legitimacy and continual, ongoing, authority for it and its economic surrogates to govern.*

A Conflict of Interest

Who is in control? Many fear that our economic institutions are running amok. Too often their only concern seems to be "the bottom line," or making a dollar profit. Where is the moral and ethical restraint in the system? A way needs to be found to help legitimize the rule of economic managers so as to strengthen the concept of the free enterprise system and the ownership of private property that provide the natural incentives for people to produce.

One must remember that, theoretically speaking, the corporation is not a real person but is instead a legal fiction that was created by the state. States are empowered by law to charter corporations. *However, neither the state, nor the federal government which empowers the state, has the power to create an instrumentality, i.e., the public corporation, and grant it more powers or permit it to acquire more powers than it itself has. That is a conflict of interest.* For example, the maximum annual pay of a civic bureaucrat working for government is the $400,000 paid to the President, the highest-ranking employee. This was raised in 2001. Before key "government bureaucrats" can get raises, however, they must be approved by Congress, which is open to the scrutiny of the media and public. It would not be appropriate for government to create a new entity, i.e., a public corporation, *basically funded by the public at large,* and then say to the "economic bureaucrats" running it, "set your own salaries and pensions and perks. Whatever you can get is OK as long as you pay yourself from 'corporate profits.'"

That is a conflict of interest. Yet that, in effect, is what has been done by default. Furthermore, bureaucrats transfer back and forth between government jobs (where they enjoy power and prestige and gain new credentials) and public corporations (where they enjoy much larger salaries). One experience enriches the other. While corporations have been considered as "immortal individuals" since the epoch making case of *Dartmouth College v. Woodward,* Justice John Marshall and the Supreme Court's decision, "had the long-range effect of keeping corporations safe from capricious interference by legislators .... After the *Dartmouth College* decision, the number of corporations would rise exponentially till, by the end of the 19th Century, they dominated the American economy."[122] *Today large, multi-national corporations need to be concerned with the growing issue of their exercising "legitimate" power.*

With the Internet explosion and world markets, there is greater and greater concentration of corporate ownership through mergers and acquisitions. Right now it is a consumer's market; but in the future it will be a seller's market if such trends continue. Without restraint and recognition of the need to make our economic institutions "legitimate," our society runs the grave risk of "killing the goose that laid the golden egg." *It is in the overall best interests of the country and multi-corporations, themselves, to be aware of this problem and address this conflict of interest responsibly for the benefit of all.*

Government now recognizes this conflict of interest in the case of non-profit, tax-exempt corporations. In this case the annual tax returns to the IRS must show if there are any family members of the CEO employed by the corporation. Such circumstances are flagged by the IRS for special scrutiny to assure that payments are for valid services rendered and not just an income diversion scheme.

Under the present circumstances, responsibility to correct these economic conditions, in which the leadership of most public corporations is not exercising legitimate power, must default to the federal government. It must create legitimate power for managers of public, domestic and multi-national corporations in order to legitimize the free enterprise system itself. This system is the major supplier of the nation's and the world's goods and services to the people.

One way would to be to recognize these theoretical problems and for Congress to set the maximum salaries that can be paid to CEOs of public corporations as well as to non-profit, tax-exempt corporations with similar circumstances. Perhaps Drucker's recommended ratio of 20 times the highest paid in government (the President) or $8 million dollars per year would be appropriate. There should be some kind of incentive to encourage performance in the private sector, which pays its own way, over the public sector, which must be supported directly by the taxes of its citizens.

This plan would not penalize in any way the Bill Gates and Paul Allens of the world, who through their Microsoft Corporation, earned their main wealth through their creativity, entrepreneurship, and subsequent ownership of stock. It would only affect those CEOs and key personnel of large public corporations who are not owners taking risks, but control the corporations by their insider positions. Because of a conflict of interest, these corporate leaders are in a position where they could abuse their fiduciary relationship. What is the cutoff point? We would think that if a CEO and/or his related family owned 51% of the stock of a large public corporation (or if they own a small closely held corporation not soliciting funds from the general public), they would be exempt and could pay themselves anything they feel appropriate. Anyone else who buys stock in such a corporation knows they have no control and so are forewarned of possible abuses. Their purchase would take this into account. Any CEO or other key persons of large, publicly owned corporations owning below 50% of the stock would be subject to the public policy guidelines.

Theoretical Tax Strategy Implications

Theoretically, if public corporations in reality are the state, they should not be taxed. The state does not tax itself. Under the free-enterprise system, the purpose of public corporations is to provide goods and services to the people and to create jobs so people can do work and receive income. Every tax that is imposed by government on a business is just passed along to the customer in terms of higher prices. This makes the product or service less competitive in the world and causes the business activity and employment to decline. Businesses do not pay taxes—only people pay taxes. Theoretically, the goal in the free-enterprise system is to deliver goods and services to the public at the lowest possible costs while maximizing employment and employment income. These seem to be contradictory, but they are really a form of checks and balances to the system as a whole. The whole system must consider the markets of the world.

So public corporations should not be taxed; they are really the state. Rather, people should be taxed, e.g., employees who receive a higher income and stockholders who receive a higher dividend because of the lowered corporate taxes. Overall the tax effect sought should be revenue neutral to the government, but the societal effect should be increased pay and productivity in the free-enterprise system as a whole with increased physical and societal rewards accruing synergistically to the people.

In support of this conclusion is a four-year study by the congressional Office of Technology Assessment in a report released May 14, 1988 and titled "Technology and the American Economic Transition." It was reported: *For the country to take full advantage of emerging technologies, Congress should consider making fundamental changes in its tax laws and various government regulations.... In the tax area, the study urged reducing or abolishing the tax on capital gains and reforming or abolishing the corporate income tax.*[123]

In today's political climate, the federal government could hardly reduce corporate taxes let alone eliminate them, but they should. *It is doubtful that government will rethink the problem, but the people should.*

All the rights of citizenship remain to every person employed by or relating to a public corporation; their rights are not diluted simply because they are working in the "private" sector. What is being seen today in the economic marketplace of the United States is probably a final playing out of the rights of people as they are enumerated in the Declaration of Independence and the Constitution, including the "right to be heard" (which was not included in the Constitution so therefore is still a "right" retained by the people under the 9th Amendment). For these reasons Many-To-Many Communication is well grounded in both social and legal theory if its open processes are ever challenged.

Again, when one looks at a public corporation today, one is really looking at the state—the government. People should expect no more, but neither should they expect less. The government and its citizens, together with Chambers of Commerce and other such related business and employee associations and unions, should be equally concerned with the vitality of the overall business and free-enterprise environment. *Everyone must work together at strategies to make the power of economic managers in public corporations of the state legitimate.* This will not be easy to understand how this can best be done. But the success of this endeavor, *which will be an act of statesmanship*, will set the keystone for private ownership, capitalism, and the free enterprise system in the future not only in the United States but in the world. This, in turn, will best assure the incentives, vitality, economic freedom, that domestic and global businesses require to fill the physical needs for goods and services of the people in our society and in the world. *This is what the free-enterprise system is all about.*

Hopefully, elected officials everywhere in the world will be attentive to the similar problem with multi-national corporations which it would appear, from a theoretical viewpoint, should be chartered by the United Nations to achieve the economic legitimacy required. If lawmakers prove to be politically incapable of exercising the statesmanship that will be required, then citizens themselves will inevitably take the responsibility through use of their powers in initiatives and referendums and at regular elections. "The people are more the creators of their own destiny, rather than the victims of it."[124] *That is, the people's "manifest destiny" is civilization building!*

Questions to Consider for Political Leaders

Do you think that there is a problem with the legitimacy of public corporate power?

Is so, why? If not, why not?

If you agree that there is a problem, what solutions do you propose?

Appendix B

Forum Foundation Machine
Scannable Response Sheet, Form L

FORUM FOUNDATION *COUNCILOR*™ RESPONSE SHEET*
(A *FAST FORUM*® MACHINE-SCANNABLE SOCIALWARE PRODUCT)

E-Mail: fastforum@aol.com   **SIDE A**   WWW: http://ForumFoundation.org

Mark Reflex® by NCS MM217043-2   654321   HR04   Printed in U.S.A.

INSTRUCTIONS: 1. Make a dark mark, using only a regular No. 2 pencil.
2. Do not use ink pens.
3. Make a dark mark that fills the bubble completely.   (RIGHT ● WRONG ⊘⊗◐⊙)
4. Cleanly erase any mark you wish to change.
5. Do not fold or write comments on this sheet; write all comments on a separate sheet.
6. It's IMPORTANT that you indicate your personal and organizational categories as requested.
7. Please respond to each statement or question, as follows:

FILL IN: ⓨ (Yes) if you can identify with the statement or question without reservation – <u>a clear Yes</u>.

ⓝ (No) if you cannot identify with the statement or question, also without reservation – <u>a clear No</u>.

● (The <u>One</u> Best Choice) if the statement or question is multiple choice.

⊛ (Object) if you believe that the statement or question is misleading or inappropriate in some manner.

MAKE NO MARK IF YOU <u>ABSTAIN</u> TO A QUESTION OR STATEMENT, i.e., if you are undecided or feel unable to respond at this time. For example, if you feel you need more information before answering, you should abstain.

YOUR PERSONAL AND ORGANIZATIONAL CATEGORIES:

1 SEX	MALE ① · FEMALE ②	**6**	①②③④⑤⑥⑦⑧⑨⓪	**11**	①②③④⑤⑥⑦⑧⑨⓪
2 AGE	10 20 30 40 50 60 70 80+ ①②③④⑤⑥⑦⑧ 19 29 39 49 59 69 79	**7**	①②③④⑤⑥⑦⑧⑨⓪	**12**	①②③④⑤⑥⑦⑧⑨⓪
3	①②③④⑤⑥⑦⑧⑨⓪	**8**	①②③④⑤⑥⑦⑧⑨⓪	**13**	①②③④⑤⑥⑦⑧⑨⓪
4	①②③④⑤⑥⑦⑧⑨⓪	**9**	①②③④⑤⑥⑦⑧⑨⓪	**14**	①②③④⑤⑥⑦⑧⑨⓪
5	①②③④⑤⑥⑦⑧⑨⓪	**10**	①②③④⑤⑥⑦⑧⑨⓪	**15**	①②③④⑤⑥⑦⑧⑨⓪

YOUR OPINION OF EACH QUESTION OR STATEMENT:

Columns (header: 1 2 3 4 5 6 / A B C D E):

1 ⓨⓝ○○○⊛   11 ⓨⓝ○○○⊛   21 ⓨⓝ○○○⊛   31 ⓨⓝ○○○⊛   41 ⓨⓝ○○○⊛
2 ⓨⓝ○○○⊛   12 ⓨⓝ○○○⊛   22 ⓨⓝ○○○⊛   32 ⓨⓝ○○○⊛   42 ⓨⓝ○○○⊛
3 ⓨⓝ○○○⊛   13 ⓨⓝ○○○⊛   23 ⓨⓝ○○○⊛   33 ⓨⓝ○○○⊛   43 ⓨⓝ○○○⊛
4 ⓨⓝ○○○⊛   14 ⓨⓝ○○○⊛   24 ⓨⓝ○○○⊛   34 ⓨⓝ○○○⊛   44 ⓨⓝ○○○⊛
5 ⓨⓝ○○○⊛   15 ⓨⓝ○○○⊛   25 ⓨⓝ○○○⊛   35 ⓨⓝ○○○⊛   45 ⓨⓝ○○○⊛
6 ⓨⓝ○○○⊛   16 ⓨⓝ○○○⊛   26 ⓨⓝ○○○Ⓡ   36 ⓨⓝ○○○⊛   46 ⓨⓝ○○○⊛
7 ⓨⓝ○○○⊛   17 ⓨⓝ○○○⊛   27 ⓨⓝ○○○⊛   37 ⓨⓝ○○○⊛   47 ⓨⓝ○○○⊛
8 ⓨⓝ○○○⊛   18 ⓨⓝ○○○⊛   28 ⓨⓝ○○○⊛   38 ⓨⓝ○○○⊛   48 ⓨⓝ○○○⊛
9 ⓨⓝ○○○⊛   19 ⓨⓝ○○○⊛   29 ⓨⓝ○○○⊛   39 ⓨⓝ○○○⊛   49 ⓨⓝ○○○⊛
10 ⓨⓝ○○○⊛   20 ⓨⓝ○○○⊛   30 ⓨⓝ○○○⊛   40 ⓨⓝ○○○⊛   50 ⓨⓝ○○○⊛

YOUR COMMENTS: If you have any comments or suggestions, please use <u>a separate sheet</u>, or the comments page of the Opinionnaire® and return it to your convener or mail directly to the Forum Foundation. Please print or write clearly. *Thank You!*

*"Councilor" is defined by Webster as "an official advisor to a sovereign or chief magistrate."

FORUM FOUNDATION *TIME & TALENT*™ RESPONSE SHEET
(A *FAST FORUM*® MACHINE-SCANNABLE SOCIALWARE PRODUCT)

SIDE B

RIGHT ●   WRONG ⊘ ⊗ ⊖ ⊙

LAST NAME   **FIRST NAME**   MI

PHONE NUMBER

BIRTH DATE

Month	Day	Year
Jan.		
Feb.		
Mar.		
Apr.		
May		
June		
July		
Aug.		
Sept.		
Oct.		
Nov.		
Dec.		

CLASS YEAR

SPECIAL CODES

A B C D E F G H I J

TIME & TALENT RESPONSES:

E-Mail: fastforum@aol.com   WWW: http://ForumFoundation.org

Appendix C

Forum Foundation Reproducible Response Sheet

COUNCILOR™ **REPRODUCIBLE RESPONSE SHEET**

(A *FAST FORUM*® GROUPWARE PRODUCT)*

INSTRUCTIONS: 1. Please indicate your personal and organizational categories as requested.   * | *Councilor is defined by Webster as: "an official advisor to a sovereign or chief magistrate."*
   2. Please respond to each statement or question, as follows:

FILL IN (Y) (Yes) if you can identify with the statement or question without reservation -- a clear Yes.

(N) (No) if you cannot identify with the statement or question, also without reservation -- a clear No.

● (The <u>One</u> Best Choice) if the statement or question is multiple choice.

(OBJ) (Object) if you believe that the statement or question is misleading or inappropriate in some manner.

MAKE NO MARK IF YOU <u>ABSTAIN</u> TO A QUESTION OR STATEMENT, i.e., if you are undecided or feel unable to respond at this time.   For example, if you feel you need more information before answering, you should abstain.

YOUR PERSONAL AND ORGANIZATIONAL CATEGORIES:

| 1 SEX | ① MALE   ② FEMALE |
| 2 AGE | 10/19 ① 20/29 ② 30/39 ③ 40/49 ④ 50/59 ⑤ 60/69 ⑥ 70/79 ⑦ 80+ ⑧ |

3 ⓪①②③④⑤⑥⑦⑧⑨
4 ⓪①②③④⑤⑥⑦⑧⑨
5 ⓪①②③④⑤⑥⑦⑧⑨

6 ⓪①②③④⑤⑥⑦⑧⑨
7 ⓪①②③④⑤⑥⑦⑧⑨
8 ⓪①②③④⑤⑥⑦⑧⑨
9 ⓪①②③④⑤⑥⑦⑧⑨
10 ⓪①②③④⑤⑥⑦⑧⑨

11 ⓪①②③④⑤⑥⑦⑧⑨
12 ⓪①②③④⑤⑥⑦⑧⑨
13 ⓪①②③④⑤⑥⑦⑧⑨
14 ⓪①②③④⑤⑥⑦⑧⑨
15 ⓪①②③④⑤⑥⑦⑧⑨

YOUR OPINION OF EACH QUESTION OR STATEMENT:

Columns of response bubbles (A=Y, B=N, C, D, E, and OBJ) for statements numbered 1–50.

YOUR COMMENTS: If you have any comments or suggestions, please outline your key points and explain your position below or continue on reverse side. Please print or write clearly. *Thank You!*

General Area of Comment: _____

OPTIONAL: Name _____ Day Phone ( ) _____ Time Zone _____ Date _____

Outline of Key Points : 1. _____ 2. _____ 3. _____

Detailed Explanation: _____

Appendix D

Select Examples of the Fast Forum Document Formats

1. Viewspaper, Topic #9 Evaluation WUMB (March 13, 1994)

WHAT UNITED METHODISTS BELIEVE

Viewspaper®

Volume 2, Number 9 (March 13, 1994)

Topic #9: Evaluation

[United Methodist *Councilor* Network Proposal]
<Example for PNW Conference, UMC, of Sample Format>

On March 13, 1994 United Methodists from churches around the country met to participate in a discussion of the last topic, Evaluation, in our project on "What United Methodists Believe." The purpose is to take a first step toward developing a new communication process, based on new participation and administrative theories, and thereby enable large numbers of people to communicate with each other over large distances. 380 people participated in small, four-person, "Future Molding Game" groups. They listened to a cassette tape regarding a UM *Councilor* Network proposal. Each participant was then invited to present his or her views in a two minute "Day-In-The Sun" process while others listened without interruption, comment, or question. Following an open discussion in their groups, participants then responded to an *Opinionnaire* composed of questions on their topic. This *Viewspaper* partially summarizes the objective opinions of everyone who participated and completed an *Opinionnaire*.

A full, detailed, profile report (analyzing the participants' opinions by jurisdiction) was mailed to your church for later review by your discussion groups and/or for posting on your church bulletin board for further reference by the congregation at large. All profiles of gender, age, role, ethnic family etc. were sent to the General Board of Church and Society and UMCom for their information and reference.

Thank you all for participating in this national research project. It has been a first and, I believe, an important learning experience for us all.

Dick Spady, President, Forum Foundation, Co-sponsor

WHAT UNITED METHODISTS BELIEVE
Viewspaper #9 Evaluation, Page 1

A CLOSER LOOK AT THE PARTICIPANTS

The first 15 questions of *Opinionnaire* #9 were demographic questions. We use these to better understand the answers. In this case, the "typical" participant is between 40 and 49 years old (28%); female (52%); Caucasian (92%); lives in the Central time zone (44%); has been a member of the United Methodist Church for over 20 years (59%); are Ordained Ministry (3%), Local Church Laity (54%), Officers (15%), or a member of local Church, District, Conf., or General Boards of Church and Society (19%), and Unidentified (8%).

Why Talk About "What United Methodists Believe"?

In our tradition as Protestants, we do not believe in the infallibility of the church. We are taught that our responsibility is directly to God through Christ and there is no institution or person between us. Accordingly, I believe that the Social Principles and The Book of Resolutions are the greatest treasures of our church after the Bible. However, we treat The Book of Resolutions as a "finished document." It is not. But it is a "great beginning document" if we can learn to use it. Perhaps this series is a start. Thank you for participating toward building the Kingdom of God!

Dick Spady, Lay Speaker, St. Peter's UMC, Seattle District, Editor

DISCLAIMER CLAUSE: The purpose of this report is to communicate ideas, issues, and problems among people as a platform for future, meaningful discussions of concerns. Participants are assisted in becoming aware of their own beliefs as well as of those intellectual and moral beliefs of others at a point in time--the "Zeitgeist," or "Spirit of the Time." The views and opinions expressed herein are those of the individuals who participated and do not necessarily represent the official views of the parent group or sponsoring organization. Nor will the views expressed necessarily represent those of the same participants at a later period of time; as humans we each have the ability to receive new information, consider it, and change.
-- FORUM FOUNDATION.

"Opinionnaire" and "Viewspaper" and "Fast Forum" are registered trademarks of the Forum Foundation, a non-profit, educational and research foundation located at 4426 Second Avenue NE, Seattle, WA 98105-6191. All trademarks are used with permission.

WHAT UNITED METHODISTS BELIEVE
Viewspaper #9: Evaluation , Page 4

PARTIAL SUMMARY OF OPINIONS

[Editor: The Polarization Rating is the % of 380 participants answering only yes or no. The Consensus Rating is the % positive of those polarized. So 42 out of 100 answered "yes" in this first question—the balance "No."]

1. At the start of this series were you familiar with the UMC Social Principles? [Rounding can affect totals + or - 1%.]
Yes (40%) No(56%) Abstain (3%) Object (2%); PC Rating (96%— 42)

2. Do you feel that you are familiar with the UMC Social Principles now?
Yes (78%) No(14%) Abstain (6%) Object (2%); PC Rating (92%—85)

3. At the start of this series were you familiar with UMC Book of Resolutions?
Yes (27%) No(69%) Abstain (3%) Object (1%); PC Rating (96%—28)

4. Do you feel that you are familiar with the UMC Book of Resolutions now?
Yes (71%) No(18%) Abstain (8%) Object (3%); PC Rating (89%—80)

6. Each week in the Viewspaper® the editor wrote, "We are taught that our responsibility is directly to God through Christ and there is no institution or person between us." Do you believe this theology is true?
Yes (88%) No(6%) Abstain (5%) Object (1%); PC Rating (94%—94)

7. Do you believe in the infallibility of the church?
Yes (9%) No(81%) Abstain (9%) Object (2%); PC Rating (2%)

8. Each week in the Viewspaper® the editor wrote, "Accordingly, I believe that the Social Principles and The Book of Resolutions are the greatest treasures of our church after the Bible." Do you share this enthusiasm?
Yes (22%) No(60%) Abstain (12%) Object (6%); PC Rating (82%—26)

9. Each week in the Viewspaper® the editor wrote, "However, we treat The Book of Resolutions as a 'finished document.' It is not. But it is a 'great beginning document' if we can learn to use it." Do you share this belief?
Yes (77%) No(9%) Abstain (10%) Object (3%); PC Rating (86%— 90)

21. It was recommended to the General Board of Church and Society that they basically replicate this series on What United Methodists Believe

WHAT UNITED METHODISTS BELIEVE
Viewspaper #9: Evaluation Page 2

---

beginning in January, 1995 "to help introduce the Social Principles and Book of Resolutions to other church groups interested and further evolve in our efforts to learn how better to communicate and create a new social context." Do you agree?
Yes (60%) No(23%) Abstain (11%) Object (6%); PC Rating (83%— 72)

22. It was recommended to the General Board of Church and Society that they "establish a United Methodist *Councilor* Network as a two-year, *national research program* to provide member and constituent responses to the General Board of Church and Society and thus the General Conference concerning social issues." Do you agree?
Yes (64%) No(19%) Abstain (11%) Object (5%); PC Rating (83%—78)

23. Would you be supportive of an additional paragraph similar to the following in italics to further clarify authority in our church?

3. *We acknowledge from our Protestant tradition that we do not believe in the infallibility of the church. Accordingly, the General Conf, in its turn, does not have the authority to speak for any individual United Methodist. We believe that our individual responsibility is directly to God through Christ and there is no other institution or person between us. Thus, any individual United Methodist is free to dissent in accordance with the Holy Spirit within himself or herself from passages in the Social Principles and The Book of Resolutions without being ostracized from the church.*
Yes (72%) No(6%) Abstain (18%) Object (4%); PC Rating (78%—93)

COMMENTS & ANSWERS

Thanks to all who submitted comments.

"It has been an interesting and meaningful project for us to participate in this, and the one thing that is sure is that more local members know about 'United Methodists Social Principles' and 'The Book of Resolutions' than before."

"Having served the Church as layman and minister, I found this project very interesting and helpful. I feel we have the machinery to make the UMC the outstanding denomination in the world. This will be a good start in dealing with the 'grassroots.'"

"With regard to the Councilor Network, what assurance is there that the responses will be heeded?" [Editor: None, the General Conference will still retain all its prerogatives. The first step in solving a problem, however, is to be aware of it; with better diagnosis, better solutions should follow.]

WHAT UNITED METHODISTS BELIEVE
Viewspaper #9 Evaluation, Page 3

2. Jan Cate's International Women's Conference Opinionnaire® in China

U.N. FOURTH WORLD WOMEN'S CONFERENCE
BEIJING, SEPTEMBER 4-15, 1995
Opinionnaire®

Background Information: This Opinionnaire® was created by the Everywoman's Delegation of Seattle, Washington, USA. The delegation is sponsored by the Institute of Global Security Studies. The value statements relate to the eleven concerns outlined by the Beijing Platform for Action and are concerns voiced from writings, conferences, plans of action and statements made by women since the beginning of the United Nation International Women's conference, 1975. [*This is a research project to inform women of a new "Many-to-Many" communication technique called the "Fast Forum®" developed in the Seattle area. (Please refer to the "Forum Foundation Fact Sheet" available from delegation members.)]

INSTRUCTIONS. PLEASE READ CAREFULLY.

The purpose of this *Opinionnaire* is to find out how women feel about the representative comments that come from a cross section of women's issues and to demonstrate as noted* above using mass communication techniques.
- Identify your demographic categories , then share your opinions as follows:
- Circle the <u>one number</u> (from 1 to 5) that reflects your opinion most closely.
- Circle <u>Abstain</u> if you are undecided or feel unable to respond.
- Circle <u>Object</u> if you believe a statement is misleading or inappropriate.

YOUR DEMOGRAPHIC CATEGORIES

- **Your Gender:** (1) Female   (2) Male
- **Your Age:** (1) 10-17,   (2) 18-35,   (3) 36-49,   (4) 50-64,   (5) 65-79,   (6) 80-over
- **Your Ethnic Family:** (1) African, (2) Asian, (3) Caucasian, (4) Latina, (5) Indian, (6) Mixed, (7) Other
- **Your Region:** (1) Asia,   (2) North America ,   (3) Central America,   (4) South America,
         (5) Europe,   (6) Africa,   (7) Mid-East,   (8) Australia,   (9) Pacific Islands, (0) Other
- **Your Profession:** (1) Religious,   (2) Education   (3) Medical,   (4) Administrator,   (5) Legal,
         (6) Political,   (7) Media,   (8) Prostitution,   (9) Student,   (0) Other
- **Your Vocation:** (1) Homemaker,   (2) Agriculture, (3) Engineer,   (4) Factory,   (5) Trades Person
         (6) Shopkeeper,   (7) Artist,   (8) Social Worker,   (9) Cottage Industry, (0) Other
- **Years of Education:**   (1) Zero,   (2) 1-4,   (3) 5-8,   (4) 9-12   (5) 13-16   (6) 17+

YOUR OPINIONS

Equality

1. It is self-defeating to achieve equality in a dysfunctional institution with negative values of racism, sexism, elitism and militarism.

Strongly Agree	Agree	Neutral	Disagree	Strongly Disagree		
1	2	3	4	5	Abstain	Object

2. Decision-making and responsibility are shared equally in my family by the adults.

Strongly Agree	Agree	Neutral	Disagree	Strongly Disagree		
1	2	3	4	5	Abstain	Object

3. Women's health will improve if men assume greater responsibility for their sexual behavior.

Strongly Agree	Agree	Neutral	Disagree	Strongly Disagree		
1	2	3	4	5	Abstain	Object

4. Women's control over their reproductive choices should be viewed as a human right.

Strongly Agree	Agree	Neutral	Disagree	Strongly Disagree		
1	2	3	4	5	Abstain	Object

5. Both sexes receive equal access to educational and training resources in my community.

Strongly Agree	Agree	Neutral	Disagree	Strongly Disagree		
1	2	3	4	5	Abstain	Object

--OVER--

6. There is discrimination and prejudice against women entering public life in my community.

Strongly Agree	Agree	Neutral	Disagree	Strongly Disagree		
1	2	3	4	5	Abstain	Object

7. Discrimination against lesbians is a violation of human rights.

Strongly Agree	Agree	Neutral	Disagree	Strongly Disagree		
1	2	3	4	5	Abstain	Object

Economic Development

8. Feminization of poverty exists because governments fail to respond to the human rights of women.

Strongly Agree	Agree	Neutral	Disagree	Strongly Disagree		
1	2	3	4	5	Abstain	Object

9. Free market capitalism depends on the domestication of women, exploitation of a low-paid labor base made up of minorities and women as well as unlimited access to national resources.

Strongly Agree	Agree	Neutral	Disagree	Strongly Disagree		
1	2	3	4	5	Abstain	Object

10. Training in the areas of agriculture, forestry and fishing is key to women's economic development.

Strongly Agree	Agree	Neutral	Disagree	Strongly Disagree		
1	2	3	4	5	Abstain	Object

11. Childhood sex education and contraception would help to ensure young women academic success and economic security.

Strongly Agree	Agree	Neutral	Disagree	Strongly Disagree		
1	2	3	4	5	Abstain	Object

12. Free Trade Zones expand employment opportunities for women.

Strongly Agree	Agree	Neutral	Disagree	Strongly Disagree		
1	2	3	4	5	Abstain	Object

13. Establish an international tribunal where indigenous women may testify and present crimes against them and/or violation of collective rights.

Strongly Agree	Agree	Neutral	Disagree	Strongly Disagree		
1	2	3	4	5	Abstain	Object

14. The interest on international debts owed by economically poor countries should be forgiven if such debts exceed 10% of their gross national product.

Strongly Agree	Agree	Neutral	Disagree	Strongly Disagree		
1	2	3	4	5	Abstain	Object

Peace

15. Conclude by the end of the year 2000 a negotiated binding schedule for the phased elimination of nuclear weapons within a time frame, and with provisions for effective verification and enforcement.

Strongly Agree	Agree	Neutral	Disagree	Strongly Disagree		
1	2	3	4	5	Abstain	Object

16. The UN should establish a permanent war crimes tribunal to prosecute rape in war as a war crime. Governments should be held responsible.

Strongly Agree	Agree	Neutral	Disagree	Strongly Disagree		
1	2	3	4	5	Abstain	Object

17. Borders should be open to all refugees fleeing political persecution.

Strongly Agree	Agree	Neutral	Disagree	Strongly Disagree		
1	2	3	4	5	Abstain	Object

Thank you for participating! Return to Everywoman's Delegation
or mail to Forum Foundation address below:

The design and tabulation of this survey is being accomplished with the generous assistance of the Forum Foundation: a non-profit, educational, and research foundation. For more information, you may write the Foundation at 4426 Second Ave NE; Seattle, WA 98105-6191; USA.   •Fax (206) 633-3561   •Phone (206) 634-0420. "Fast Forum," "Opinionnaire," and "Viewspaper" are registered trademarks of the Forum Foundation. Used by permission.

3. Profile Report, Issaquah Middle School (Dec. 12, 1986)

```
                Many-to-Many  Communications
    ***** [EXAMPLE SHEET WITH SAMPLE QUESTIONS AND FORMATS] *****
              ----- Fast Forum (R) Technique -----
              Attitudinal Profile Report  DEC 12, 1986

Issaquah, WA Middle School                       Class Profile
```

Disclaimer clause: The purpose of these informal reports is to communicate ideas, issues, and problems among people as a platform for future,
meaningful discussions of concerns. Participants are assisted in be
coming aware of their own beliefs as well as of those intellectual and
moral beliefs of others at a point in time--the Zeitgeist. The views
and opinions expressed herein are those of the individuals who participated and do not necessarily represent the official views of the parent
group or sponsoring organization. Nor will the views expressed necessarily represent those of the same participants at a later period of
time; as humans we each have the ability to receive new information,
consider it, and change. -- The Forum Foundation

*Legend: Example of a Polarization-Consensus Rating for yes/no questions
                              PC Rating
    "Polarization Rating"   (75% -- 80)   "Consensus Rating"
A measure of the WEIGHT given an   A measure of the OPINION given by
idea or question by the people   those people answering yes or no.
participating. The polarization   The consensus rating is the per-
rating is the percentage of people   centage of people answering yes of
participating who answered yes or   those who answered yes or no, i.e.
no (excluding those who abstained   The % positive response (excluding
or objected)   those who abstained or objected)

Thus: A polarization rating of   Thus: A consensus rating above 50
100% means everyone participating   means the people answering favored
answered yes or no. A rating of   the idea--up to 100 which means
50% means half answered yes or no.   unanimously favorable. A rating
A rating of 0% means no one   below 50 means they were against
answered yes or no (thus, everyone   the idea, down to zero which means
abstained or objected)   they were unanimously against it.

Read the PC rating cited above as "75% had 80 consensus" meaning: 75% of
those persons participating were polarized and answered either yes or
no. Therefore, of those persons who answered yes or no, 80 out of 100
answered yes (thus 20 out of 100 answered no). The P/C Rating, therefore, allows accurate and easy comparison of responses between differ-
ent-sized groups and also total responses.

For further insights on the kinds of questions people feel able to answer within a grouping of related questions, questions can be ranked and
reordered by the P/C rating showing the weight. That is, both yes/no
and multiple-choice questions can be ranked and reordered by the percentage of people who answered the question with clear yes/no or multiple-choice responses--excluding those who abstained or objected. This
magnifies the analysis of the data to better resolve the social attitudes of those who participated, i.e., "Social Resolving Power."
 Computer Program & Report copyright © 1998 Forum Foundation.

[Appendix G-2: Example of Yes/No/Abstain Questions   Class Profile Report]

1 QUESTIONS ABOUT DRUGS   [Gender Profile}

1-1 (Original Question no. 6)
Have you ever been pressured into taking drugs?

Total	Yes	No	Abstain	Object	PC Rating *	Category
110	14%	81%	5%	0%	(95%-- 14)	MALE
135	10%	89%	1%	0%	(99%-- 10)	FEMALE
73	19%	78%	3%	0%	(97%-- 20)	Not Identified
318	13%	84%	3%	0%	(97%-- 14)	Total

2-1 (Original Question no. 2)
Does your best friend take drugs?

Total	Yes	No	Abstain	Object	PC Rating *	Category
110	12%	83%	5%	0%	(95%-- 13)	MALE
135	5%	90%	4%	0%	(96%-- 5)	FEMALE
73	8%	82%	8%	1%	(90%-- 9)	Not Identified
318	8%	86%	6%	0%	(94%-- 9)	Total

3-1 (Original Question no. 3)
Do you have any friends who take drugs?

Total	Yes	No	Abstain	Object	PC Rating *	Category
110	27%	60%	12%	1%	(87%-- 31)	MALE
135	36%	52%	10%	2%	(88%-- 41)	FEMALE
73	34%	52%	14%	0%	(86%-- 40)	Not Identified
318	33%	55%	11%	1%	(87%-- 37)	Total

4-1 (Original Question no. 4)
Do you feel uncomfortable with people who take drugs?

Total	Yes	No	Abstain	Object	PC Rating *	Category
110	45%	36%	17%	1%	(82%-- 56)	MALE
135	41%	34%	23%	1%	(76%-- 55)	FEMALE
73	42%	38%	15%	4%	(81%-- 53)	Not Identified
318	43%	36%	19%	2%	(79%-- 55)	Total

1 QUESTIONS ABOUT DRUGS   [Class Profile]

1-1 (Original Question no. 6)
Have you ever been pressured into taking drugs?

Total	Yes	No	Abstain	Object	PC Rating *	Category
65	6%	91%	3%	0%	(97%-- 6)	6TH GRADE
98	10%	85%	5%	0%	(95%-- 11)	7TH GRADE
84	18%	81%	1%	0%	(99%-- 18)	8TH GRADE
71	18%	79%	3%	0%	(97%-- 19)	Not Identified
318	13%	84%	3%	0%	(97%-- 14)	Total

2-1 (Original Question no. 2)
Does your best friend take drugs?

Total	Yes	No	Abstain	Object	PC Rating *	Category
65	6%	89%	5%	0%	(95%-- 6)	6TH GRADE
98	4%	94%	2%	0%	(98%-- 4)	7TH GRADE
84	14%	77%	8%	0%	(92%-- 16)	8TH GRADE
71	8%	82%	8%	1%	(90%-- 9)	Not Identified
318	8%	86%	6%	0%	(94%-- 9)	Total

3-1 (Original Question no. 3)
Do you have any friends who take drugs?

Total	Yes	No	Abstain	Object	PC Rating *	Category
65	25%	58%	17%	0%	(83%-- 30)	6TH GRADE
98	26%	65%	9%	0%	(91%-- 28)	7TH GRADE
84	46%	42%	7%	5%	(88%-- 53)	8TH GRADE
71	34%	52%	14%	0%	(86%-- 39)	Not Identified
318	33%	55%	11%	1%	(87%-- 37)	Total

4-1 (Original Question no. 4)
Do you feel uncomfortable with people who take drugs?

Total	Yes	No	Abstain	Object	PC Rating *	Category
65	48%	34%	18%	0%	(82%-- 58)	6TH GRADE
98	47%	29%	23%	1%	(76%-- 62)	7TH GRADE
84	37%	43%	18%	2%	(80%-- 46)	8TH GRADE
71	41%	39%	15%	4%	(80%-- 51)	Not Identified
318	43%	36%	19%	2%	(79%-- 55)	Total

. . . .

The Forum Foundation is a non-profit educational/research corporation dedicated toward strengthening the democratic processes of our society through improved feedback communications from people. This Fast
Forum (R) technique assists interested persons in our society and
among its institutions and organizations to participate more meaningfully by expressing their individual opinions. Through written reports,
as attached, these opinions assist those persons participating to illustrate to themselves, as well as to parent/teacher/school/church/
business/community and government establishments, the values in which
they believe. It is hoped that the overall communication process established will reduce apathy among people, improve community mental health,
and assist in solving the human problems we face together in our society
and world.

Confrontation of ideas is the mortar which binds a creative society
actively searching for solutions to its problems. It leads to better
diagnosis in the decision-making process which inevitably follows and to
improved collaboration by members toward organizational objectives. Any
organization or society which inhibits (innocently or not) the free
movement of ideas among the people who comprise it--up, down, and across
their organizational structures--is depriving itself of its full measure
of its greatest resource, human thought, and is in grave danger of being
buried in history by the avalanche of the creativity of others.

The data utilized in this report was submitted on individual Forum
Foundation or other response sheets by the user organization and recorded
by optical scanning or was keypunched from Opinionnaires (R) provided.
The information contained herein is certified correct barring unintentional errors.

Inquiries are invited from interested organizations and persons who
may wish to establish, experiment, or participate in this Many-to-Many
Communication process and Fast Forum (R) technique. "Zeitgeist" and
"PC rating" are registered trademarks. "Fast Forum", "Opinionnaire", and
"Viewspaper" are registered trademarks of the Forum Foundation, United
States Patent Office.

> Richard J. Spady,
> President
> Forum Foundation

4. "Make Ideas Count" flyer for "State of the Union Address"

MAKE IDEAS COUNT

• **Use the Inaugural and State-of-the-Union addresses to teach citizenship skills and receive a report on the response of the class for their discussion.**

• **In one class period present the Inaugural Address or an abridged State-of-the-Union Address, students engage in reaction in "Future Molding Game" foursomes, and collect their anonymous opinions using the Fast Forum® technique. (No cost if internet access available.)**

• **Join classrooms across the country in a "conversation" with the President of the United States using "symbolic dialogue" [This enables youth to think about the future in a process of: Psychosocial Moratorium (Erik Erikson—" A timeout place to talk") which Robert Pranger writes in *The Eclipse of Citizenship* "is so important, it is of equal importance to the need of a small child for maternal care."]**

• **Students engage in reflective discussion of reports later with classmates and finally with their own parents when possible.**

Forum Foundation

Enhancing Communication in Organizations and Society

Enroll at: www.ForumFoundation.org

Lesson Plan for "State of the Union Address"

2001 Inaugural Address and the Youth of America Opinionnaire®

Teacher's Lesson Plan

This class project is open to public and religious school teachers who enroll. The project demonstrates an instrument for mass communication using "symbolic dialogue" and has been endorsed by the Professional Members Forum of the World Future Society (scientific-educational, non-profit to assist persons interested to think about the future; they take no advocacy position on issues.) Here is a suggested class outline, which we hope you and your students, as well as their parents can use.

Class Objectives

To allow students to participate in a "symbolic dialogue" with the President of the United States in the exercise of their "right to be heard" in a process of "intellectual gaming" and citizenship to develop critical thinking skills through use of the Fast Forum® technique. This is a project that can provide *a social audit* (of the nation's intangible youth assets) to assist youth in thinking about the future through a process of *Psychosocial Moratorium* as theorized by school psychologist Erik Erikson. It utilizes the dynamics of the Socratic Method, one of history's proven learning techniques.

The Opinionnaires® can be administered in one classroom experience March through October each year. Public school teachers can enroll without cost if their class has computer facilities to participate. Go to website ForumFoundation.org. Other public school and religious teachers can enroll by mailing a check for $35 to the Forum Foundation (Washington state teachers add 8.8% sales tax) at 4426 Second Ave. N.E., Seattle, WA 98105-6191. A packet will be mailed with this lesson plan, an Opinionnaire®, audio tape, and 100 machine-scannable response sheets.

Class Activity

(A) Give a copy of the Inaugural or State-of-the-Union Address Opinionnaire® to each youth and ask them to read it the day before they have their next meeting so it is fresh in their mind. They should note informally the issues about which they have an opinion, and they should prepare to speak briefly about one issue.

(B) At the meeting play the 15-20 minute audio tape of the President's Inaugural or State-of-the-Union Address.

(C) Ask students to sit almost kneecap to kneecap in <u>foursomes</u> to play the "Future Molding Game."

(D) Suggest a method to select who starts first in each group and who follows. (For example, "The person nearest the door in each group goes first followed by others clockwise.")

(E) Each student gets a two-minute "Day-in-the-Sun" to talk about a question raised by the President's address while others listen respectfully and without interruption, comment, question, or "body English," i.e., thumbs up or down. The teacher keeps time and announces the time intervals at one minute, 1-1/2 minutes, and two minutes. (Students do not need to stop abruptly at the end but should wind up their idea so that the next students in the groups can begin together.)

(F) Open discussion is then held in each foursome on the first student's issue. When the teacher judges the time is appropriate (usually two to four minutes), the teacher then starts the second student in each foursome similarly until all students have had a chance for their issue to be reflected by their group in open discussion.

(G) Students respond to the Address Opinionnaire® recording their answers individually directly into the computer. (Forum Foundation machine-scannable response sheets are required if class computers are not available.)

(H) Students take home to each parent an unmarked copy of the Address Opinionnaire and one Forum Foundation response sheet. Place all in a large envelope (unfolded if machine-scannable) and seal on return so responses are anonymous.

(I) Ask each parent to respond individually without discussion with the student or spouse regarding the issues at this time. This is a QUEST Forum (QUick Environmental Scanning Test with no talking.) Parents then seal their completed response sheets in the large envelope provided for anonymous return to the teacher.

(J) Teacher (1) distributes anonymous parent response sheets to class for entry into the class file of responses and transmits all responses via E-mail to the Forum Foundation website at ForumFoundation.org or (2) mails machine-scannable sheets to the Forum Foundation at 4426 Second Ave. NE, Seattle, WA 98105-6191 (with envelope marked for: Inaugural or State-of-the-Union Address). A profile report showing gender responses by students and parents will be returned usually within a one-week turnaround.

(K) Teacher and youth discuss results and reflect on their possible meanings. (All reports are properly "disclaimed" and do not represent the "sponsoring organization." The reports represent only participant views—but they are 100% valid.)

(L) Copies of the profile report are returned to parents for discussion of results and reflection on their meaning with their student and themselves. [It is at this point where parents can finally resolve sensitive moral issues that might be involved. For example: "Even though all other students responded 'this way' or all parents responded 'that way,' I want to call your attention to this 'fact'" *and they lay their own value judgment on their own child—which is the parental prerogative*. And the whole process ends right there like the story "The Lady or the Tiger."]

(M) In late November, totals by all participants can be tabulated. A profile report and Viewspaper® (with summary highlights prepared) will be sent to the President with a copy sent to all school groups participating for further discussion on their meaning. [This is a process of "intellectual gaming" similar to "physical gaming" by students in their schools. As students "exercise" their minds and reasoning skills, they will get stronger and move toward emotional and political maturity leading toward improved citizenship and a strengthening of the democratic processes in our republic.]

Resources for those persons who might want more background and information can be found in the book: *The Leadership of Civilization Building (Administrative and Civilization Theory, Symbolic Dialogue, and Citizen Skills for the 21st Century)* by Richard Spady and Richard Kirby. The estimated publication date is January, 2002. The book can be ordered by calling Cokesbury Bookstore (Kirkland, WA) at 1-800-605-9403, University Bookstore in Seattle at 1-800-335-READ, or the Forum Foundation at (206) 634-0420 in Seattle.

State of the Union Address and Youth of America Opinionnaire®

2001 Inaugural Address and the Youth-of-America Opinionnaire®
A *Future Molding Game* and Youth Research Project Endorsed
by the Professional Member's Forum of the World Future Society

Sponsors: Forum Foundation, World Network of Religious Futurists,
and Stuart C. Dodd Institute for Social Innovation (Seattle, WA)

Based on the January 20, 2001 Inaugural Address by President George W. Bush

To teachers/students/parents: Thank you for participating in this important national educational project to help build "social capital" in America (ref. *Bowling Alone* by Robert Putnam, 2000). This is a research project utilizing symbolic dialogue and the Fast Forum® technique to provide American youth with a *Psycho-social Moratoria* (Erik Erikson), "which is so important [to an adolescent], it is equal to the importance of a small child for maternal care" (Robert Pranger, *The Eclipse of Citizenship,* University of Washington, 1968). This is a project that can provide *a social audit* (of the nation's intangible youth assets) to assist American youth in thinking about their future and that of the nation in a process of Psycho-social Education. It utilizes the dynamics of the Socratic Method, one of history's proven learning techniques. As students struggle with questions about real problems in their world they achieve insight and grow psychologically as they learn and move toward emotional maturity. Results will be reported to teachers/student/parents, participating groups, World Future Society members, and to the President in December, 2001. **PLEASE READ THE INSTRUCTIONS on your Forum Foundation** *Councilor*™ **Response Sheet** and mark your response categories as follows:

[1] **Gender:** (1) Male, (2) Female

[2] **Your Age Range:** (1) 10-19, (2) 20-29, (3) 30-39, (4) 40-49, (5) 50-59, (6) 60-69, (7) 70-79, (8) 80 and over

[3] **Mark Your One Most Exclusive Group:** (1) High School Youth/Student, (2) Adult Parent of a High School Youth/Student, (3) A Senior Citizen 60 Years and over, (4) World Future Society Member, (5) All others

[4] **Your High School Class:** (1) Freshman, (2) Sophomore, (3) Junior, (4) Senior, (5) Not a High School Student

[5] **Mark Your One Closest subject of your current high school class** (1) U.S. Government, (2) U.S. History, (3) World History, (4) Other Social Studies, (5) Any Other Class, (6) Not a High School Student

[6] **Your Ethnic Family:** (1) African Descent, (2) Asian Descent, (3) Native American Descent, (4) European/Caucasian Descent, (5) Hispanic/Chicano/Latino Descent, (6) Pacific Islander Descent, (7) Other Ethnic Descent, (8) Blended Ethnic Family

[7] **Your Time Zone:** (1) Eastern, (2) Central, (3) Mountain, (4) Pacific, (5) Alaska/Hawaii, (6) All Others

[8] **Current Year:** (1) 2001, Inaugural and State-of-the-Union Addresses of President George W. Bush

"Our children long for realistic maps of a future they can be proud of. Where are the cartographers of human purpose?" **(Carl Sagan, *People Digest*, Nov. 21, 1987).**

Students Please Note: The President of the United States is Chief-of-State of our nation and is the one official who represents everyone. Functionally, a "Chief-of-State" is anyone elected (or duly appointed—public or private) as he or she alone best represents the interests overall of his or her constituents. This includes governors, county executives, mayors corporate CEOs, schools, religious groups, civic groups, community service groups, associations, unions etc.

The following statements are related to President Bush's 2001 Inaugural Address. You can expect to experience frustration as you grapple with your responses. It is hard to think, not easy; there is ambiguity, but that's the purpose. "Physical gaming" in schools is to help your body get stronger physically. Similarly, "intellectual gaming" will help your mind get stronger and help you to mature emotionally by practicing your reasoning and critical thinking skills about real problems in life. The process of *responding to questions* is known as the Socratic Method; it is one of history's proven learning techniques. In this case you are engaging in a "symbolic dialogue" with the President of the United States and with your parents and with other adults—especially senior adults. "To every one else life is just hearsay" (Erik Erikson). It is an elected or duly appointed public official's job to articulate public issues and try to suggest future solutions for the public good in acts of statesmanship. **Your job, as a citizen engaged in** *civilization building*, **is to always listen to such an official and then: reflect, discuss with your citizen peers, and** *respond with your opinion.* Trust your own instincts; secondary insights will come later when you and your teacher, parents, or other leader reflects on the overall responses of all participants. We are trying to learn how to distill *knowledge* into the *wisdom* society needs to govern itself and to create a new social context in which individual citizens can be responsible. **Most of the knowledge in the world is in books and computer data banks. But most of the wisdom of the world is in the minds of people walking the earth. We have to learn how to reach it.** Remember, if you cannot make a clear choice to a question—just Abstain, i.e., if you are undecided or feel unable to respond—just abstain and continue. You can "Object" if you feel a question is misleading or inappropriate in some manner.

PAGE 1

1. President Bush characterized the United States—"as the new world that became a friend and liberator of the old—as a slave society that became a servant of freedom—a power that went into the world to protect—to defend but not to possess—to defend but not to conquer." To what extent do you agree with these basic assumptions?

Strongly Agree   1 2 3 4 5   Strongly Disagree
Abstain   Object

2. "Everyone belongs, everyone deserves a chance, no insignificant person was ever born." To what extent do you agree with Bush, that these ideals are strong motivating factors to work toward a more equitable society?

Strongly Agree   1 2 3 4 5   Strongly Disagree
Abstain   Object

3. "And though our nation has sometimes halted and sometimes delayed [in reaching the above ideals in question 2], we must follow no other course." To what extent do you agree?

Strongly Agree   1 2 3 4 5   Strongly Disagree
Abstain   Object

4. President Bush suggests that our democracy is a "seed in the wind" taking root in many nations. Others have suggested that we are moving toward an economic colonialism. To what extent do you agree with Bush or with others?

Agree with Bush   1 2 3 4 5   Agree With Others
Abstain   Object

5. "The ambitions of some Americans are limited by failing schools and hidden prejudice and the circumstances of their birth." Bush implies that government has responsibility for correcting some of the limitations that people experience. To what extent do you agree?

Strongly Agree   1 2 3 4 5   Strongly Disagree
Abstain   Object

6. "Hidden prejudice and limitations of birth" hinder democracy. Looking back, do you think you have had hidden prejudices that have hindered democracy from righting the wrong?

Had Many Prejudices   1 2 3 4 5   Had No Prejudices
Abstain   Object

7. The President has identified education and better schools as his strongest priority. In view of other concerns, to what extent do you agree that education should be the highest priority?

Strongly Agree   1 2 3 4 5   Strongly Disagree
Abstain   Object

8. "I want to build a single nation of justice and opportunity." To what extent do you agree that Bush can move the nation effectively in this direction?

Strongly Agree   1 2 3 4 5   Strongly Disagree
Abstain   Object

9. "I know this is within our reach because we are guided by a power larger than ourselves who creates us equal in His image." Our history suggests we share our constitution with people of religious faith and of no faith. To what extent do you agree with Bush in his emphasizing religious faith?

Strongly Agree   1 2 3 4 5   Strongly Disagree
Abstain   Object

10. "America has never been united by blood or soil. We are bound by ideals that move us beyond our backgrounds, lift us above our interests, and teach us what it means to be citizens." To what extent do you agree that our diversity makes us more rather than less American?

Strongly Agree   1 2 3 4 5   Strongly Disagree
Abstain   Object

11. "America at its best, matches a commitment to principle with a concern for civility." In the light of the recent election, to what extent do you agree it is possible for Republicans and Democrats to move toward civility?

Strongly Agree   1 2 3 4 5   Strongly Disagree
Abstain   Object

12. "Our unity, our union is the serious work of leaders and citizens in every generation." To what extent do you agree that Bush can generate enthusiasm for citizen participation?

Strongly Agree   1 2 3 4 5   Strongly Disagree
Abstain   Object

13. "Civility, courage, compassion, and character—a civil society demands that from each us—good will and respect, fair dealing, and forgiveness." To what extent do you feel these qualities are operative in your community?

Are Available   1 2 3 4 5   Limited Availability
Abstain   Object

PAGE 2

14. "We will reform Social Security and Medicare." Some in society feel these are the best services of government to seniors and those with special needs. To what extent do you feel there needs to be reform?

Major Reform Needed   1 2 3 4 5   Limited Reform

Abstain   Object

15. "We will reduce taxes." There is considerable disagreement as to how reduced taxes will benefit those who need education opportunities and those who are left out of economic good times. To what extent do you agree with President Bush that a tax reduction at this time will benefit those most in need?

Strongly Agree   1 2 3 4 5   Strongly Disagree

Abstain   Object

16. "We will build our defense beyond challenge." Some suggest that since our nation is the most powerful in the world and will be in the foreseeable future, that defense spending should be reduced rather than increased. To what extent do you agree with President Bush that we must build our defenses?

Strongly Agree   1 2 3 4 5   Strongly Disagree

Abstain   Object

17. "America remains engaged in the world by history and by choice." In the Bush campaign there was relatively little said about our overseas relationships. To what extent do you agree Bush will challenge isolationist thinking?

Strongly Agree   1 2 3 4 5   Strongly Disagree

Abstain   Object

18. "America at its best is compassionate. . . .In the American conscience, we know that deep, persistent poverty is unworthy of our nation's promise. . . . And whatever the cause, we can agree that children at risk are not at fault." To what extent do you believe Bush will challenge both Republicans and Democrats in moving toward more social responsibility?

Strong Challenge   1 2 3 4 5   Limited Challenge

Abstain   Object

19. "And the proliferation of prisons, however necessary, is not a substitute for hope and order in our souls." This statement suggests Bush may seek beyond punishment for ways to reduce crime. To what extent would you support Bush in preventive measures?

Strongly Support   1 2 3 4 5   Limited Support

Abstain   Object

20. "And I can pledge our nation to a goal: when we see the wounded traveler on the road to Jericho, we will not pass on the other side." The use of the story of the Good Samaritan from the Christian tradition suggests possible bias toward one faith. In other statements Bush affirms the work of the church, the synagogue, and the mosque. To what extent do you agree with Bush that the inclusion of faith communities is important in social service roles?

Strongly Agree   1 2 3 4 5   Strongly Disagree

Abstain   Object

21. "Government has great responsibilities for public safety and public health, for civil rights, and common schools. Yet compassion is the work of the nation, not just the government." To what extent would you agree that the private sector and the government should cooperate toward these ends?

Strongly Agree   1 2 3 4 5   Strongly Disagree

Abstain   Object

22. "America at its best is a place where personal responsibility is valued and expected." Many feel there should be more personal responsibility exercised rather than more government responsibility exercised for the common good. To what extent do you agree responsibilities should be exercised primarily personally or by governments?

Personally   1 2 3 4 5   By Governments

Abstain   Object

23. "Our public interest depends on private character, on civic duty, and family bonds and basic fairness." To what extent do you agree with President Bush?

Strongly Agree   1 2 3 4 5   Strongly Disagree

Abstain   Object

24. "I ask you to seek a common good beyond your comfort: to defend needed reforms against easy attacks, to serve your nation, beginning with your neighbor. I ask you to be citizens, not spectators, citizens not subjects, responsible citizens building communities of service and a nation of character." Are you ready to be such a citizen?

Yes   1 2 3 4 5   No

Abstain   Object

25. Many people suggest that we need to appeal to people from their selfish rather than their altruistic motives. To what extent do you believe the appeal to altruism will receive much positive response?

Strong Response   1 2 3 4 5   Little Response

Abstain   Object

26. Generally President Bush in his inaugural address dealt with generalities rather than specifics. To what extent do you agree that this was the best way to introduce his agenda to the nation?

Strongly Agree   1 2 3 4 5   Strongly Disagree

Abstain   Object

27. Bush recognizes the importance of the individual citizen. To what extent do you agree programs should be proposed which will help give the majority of persons opportunities to participate more fully in the decision-making processes that affect their lives in local, state, and federal arenas?

Strongly Agree   1 2 3 4 5   Strongly Disagree

Abstain   Object

28. Overall the Bush inaugural appeals to citizens across political spectrums. To what extent do you agree it was an adequate and challenging statement to begin a new administration?

Strongly Agree   1 2 3 4 5   Strongly Disagree

Abstain   Object

29. To what extent do you agree or disagree with the statement, "Participation of citizens in a valid 'visioning process' in their governments [such as this symbolic dialogue to the Inaugural Address] is essential if our democratic republic is to survive as a decision-making process?"

Strongly Agree   1 2 3 4 5   Strongly Disagree

Abstain   Object

30. How do you as a student or adult feel about growing up and/or living in the United States of America?

It is a wonderful country   1 2 3 4 5   I am disappointed

Abstain   Object

For further information contact the Forum Foundation.

Resources for those interested in "Psycho-social Education" can be found in the book: *The Leadership of Civilization Building (Administrative and Civilization Theory, Symbolic Dialogue, and Citizen Skills for the 21st Century)*. The estimated publication date is May, 2001. The book can be ordered by calling University Bookstore in Seattle at 1-800-335-READ, Cokesbury Bookstore (Kirkland, WA) at 1-800-605-9403, or the **Forum Foundation, 4426 Second Ave. N.E., Seattle, WA 98105-6191; Fax. (206) 633-3561; Tel. (206) 634-0420; ForumFoundation.org or FastForum@aol.com.**

To Tabulate Data and Receive A Gender Youth/Parent/Adult Profile Report of Class Responses

If not using e-mail for tabulation of data, please return your completed machine-scannable response sheets by mail to: Forum Foundation, 4426 Second Ave. N.E., Seattle, WA, 98105-6191 marked: 2001 Inaugural Address. A detailed profile report of the class/parent responses will be returned within about one week.

Please include a cover sheet using school or organizational stationery to authenticate the response sheets together with the name and phone number of the teacher, convener, or sender.

A profile report showing detailed responses by percentages and by gender for students, parents, senior adults, and members of the World Future Society (nonprofit, scientific-educational) will also be returned to participating teachers for discussion by their students and parents, to participating groups, to *The Futurist* magazine of the World Future Society, and to the President in December, 2001. Thank you.

5. Pastor's Letter for Time and Talent Survey

UNITED METHODIST CHURCH
17222 N.E. 8th Street • Bellevue, WA 98008

September 20, 2000

Dear Church Friends:

As your pastor, I am also the chair of the Committee on Nominations and Personnel. It is our job to find a place in the Church for you to serve God and others.

The best possible way for this committee to operate is to have some advance information as to where you prefer to serve. The Time and Talent Survey, filled out by you and others, can be the needed tool for us to get at this data.

So, I am asking you to take a few minutes and review the survey and check the sections you wish. You can be assured that my committee will be grateful for any help we receive from the survey.

Sincerely yours,

Pastor Tom

Pastor Tom Carlson

A. Thomas Carlson, Pastor   Office: 747-3210 • Residence: 746-3708

Household Survey and Report

St. Peter's United Methodist Church
Seattle District, PNW Annual Conference
September10, 2000

Time & Talent Household Survey
Please Help Us to Update Our Records of Your Family's Interests at St. Peter's

PLEASE PRINT:　　　　　　　　　　　　　　**Current Date:**_____

ADULT PERSON(S) IN HOUSEHOLD:

(1) _____　_____　_____　_____
　　(last name)　　　　　　　(first name)　　　　M/Initial　　　(birthday)
_____　_____　　　　　[If you prefer your
　　(street address)　　　　　(if needed)　　　　　　　　　year of birth be
_____　_____　_____　-　unknown, do not
　　(city)　　　　(state)　　(ZIP code)　　　　　　　　show it here.]
_____　_____
　　(residence phone)　　　　(other phone)

(2) _____　_____　_____　_____
　　(last name)　　　　　　　(first name)　　　　M/Initial　　　(birthday)

CHILDREN AND YOUTH IN HOUSEHOLD:

(3) _____　_____　_____
　last name,　(first name, MI)　　Birthdate　　High School Graduation Year

(4) _____　_____　_____
　last name,　(first name, MI)　　Birthdate　　High School Graduation Year

(5) _____　_____　_____
　last name,　(first name, MI)　　Birthdate　　High School Graduation Year

(6) _____　_____　_____
　last name,　(first name, MI)　　Birthdate　　High School Graduation Year

(7) Note: Use if another adult or more children are in the Household.

"Yes, as opportunities arise, I am interested in sharing my time and talents or participating in furthering the mission of our church in the following areas." (Please write "A," "B," "C," or "D" as applicable.)

A = **Presently Serving or Active;**
B = **Interested** (but not serving, participating, or experienced);
C = **Interested and experienced** (but not currently serving);
D = **Experienced** (but not currently interested)

Note: Where shown, please add the underlined letter(s) indicating a further status. For example: "8. Membership Records Secretary/Helper " show "A-S" to indicate you are presently serving as Membership Secretary or "B-H" to indicate you are interested in helping.
PLEASE DO NOT FOLD SURVEY

Household Time and Talent Survey, September 10, 2000   Page 2

Church Leadership/Administration   **Household person(s)**
1. Administrative Council Member   (1)___; (2)___; (3) __; (4) __; (5) __; (6) __ (7) __
2. Lay Leader   (1)___; (2)___; (3) __; (4) __; (5) __; (6) __ (7) __
3. Lay Member to Annual Conf.   (1)___; (2)___; (3) __; (4) __; (5) __; (6) __ (7) __
4. Lay Speaker (Training/Program Support) (1)___; (2)___; (3) __; (4) __; (5) __; (6) __ (7) __
5. Trustees (Building and Grounds)   (1)___; (2)___; (3) __; (4) __; (5) __; (6) __ (7) __
6. Staff-Parish Committee   (1)___; (2)___; (3) __; (4) __; (5) __; (6) __ (7) __
7. Membership & Evangelism Area   (1)___; (2)___; (3) __; (4) __; (5) __; (6) __ (7) __
8. Membership Records Secretary/Helper   (1)___; (2)___; (3) __; (4) __; (5) __; (6) __ (7) __
9. Outreach and Mission Work Area   (1)___; (2)___; (3) __; (4) __; (5) __; (6) __ (7) __
10. Financial Secretary   (1)___; (2)___; (3) __; (4) __; (5) __; (6) __ (7) __
11. Treasurer   (1)___; (2)___; (3) __; (4) __; (5) __; (6) __ (7) __
12. Stewardship Chair   (1)___; (2)___; (3) __; (4) __; (5) __; (6) __ (7) __
13. Finance Committee   (1)___; (2)___; (3) __; (4) __; (5) __; (6) __ (7) __
14. Memorials Committee   (1)___; (2)___; (3) __; (4) __; (5) __; (6) __ (7) __
15. Church Historian   (1)___; (2)___; (3) __; (4) __; (5) __; (6) __ (7) __
16. Church Librarian   (1)___; (2)___; (3) __; (4) __; (5) __; (6) __ (7) __
17. Communicator (Time/Talent data/E-mail) (1)___; (2)___; (3) __; (4) __; (5) __; (6) __ (7) __

Worship and Music Program
20. Greeter   (1)___; (2)___; (3) __; (4) __; (5) __; (6) __ (7) __
21. Usher   (1)___; (2)___; (3) __; (4) __; (5) __; (6) __ (7) __
22. Acolyte (Children, Candle Lighters)   (1)___; (2)___; (3) __; (4) __; (5) __; (6) __ (7) __
23. Liturgist   (Read Scripture)   (1)___; (2)___; (3) __; (4) __; (5) __; (6) __ (7) __
24. Chancel Choir   (1)___; (2)___; (3) __; (4) __; (5) __; (6) __ (7) __
25. Bell Choir   (1)___; (2)___; (3) __; (4) __; (5) __; (6) __ (7) __
26. Contemporary Worship Praise Team   (1)___; (2)___; (3) __; (4) __; (5) __; (6) __ (7) __
27. Joyfull Noise   (1)___; (2)___; (3) __; (4) __; (5) __; (6) __ (7) __
28. Children's Choir   (1)___; (2)___; (3) __; (4) __; (5) __; (6) __ (7) __
29. Youth Band   (1)___; (2)___; (3) __; (4) __; (5) __; (6) __ (7) __
30. Soloist: _____ (list) (1)___; (2)___; (3) __; (4) __; (5) __; (6) _. (7) __
31. Musical Instrument: _____ (list) (1)___; (2)___; (3) __; (4) __; (5) __; (6) __ (7) __
32. Sacred Dance   (1)___; (2)___; (3) __; (4) __; (5) __; (6) __ (7) __
33. Sunday Fellowship Family Coord./Helper (1)___; (2)___; (3) __; (4) __; (5) __; (6) __ (7) __
34. Altar Flower Arranging/Banners   (1)___; (2)___; (3) __; (4) __; (5) __; (6) __ (7) __
35. Communion, (preparation of)   (1)___; (2)___; (3) __; (4) __; (5) __; (6) __ (7) __
36. Worship Committee   (1)___; (2)___; (3) __; (4) __; (5) __; (6) __ (7) __

Household Time and Talent Survey, September 10, 2000   Page 3

Sunday School
40. Sunday School Supt.   (1)____; (2)____; (3) ___; (4) __; (5) __; (6) __ (7) __
41. Coordinator, Adult Ed.   (1)____; (2)____; (3) ___; (4) __; (5) __; (6) __ (7) __
42. Teacher, Pre-school   (1)____; (2)____; (3) ___; (4) __; (5) __; (6) __ (7) __
43.   Elementary   (Grades 1-5)   (1)____; (2)____; (3) ___; (4) __; (5) __; (6) __ (7) __
44.   Middlers   (Grades 6-8)   (1)____; (2)____; (3) ___; (4) __; (5) __; (6) __ (7) __
45.   Senior High (Grades 9-12)   (1)____; (2)____; (3) ___; (4) __; (5) __; (6) __ (7) __
46.   Adult   (1)____; (2)____; (3) ___; (4) __; (5) __; (6) __ (7) __
47. Student, Pre-school   (1)____; (2)____; (3) ___; (4) __; (5) __; (6) __ (7) __
48.   Elementary   (1)____; (2)____; (3) ___; (4) __; (5) __; (6) __ (7) __
49.   Middlers   (1)____; (2)____; (3) ___; (4) __; (5) __; (6) __ (7) __
50.   Senior High   (1)____; (2)____; (3) ___; (4) __; (5) __; (6) __ (7) __
51.   Adult Sunday Class   (1)____; (2)____; (3) ___; (4) __; (5) __; (6) __ (7) __
52. Sunday Morning Prayer Circle   (1)____; (2)____; (3) ___; (4) __; (5) __; (6) __ (7) __
53. Adult Bible Study (Sunday Morning)   (1)____; (2)____; (3) ___; (4) __; (5) __; (6) __ (7) __
54. Weekday Noon Adult Text Bible Study   (1)____; (2)____; (3) ___; (4) __; (5) __; (6) __ (7) __
55. Assist in Daily Vacation Bible School   (1)____; (2)____; (3) ___; (4) __; (5) __; (6) __ (7) __
56. Education Committee   (1)____; (2)____; (3) ___; (4) __; (5) __; (6) __ (7) __

Children and Youth Groups
60. Child Drop-In Center   (1)____; (2)____; (3) ___; (4) __; (5) __; (6) __ (7) __
61. Kids' Club Participant   (1)____; (2)____; (3) ___; (4) __; (5) __; (6) __ (7) __
62. Kid's Club Volunteer   (1)____; (2)____; (3) ___; (4) __; (5) __; (6) __ (7) __
63. Middler Youth Group   (1)____; (2)____; (3) ___; (4) __; (5) __; (6) __ (7) __
64. Senior Youth Group   (1)____; (2)____; (3) ___; (4) __; (5) __; (6) __ (7) __
65.Youth Band   (1)____; (2)____; (3) ___; (4) __; (5) __; (6) __ (7) __
66. Youth Drama Group   (1)____; (2)____; (3) ___; (4) __; (5) __; (6) __ (7) __
67. Scouting   (1)____; (2)____; (3) ___; (4) __; (5) __; (6) __ (7) __
68. Youth Volunteer   (1)____; (2)____; (3) ___; (4) __; (5) __; (6) __ (7) __
69. Youth Council   (1)____; (2)____; (3) ___; (4) __; (5) __; (6) __ (7) __

Adult Participant Groups
80. United Methodist Men   (1)____; (2)____; (3) ___; (4) __; (5) __; (6) __ (7) __
81. United Methodist Women   (1)____; (2)____; (3) ___; (4) __; (5) __; (6) __ (7) __
82. Young Adults (College Age and Up)   (1)____; (2)____; (3) ___; (4) __; (5) __; (6) __ (7) __
83. M & M (Mature Methodists)   (1)____; (2)____; (3) ___; (4) __; (5) __; (6) __ (7) __
84. Dinners-For-Eight   (1)____; (2)____; (3) ___; (4) __; (5) __; (6) __ (7) __

Wesley Wellness Center Activities
90. Nutrition Seminars (Participant/Speaker)   (1)____; (2)____; (3) ___; (4) __; (5) __; (6) __ (7) __
91. Healing Seminars (Participant/Speaker)   (1)____; (2)____; (3) ___; (4) __; (5) __; (6) __ (7) __
92. Parenting Seminars (Participant/Speaker)   (1)____; (2)____; (3) ___; (4) __; (5) __; (6) __ (7) __
93. Investment Club (Participant/Speaker)   (1)____; (2)____; (3) ___; (4) __; (5) __; (6) __ (7) __
94. Financial Planning (Participant/Speaker)   (1)____; (2)____; (3) ___; (4) __; (5) __; (6) __ (7) __
95. Adult Bible Study & Care Dialogue Group   (1)____; (2)____; (3) ___; (4) __; (5) __; (6) __ (7) __
96. Lay Councilor Dialogue Group*   (1)____; (2)____; (3) ___; (4) __; (5) __; (6) __ (7) __

*Lay Councilors will study in homes or the church the UMC *Social Principles* and the new 2000 *Book of Resolutions* in a small group(s) of 4-12 persons, March-May, 2001.

Household Time and Talent Survey, September 10, 2000   Page 4

Helping Hands and Other Activities
100. Receptions (Weddings/Funerals)   (1)____; (2)____; (3) ___; (4) ___; (5) ___; (6) __ (7) ___
101. Shut-ins (Adm./Phone./Visitation)   (1)____; (2)____; (3) ___; (4) ___; (5) ___; (6) __ (7) ___
102. Meals (Providing/Need)   (1)____; (2)____; (3) ___; (4) ___; (5) ___; (6) __ (7) ___
103. Meals—Providing at Seasonal events   (1)____; (2)____; (3) ___; (4) ___; (5) ___; (6) __ (7) ___
104. Drive Van, Sundays   (1)____; (2)____; (3) ___; (4) ___; (5) ___; (6) __ (7) ___
105. Drive Van, Kid's Club, Weekday   (1)____; (2)____; (3) ___; (4) ___; (5) ___; (6) __ (7) ___
106. Office: Help/Typing   (1)____; (2)____; (3) ___; (4) ___; (5) ·___; (6) __ (7) ___
107.   Telephoning   (1)____; (2)____; (3) ___; (4) ___; (5) ___; (6) __ (7) ___
108.   Keys/Newsletter Preparation   (1)____; (2)____; (3) ___; (4) ___; (5) ___; (6) __ (7) __
109.   Mailings   (1)____; (2)____; (3) ___; (4) ___; (5) ___; (6) __ (7) ___
110.   Vacation/Illness Secretarial Substitute (1)____; (2)____; (3) ___; (4) ___; (5) ___; (6) __ (7) ___
111. Gardening/Landscaping   (1)____; (2)____; (3) ___; (4) ___; (5) ___; (6) __ (7) ___
112. Adult and Family Retreats   (1)____; (2)____; (3) ___; (4) ___; (5) ___; (6) __ (7) ___
113. Computer Host (church library)   (1)____; (2)____; (3) ___; (4) ___; (5) ___; (6) __ (7) ___
114. Active Hobbies   (1)____; (2)____; (3) ___; (4) ___; (5) ___; (6) __ (7) ___
     (list:_____
     _____
     _____

115. Other skills/activities   (1)____; (2)____; (3) ___; (4) ___; (5) ___; (6) __ (7) ___
     (list:_____
     _____
     _____

Church Athletic Activities
120. Softball   (1)____; (2)____; (3) ___; (4) ___; (5) ___; (6) __ (7) ___
121. Basketball   (1)____; (2)____; (3) ___; (4) ___; (5) ___; (6) __ (7) ___
122. Volleyball   (1)____; (2)____; (3) ___; (4) ___; (5) ___; (6) __ (7) ___
123. Golfing   (1)____; (2)____; (3) ___; (4) ___; (5) ___; (6) __ (7) __
124. Tennis   (1)____; (2)____; (3) ___; (4) ___; (5) ___; (6) __ (7) ___
125. Bowling   (1)____; (2)____; (3) ___; (4) ___; (5) ___; (6) __ (7) ___

Any other comments about the family household that the church should know about?
(If it's personal, please tell the pastor.)

_____
_____

You have been participating in a process of **Civilization Building on behalf of God's
Kingdom!** Please thank all members of the household for their help in completing this survey
of their religious journey.

Please return or mail this Household Survey to the church office for tabulation.
Please do not fold this survey. Thank you

St. Peter's United Methodist Church   **Administrative Council and**
17222 NE 8th Street   **Pastor Tom Carlson**
Bellevue, WA 98008   **Heather Baker, Youth Minister**
[If you have a question, please call the church office: (425) 747-3210 or
Dick Spady, Communicator, 747-8373.]

Household Survey and Report

Local Church TIME & TALENT

Last Name	First Name	MI	Area	Phone Number	Church Leadership	Birth Month	Birth Day	Birth Year	Class Year	Special Codes	1	2	3	4	5	6	7	8
Family 1	Father		425		Praise Team						1							
Family 1	Mother										1							
Family 1	Son		425			2	1	85	2003									
Family 1	Daughter		425			7	26	82	2000									
Family 2	Father		425			9	7											
Family 2	Mother		425			7	31											
Family 2	Son		425			11	15	85	2004									
SPADY	RICHARD	J	425		Lay Speaker	10	15	23			1	4	4	1		4		
Member			425			5	8	38			1	4	4		4	4		
Member			425			9	12	25										
Member			425			4	2	26										
Member			425															
Member			425		Chair, Outreach	8	5	29			1					3		
Member			425			10	16	20								3		
Member			425			4	13	88	2006									
Member			425			5	14	90	2008									
Member			425			5	2	59										
Member			425		Pastor													
Member																		
Member																		
Member																		
Member																		
Member																		
Member			425			8	27				1							
Member			425		Chair, Ad Council													
Member			425			5	28				1	2				2	2	
Member																		
Member																		

6. Flyer from Rev. Joe Harding, Rev. Bill Ellington, and Dick Spady, to United Methodist Pastors

Forum
oundation
Enhancing Communication in Organizations and Society
Symbolic Dialogue, Opinionnaire®, Viewspaper®, and Fast Forum® Services

Founded in 1970
Non-Profit

January 26, 2001

To: United Methodist Pastors   Re: "Focus on the Issues" Project—A Study of 2000
                                   Social Principles and *The Book of Resolutions, UMC*
Dear Colleagues:

Humanity longs for spiritual relevancy. Parishioners and pastors of our churches long for spiritual relevancy. "Man is a being in search of meaning" (Plato). The religious questions of the millennium may well be the Identity Questions—Who am I? What is my role in life? Where do I fit in? With current events in their present state in our nation and the emphasis on citizenship, America needs a "time-out place to talk." This can be accomplished in non-confrontational processes by the use of the new "Fast Forum®" technique.

The United Methodist Church is uniquely situated to provide America with the leadership to organize and conduct such dialogue through its long and close affiliation with the Forum Foundation. The Seattle District Board of Laity conducted research in how to improve communication in churches from 1965 to 1968. Rev. Joe A. Harding was District Supt. and Mr. Richard J. Spady was District Lay Leader. The foundation was founded as a non-profit Washington state educational research organization in 1970 by United Methodist laity and clergy including Rev. Dr. William D. Ellington, theologian, and subsequently a Director of Evangelism, GBOD. Joe Harding followed Ellington at the GBOD and last served as Director of the *Vision 2000* project of our church. Both pastors are now retired but remain active with the foundation.

Enclosed is a flyer which tells of a new program to study the 2000 *Social Principles* and *The Book of Resolutions*. This is a wonderful opportunity for your people to study and understand better the *Social Principles* of our church. For further information see our website at www.ForumFoundation.org or phone (206) 634-0420.

Churches can participate in one or more small groups of 4-12 persons meeting monthly for about two hours to discuss a single subject, e.g., families, children, aging etc., or spread weekly or bi-monthly during the month with one or more hour meetings. Each meeting will start with a 5 to 15 minute "theological conversation" on audio tape between Harding and Ellington to provide scriptural and theological context. Our church will have taken the first steps in implementing "Zeitgeist Communication." All of this will be more fully explained by UM lay speaker, Dick Spady, in his new book to be released in April, 2001 titled: *The Leadership of Civilization Building (Administrative and Civilization Theory, Symbolic Dialogue, and Citizen Skills for the 21st Century)*. Mr. Spady will present "New Learnings in Leadership" at the United Methodist Men's Congress at Purdue next July 13-15, 2001 with Timothy E. Moss, Director, Lay Leadership Development, GBOD. Join us in understanding the wealth and integrity of our church's social and moral values.

Sincerely Yours in Service,

Rev. Dr. Joe A. Harding   Rev. Dr. William D. Ellington   Richard J. Spady, President

---

UNITED METHODIST "FOCUS ON THE ISSUES" PROJECT
5 Minute "Theological Conversations" audio tapes provided at the start of each session by these UMC theologians

Rev. Dr. Joe A Harding
Formerly Director, Vision 2000
GBOD, UMC

Rev. Dr. William D. Ellington
Formerly, A Director of Evangelism
GBOD, UMC

•Use new *Symbolic Dialogue* to discuss issues in a non-confrontational process developed by the Forum Foundation (founded in 1970, non-profit). •Contribute *Parishioner Opinions* to a National Database of United Methodists. •*Develop Experience* with a process (called the Fast Forum® Technique) that can help our church and your congregation with planning and management if desired. *"This is a new visioning process of civilization building that will help bring theological relevancy to the level of the pew."* Mr. Tim Moss, Director, Conference Leaders Team, Discipleship Ministries Unit, GBOD, UMC.

A. Additionally, the first topic, Orientation, will include questions from the President's State-of-the-Union address (or inaugural address) and will tie in with a national research project involving high school Social Studies students in schools and churches and members of the World Future Society (non-profit, scientific-educational).

B. The sooner groups sign up the better chance they have to receive the packet for free and the more time they have to do the project.

— Cut along this line —

"FOCUS ON THE ISSUES"
(PROJECT)
FORUM FOUNDATION

Forum Foundation
4426 Second Ave. N. E.
Seattle, WA 98105-6191

UNITED METHODIST "FOCUS ON THE ISSUES" PROJECT
DEVELOP INFORMED OPINIONS ON ISSUES!
In 2001 Discuss Topics from The United Methodist Church 2000 *Book of Resolutions*

— Topics —

1. Orientation and "Inaugural Address" (Starts March, 2001)
2. Authority in the Church (April)
3. Family (May)
4. Children (June)
5. Aging (July)
6. Health Care (September)
7. Racism (October)
8. Economic Justice and Evaluation (November)

Free materials provided by the Forum Foundation are perfect for use with one or more small groups of 4-12 persons. Supplied materials provided are designed for eight topics. (Free materials are provided for the first 100 groups of 4-12 persons who enroll. Additional machine-scannable response sheets @ 25 cents are available if more than the initial small group of 4-12 persons participate.) After the first 100 churches enroll there is a nominal fee of $75 for book, audio tapes, materials, scanning, and mailings for the year's programming.

•The **FOCUS ON THE ISSUES** project is an eight-month research project in "symbolic dialogue" sponsored by the Forum Foundation. Materials provided are for 8 topics. Participants can meet anytime from weekly to monthly between March 2001 and November 2001. Dependent upon weekly/monthly meetings, participants meet and listen to a 5/15 minute "Theological Conversation" tape by UMC theologians Harding and Ellington on each of the eight topics. Every person gets a two-minute "Day-in-the-Sun" to speak—*others listen*—without comment, question, or interruption. Open discussion then follows in the group on the topic. At the end of the topic being studied, each participant can personally ratify or not each resolution studied.* Their answers are disclaimed and added to a national **UMC** database. A *Viewspaper*® will be mailed regularly to local churches participating summarizing results gathered nationally from the previous month's topic.

[*A Fast Forum® Opinionnaire® with questions drafted by Rev. Dr. John C. Gingerich, Christian Education (formerly Director, Kansas East Annual Conference, now retired). See www.ForumFoundation.org/ UMissues2001 at end of year.]

(To see a sample *Viewspaper*® from the 1994 *WHAT UNITED METHODISTS BELIEVE* research project visit: www.ForumFoundation.org/wumbview9. See also on www.ForumFoundation.org the video interview "A Time for History" of Dick Spady given at the 45th annual Creative Problem Solving Institute Conference, June, 2000, University of New York, Buffalo.)

The *Fast Forum*® process was developed by United Methodist Lay Speaker, Richard Spady, President of the Forum Foundation (Seattle), who will be conducting a workshop at the United Methodist Men's Congress at Purdue University July 13-15, 2001 with Tim Moss, Director of the Conference Leadership Team, GBOD, UMC. The Fast Forum technique can transform the way the church and you collect and use the wisdom of members of the congregation.

Note: Churches must supply their own copies of the 2000 Social Principles (over the one copy received in the packet). Order from the General Board of Church and Society (202) 488-6518 (35 cents each). Participants are encouraged to order their own personal copies of *The Book of Resolutions*, 2000 edition, from Cokesbury (1-800-605-9403). Churches should also place one or more copies in their church library for general reference of their study groups and the congregation.)

- -

Please fold, place in envelope, and mail to:

Forum Foundation
4426 Second Ave. N. E.
Seattle, WA 98105-6191

Please send me the materials I need to participate in the United Methodist **FOCUS ON THE ISSUES** project. I understand that I will receive a packet before the end of February, 2001 for one group of 4-12 persons with assignments and materials to study the year 2000 *Social Principles* and *The Book of Resolutions*. I understand that the first 100 churches enrolled will receive all materials free to help jump start the program, otherwise I will pay $75 on receipt of the materials for the year's program.

Name:_____

Address:_____

City, State, Zip:_____

Phone:_____ Fax:_____

Can we keep you informed via email?_____ If so, please give your email address:_____

Appendix E

The Converted Polarization-Consensus Rating (CPC Rating™)

This is a new social invention and indicator that is being introduced in this book; it will be first incorporated in reports for the "2001 Inaugural Address and the Youth of America" project with an Opinionnaire® and tape released for use in high schools in Year 2001. This is a symbolic dialogue between the President of the United States and the youth of America (and their parents, hopefully, and other citizens.)

The project got off the ground in August, 1999, when it received the endorsement of the Professional Members Forum of the World Future Society.[125] We are learning and will be poised to administer the project nationally in January, 2001, when President George W. Bush is inaugurated.

When the PC Rating was originally designed and published in 1969[126], the need was to better understand the responses of large numbers of participants—usually several hundred. One's mind could not comprehend the meaning of the yes/no/abstain raw data. After struggling for a month with the problem, I (RJS) hit on the Polarization-Consensus Rating. It worked,

But a new problem has arisen in administering the "State of the Union Address and the Youth of America" project. We felt it was not appropriate in our research to ask young people, their parents, and others to respond by yes/no/abstain to all questions derived from the State of the Union address. Young people needed more latitude to respond as they search in Psycho-Social Education for meaning; so we used Likert value scales of: Strongly Agree, Agree, Neutral, Disagree, and Strongly Disagree.

However, doing so introduces a new problem. Instead of the highly efficient PC Rating being used, we would now report percentages for each value chosen plus abstention and objection—seven in all. While this is accurate, it is inefficient, cumbersome, and academic for young people and the public at large. A simpler and quicker way is needed to convey the opinions of people and meaning.

We believe the CPC Rating will solve this problem. Like the alphabet, it's both simple and profound. We will *convert* the Likert scale Strongly Agree and Agree into "yes" responses; Disagree and Strongly Disagree into "no" responses; neutral responses will be converted to Abstain; and Objection will be reported as usual. Results and legends in all computer reports will be reported as usual showing percentages of response for each choice but, as a protocol, a "Converted Polarization Consensus Rating" (CPC Rating™) will also be shown.

What will be the result? The Fast Forum® computer software can reorder all questions by Polarization Rating (whether yes/no questions or not) simply by calculating the "abstains" and objections which proportionately depress or enlarge the rating. For example, if all questions receive a Polarization Rating above 70 per cent, i.e. it is "good" data, it means there is only *one* number, the Consensus Rating, to convey the meaning—instead of seven. That's a big jump, in fact a quantum jump, in efficiency as a social indicator and a real breakthrough in social science where we don't have as many discoveries as in the physical sciences. We should learn more in the future as we gain experience.[127] Reports by the full Likert value scale will still be shown for academic purposes, but it is doubtful, as a practical matter, that it will be as important once people understand the Consensus Rating as merely "the percentage positive of those polarized."

Understanding the Converted Polarization Rating, Consensus Rating, & CPC Rating™

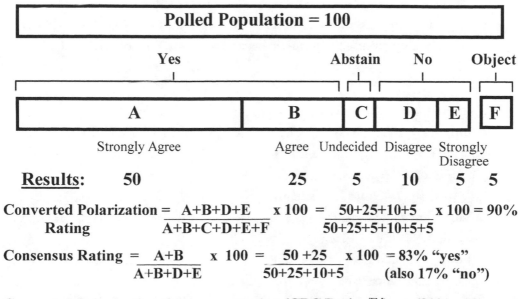

Appendix F

Entering Fast Forum® Data Records Into a File

For transmission of data to the Forum Foundation via Internet, e-mail or Diskette

Legend:

A Field is a collection of Characters.

A Record is a collection of Fields.

A File is a collection of Records.

An asterisk (*) in column one indicates a comment paragraph (not line) and can consist of several lines as follows:

*The Fast Forum® computer program will ignore comment paragraphs.

*The Fast Forum® program allows a maximum of 15 columns (1-15) for demographic and alphanumeric character responses plus a maximum of 50 more columns on Side A for numeric character responses (an additional 100 columns are available on Side B if required in special cases). The optical scanner scans both sides simultaneously. Any characters entered beyond column 65 on a line are considered comments by the program and ignored. (Note: It may be easier to use the numeric keypad to record data on each line.)

For example a Youth Opinionnaire® might be set up as follows:

Column one will designate Gender, i.e., 1=male, 2=female;

Column two will designate Age, i.e., 1=teenager, 2=20-29, 3=30-39 years, etc.

Column three could designate Ethnic Family, i.e., 1=African-American, 2=Asian-American, 3=Caucasian-American, 4=Chicano/Latino American, 5=Native-American, 6=Other Ethnic Family, 7=Pacific Islander, 8=Blended Family

Column four could designate Role, i.e., 1=Teenage Student, 2=Parent, 3=Grandparent, 4=Other Citizen

Column five could designate State Region, i.e., 1=Region One, 2=Region Two, 3=Region Three, etc., "0" (Zero)=Region Ten.

Protocol:

Any *demographic* column left unmarked, should be keyed as a blank (not identified). If the person tabulating knows the answer from other information, for example, the State Region number designated because of the return address, it should be keyed. Any *question* column left unmarked, should be keyed as a blank (abstention).

A (".")period can then be entered in column 6, for example, denoting the end of the demographic responses and the beginning of the question responses. A "+" is entered after the last character in the record denoting the end of the data string. A non-proportional font (such as Courier) should be used; the strings will all align on the right and alert all when keying errors of skipping or duplicating entries have been made.

Up to 50 numeric character responses to corresponding questions can then be entered beginning in column 7, e.g., 1=yes, 2=no; 1,2,3,4,or 5 for multiple-choice or value scale questions, i.e., 1=Strongly Agree, 2=Agree, 3=Neutral, 4=Disagree, 5=Strongly Disagree.

To denote an abstention to a question, key a space stroke or use a "0" (zero); to denote an objection to a question use a "6" (six).

Thus, for a participating local church to record a female, teenager, whose ethnic family is Caucasian, a student, who lives in jurisdiction 7 and who answers the first 5 questions Yes, the second five questions No, marks "3" on the next four multiple-choice questions except that she abstains to question number 15, and answers the last five questions "2" (Agree) except that she objects to the next to last question—a typical data setup sheet and single-spaced, keyed character string would be:

```
*Data Setup File
*To: The Forum Foundation Data Center
*4426 Second Ave. N.E.
*Seattle, WA 98105-6191
*Date: _____ Forum #_____ Subject:
*From Local Church or Organization: #xxx, City, State, Zip.
*Teacher/Church/Organization Communicator: _____
*Phone:_____ ; Fax:   e-mail:
*Comment:
*START OF DATA (Use Courier non-proportional font)
 21317.11111222223333 22262+
*etc.
*END OF DATA
*Secretary/Coordinator: _____
*Phone:_____ ; Fax: _____; e-mail _____
```

Appendix G

Senate Resolution 1993-8636

IN THE LEGISLATURE
of the

STATE OF WASHINGTON

SENATE RESOLUTION
1993-8636

By Senators Pelz and Moyer

WHEREAS, The Forum Foundation is a nonprofit, research corporation of Washington State organized in 1970 to improve the functioning of organizations and society; and

WHEREAS, Founders Richard J. Spady, President of The Forum Foundation, and Dr. Cecil H. Bell, Jr., of the University of Washington Graduate School of Business Administration and Vice-President of The Forum Foundation have worked tirelessly to promote new theories and technologies of innovative and effective communication strategies; and

WHEREAS, These new theories of administration and communication have been developed in Washington State to strengthen the effectiveness of new citizen involvement and education applications with the assistance of the late Dr. Stuart C. Dodd, professor-emeritus of sociology at the University of Washington; and

WHEREAS, A new communication technology called the "Fast Forum" technique, developed at the University of Washington Academic Computing Services beginning in 1970 and continuing there today, has emerged from these theories; and

WHEREAS, This communication technology facilitates the exchange of ideas among people in large and diverse groups, improves citizen participation, and has been used successfully by the municipalities of Redmond and Kent, and the Republic of Kryrgyzstan of the Commonwealth of Independent States; and

WHEREAS, The application of this communication technology to enhance citizenship education and critical-thinking curriculum materials for secondary schools in our state and elsewhere holds great promise;

NOW, THEREFORE, BE IT RESOLVED, By the Senate of the state of Washington, that the members of The Forum Foundation be recognized for their excellent work and research to improve communication in organizations and society, and that copies of this resolution be immediately transmitted by the Secretary of the Senate to the Governor, the Department of Community Development, the Superintendent of Public Instruction, Richard J. Spady, and Dr. Cecil H. Bell, Jr. to encourage the further innovative research of The Forum Foundation in citizenship education programs for communities and educational programs in schools.

I, Marty Brown, Secretary of the Senate,
do hereby certify that this is a true and
correct copy of Senate Resolution 1993-8636,
adopted by the Senate April 13, 1993.

Marty Brown

MARTY BROWN
Secretary of the Senate

Appendix H

Forum Foundation Fact Sheet as of January 1, 2001

Forum Foundation:

Enhancing Communication in Organizations and Society
Providing Symbolic Dialogue,
Opinionnaire®, Viewspaper®, and Fast Forum® Services
www.ForumFoundation.org
Founded in 1970, Non-Profit

Keywords:

Symbolic dialogue, social audit, social science, futures research, administrative theory, civilization theory, civilization building, social innovation, leadership, citizen participation, Many-To-Many Communication, Zeitgeist Communication, Fast Forum® Technique, Opinionnaire®, Viewspaper®, PLAN Forum®, QUEST Forum™, Dodd, Spady, Bell, Kirby, Ellington, Harding, Bedell, Gingerich, Clinton, Schreiner.

Purpose:

The Forum Foundation conducts educational and futures research in the field of Administrative Theory and Many-To-Many Communication technology to discover those dynamics which tend to move organizations and institutions, universally, toward solving their problems and anticipating or adapting to changes in their internal or external environment.

Office Address:

Forum Foundation
4426 Second Ave., N.E.
Seattle WA 98105-6191
Fax: (206) 633-3561; Tel: (206) 634-0420

Principals and associates:

Richard J. Spady, President and co-founder; also CEO of Dick's Drive-In Restaurants, Seattle, Recipient "Outstanding Philanthropic Small Business 2000" award;

Recipient of the 1993 Earl Award, World Network of Religious Futurists; Lay speaker, St. Peter's United Methodist Church, 1967-current; recipient, Bishop's Award, June, 2001, PNW Annual Conference, UMC (Bishop Elias Galvan, Resident Bishop, Seattle Area and Presiding Bishop, The United Methodist Church).

James R. Spady, Executive Vice President; also CFO Dick's Drive-In Restaurants, Attorney, Seattle.

Dr. Cecil H. Bell, Jr., Vice President and co-founder; formerly Associate Professor and Chair, Dept. of Management and Organization, School of Business Administration, University of Washington; Co-author, *Organization Development*, 6th Ed., 1998, Prentice-Hall publisher; President, Stuart C. Dodd Institute for Social Innovation.

Rev. William D. Ellington, Ph.D., Theology, co-founder and board member, retired minister, UMC, Associate Ecclesiastical Professor for United Methodist Ministries, Fuller School of Theology.

Rev. William B. Cate, Ph.D., Social Ethics, President-Director Emeritus, Church Council of Greater Seattle, and Jan Cate, Ph.D., Values Education, Board Members.

Rev. Richard S. Kirby, Ph.D., Theology, Executive Director, Stuart C. Dodd Institute for Social Innovation; Adjunct Faculty, University of Washington, School of Business Administration (1997-2001); Chair, World Network of Religious Futurists.

Rev. Kenneth L. Bedell, Ph.D., Sociology, President, Ecumenical Programs in Communications, Inc. (EPIC, Inc.); Vice President Administration, Forum Foundation.

Rev. Dr. Joe A. Harding, formerly Director, Vision 2000 program, General Board of Discipleship, The United Methodist Church (retired).

Rev. Dr. John C. Gingerich, Christian Education, formerly Director, Kansas-East Annual Conference, The United Methodist Church (retired).

Dr. Tatyana Tsyrlina, Moral Education, Professor of Education, Kursk State Pedagogical University, Kursk, Russia; associate, Forum Foundation and Stuart C. Dodd Institute for Social Innovation.

John I. Spady, M. S., Applied Information Management, Director of Research, Forum Foundation.

Gus Jaccaci, MAT, Education; MFA, Painting; Chair, Unity Scholars Foundation; associate, Forum Foundation and Stuart C. Dodd Institute for Social Innovation.

Graham Clinton, Christian Liaison to International Mensa; associate Forum Foundation and Stuart C. Dodd Institute for Social Innovation.

Len Schreiner, M.Div., Director, Namaste Peace Project; Seattle Teacher; associate, Forum Foundation and Stuart C. Dodd Institute for Social Innovation.

Writings:

"A New View of Authority and the Administrative Process (Revisited 1980)"

The Search For Enlightened Leadership (a trilogy); Vol. 1: *Applying New Administrative Theory* (1996); Vol. 2: *Many-To-Many Communication* (1998); *The Leadership of Civilization Building* (2002).

Concept:

The basic organizing principle of the human race in the present and historic past has been the Authoritarian Hierarchy, A>B>C>D ... (authoritarianism and dictatorships). It provides no checks or balances in governance and minimum societal incentives. Research indicates that the basic organizing principle of the human race actually is the Participative Heterarchy—A>B>C>A i.e., <u>A</u>dministrators over <u>B</u>ureaucrats over <u>C</u>itizens over <u>A</u>dministrators (freedom and democracy)—it provides checks and balances in governance and maximum societal incentives in civilization building!

Services:

The foundation has been primarily in a research mode and not a service delivery mode but is increasingly providing support services for participating organizations. The foundation is interested in applying the Fast Forum® groupware technique in *symbolic dialogue* and *social audits* using an "Opinionnaire®", profile reports, publications, and "Viewspaper®" to assist leaders to "talk" symbolically with constituents and for them to "talk" back. This assists in 1) *diagnosing* system problems as a first step in solving them, 2) *learning* through the dynamics of the Socratic Method by individuals and organizations participating, and 3) moving organizations and individuals participating toward organizational and societal *peace.* Some limited grants are available to support services to organizations interested in participating in the research. States, cities, schools, and organizations interested are invited to apply.

Brief History:

Between 1965 and 1968 the Seattle District Board of Laity of The Methodist Church first experimented with traditional forums. Big meetings at often-remote distances using Robert's Rules of Order to pass resolutions was not working well. These were often emotional and frustrating experiences for both people and leaders.

From this effort emerged the prototype of what today is known as the "Fast Forum" technique. There are no motions, no amendments, no win-lose situations, no contro-versy, no arguments, no talking at the point of decision-making as all talking precedes decision-making—thus there is no emotionalism or heat. Instead, there is just light, that is, swift, silent, rational, synaptic mind-to-mind, response to some idea posed in writing for objective response such as yes, no, abstain, multiple-choice, or value scales. Hence the name, Fast Forum®.

Today the question the foundation is asking is, "What is the role of a citizen, that is, what is the unique contribution of citizenship that leaders/representatives and ex-perts cannot do, no matter how great their knowledge nor how good their inten-tions?" A member of a religious or church group is a citizen of the group, a member of a union or association is a citizen of that group, a member of Rotary International or The Women's International League for Peace and Freedom is a citizen of those groups, and so forth and, of course, a member of society is a citizen of the society. What is the *unique* contribution of citizenship in all those contexts? We in the Forum Foundation believe there are three unique contributions of a citizen. *First, to contribute one's opin-ion, second, to respond to the opinions of one's peers, and third, to respond to the queries of leaders/representatives to the solution of those problems which interest and concern oneself. This is a process of civilization building.*

The Fast Forum® technique, as a new Many-To-Many Communication technol-ogy using mass means of communication, does not use random-sample, objective questionnaires based on statistical and mathematical theory. Instead it uses objective "Opinionnaires" based on participation and administrative theory. An Opinionnaire® looks much like a typical survey questionnaire, but it is not; different rules apply. We in the foundation are working with scholars to define them. Because we properly disclaim the responses on reports from all participants, the results are 100% valid for those persons participating; they are just as valid as letters and telephone calls and testimony given at public hearings. Thus reports accurately project individual opin-ions to the questions asked which is every person's right. It's as if those persons partici-pating were meeting at one place in a forum to voice their opinion but instead of meeting physically together, which is not possible, they are meeting symbolically to-gether at a point in time through computer tabulation. Usually this is done in small groups of 4-12 persons meeting at a time and place convenient for themselves such as in their own homes or workplaces. These are places where people already are; they don't have to go someplace to meetings which are often at remote distances for people.

Their conveners receive audio or video tapes from leaders by regular mail, approximately quarterly, but not more than monthly on issues of concern. People review the tape, engage in a structured "study circle" format using a process called "Day-in-the-Sun" to assure each person has an opportunity to speak while others listen. Following this there is open discussion. But before the group leaves, each person responds to an objective Opinionnaire® to questions posed for response by Yes, No, Abstain, multiple-choice, or value scale questions. Responses are marked onto Forum Foundation *Councilor*™ Response Sheets that are machine-scannable. This sheet does the same thing as a computer but for just a fraction of the cost—it allows a human being to interface directly with a machine, accurately, swiftly, and economically. These are returned by mail to the foundation for optical scanning and processing.

In this way hundreds or even thousands of people can "meet" symbolically (i.e., through *symbolic dialogue*, not in physical dialogue) to try to discover their Zeitgeist, that is, their "Spirit-of-the-Time," (which is their degree of consensus on topics being discussed). The Zeitgeist, the prevailing ideas of a group, institution, or society, is actually the *Supreme Governor;* in a democracy it is that from which is derived not only our laws but our constitutions as well. Thus citizens can participate fully in the "Administrative Process" functions of Diagnosing, Theorizing, and Reviewing. Yet the process takes nothing away from those who are legitimate leaders, either elected or appointed, i.e., "chiefs-of-state, who still retain all their prerogatives in the "Administrative Process" of Deciding and Accomplishing. Again, this is a democratic process of community and civilization building as leaders and citizens search together for a better future. The process is therapeutic and leads to a reduction in organizational and societal tensions and leads toward peace—and thus toward "happiness." *And this is a fundamental reason for forming all governments, public and private, "For Life, Liberty, and the Pursuit of Happiness!"* Governments are not charged with providing their citizens with all the amenities of life they feel they need to make them happy. But all governments are charged with enabling their citizens to pursue their own happiness.

Any organization, institution, government, or civilization which inhibits, innocently or not, the free movement of ideas and opinions about those ideas—up, down, and across its organizational and societal structures—is depriving itself of its greatest resource—*human thought*—and is in grave danger of being buried in history by the avalanche of the creativity of others.

Appendix I

Stuart C. Dodd Institute for Social Innovation Fact Sheet (SCDI)

As human systems and organizations grow ever larger, more complex, and more imper-sonal — in our schools, in our communities, in our churches, in our governments, and in industries and commerce—the individual shrinks toward facelessness, hopelessness, and frustration.

> Dr. Stuart C. Dodd,
> "Citizen Counselor Proposal,"
> *The Seattle Times,* November 10, 1974

Internet web address: www.stuartcdoddinstitute.org

Office Address: 4427 Thackeray Place NE; Seattle, WA 98105-6124

Phone: (206) 545-0547 Tel; Fax: (206) 632-1975;

Electronic mail general information:

info@stuartcdoddinstitute.org

Webmaster: Webmaster@stuartcdoddinstitute.org

Other e-mails: DrRSKirby@aol.com (Director), LUCSTEW @aol.com (Office Manager)

Stuart C. Dodd Institute for Social Innovation (SCDI/SI) is a not-for-profit, tax exempt, organization registered as such with the U.S. government. Incorporated on May 9, 1997; 501(c)(3) application approved on September 9, 1997.

Purposes:

SCDI/SI encourages scholarly, interdisciplinary research in the archives of Stuart C. Dodd (1900-1975), Professor Emeritus of Social Science at the University of Washington. Scholars and associates pursue the intellectual, moral and civic legacies of Dr. Dodd in the fields of sociology, business administration, education, urban planning, sustainable communities, cosmology, statistics, and mathematics. Topics of particular interest include organization development, administrative theory, many-to-many communication and value reporting.

Our Mission:

"The Stuart C Dodd Institute for Social Innovation is dedicated to using the full range of human knowledge to achieve a society that is democratic, equitable, just, compassionate, spiritual, sustainable, diverse, and fulfilling."

Our Methods:

We advance social innovation on the successive planes of *theory* (particularly Social Innovation Theory), *organization* (particularly The Stuart C. Dodd Institute for Social Innovation with help from the Forum Foundation), *event* (particularly our annual conferences and regional training activities), in social policy, program and experiment, and communication.

Our social experiments range from uses of the Fast Forum® technique to the establishment of civic innovation programs in entire cities such as Slidell, Louisiana. We operate with a view to doing ideally profitable social science and social philosophy research deriving from the legacy of Stuart C. Dodd. Our national and international activities collectively act as a model social science "think-tank." We explore new horizons of excellence in self-management and organizational development, in social theory, philosophy of society and political science/philosophy/art, and in the development of breakthrough social technologies. We aim to advance the theory and the practice of social innovation, as part of the legacy of Stuart C. Dodd. We conduct research in sub-fields of social innovation such as educational innovation. We are developing an in-house five-year plan for the planes on which we operate, from the pre-theoretical to the communication/publication plane. This will be published in 2001.

Dr. Stuart C. Dodd:

Dr. Stuart C. Dodd published over 200 scholarly works in his career and is recognized as one of the pioneers in his field. After earning his B.S. (1922), M.A. (1924) and Ph.D. (1926) at Princeton University, and World War II, Dr. Dodd served as a professor of sociology at American University in Lebanon for 20 years. During World War II, Dr. Dodd served as a Lieutenant Colonel on Eisenhower's staff with the American Army in Italy. After Lebanon, he was offered and accepted a position at the University of Washington in Seattle as a Walker-Ames Professor of Sociology. There he stayed and was for 14 years the director of the Washington State Public Opinion Laboratory. During this time, Dr. Dodd was the leading authority on random-sample polling in the Northwest. Among his many accomplishments, Dr. Dodd was the only pollster to predict that President Truman would defeat Governor Dewey in the 1948 election and was later called before Congress to explain what happened. Dr. Dodd's work at the University of Washington continued until his death in 1975.

Principals of the Institute:

Dr. Cecil H. Bell, Jr., President SCDI/SI; former Chair, Department of Management and Organization, School of Business Administration, University of Washington; and co-author: *Organization Development,* 6th Ed., 1998, Prentice-Hall publisher.

Rev. Dr. Richard S. Kirby, Executive Director, former adjunct faculty of the University of Washington's School of Business Administration; former Director of Administration, International Mensa; Chief Executive Officer of the World Network of Religious Futurists; and co-author: *The Temples of Tomorrow: World Religions and the Future* (Grey Seal Publishers, 1993).

James R. Spady, SCDI/SI Secretary-Treasurer; Seattle attorney; and businessman.

Dr. Kenneth A. Miller, MD: Deputy Executive Director of SCDI/SI; inventor of the Vibrational Theory of Relativity and Founder of the "I-CAN! Children for world health program." (kmiller@newnorth.net).

August Jaccaci, regional director SCDI/SI-Northeast America, 19 High Bluff Road, Cape Elizabeth, Maine 04107, tel: 207-799-0072 Fax; 207-767-4366, joannegus@msn.com.

Dr. Tatyana V. Tsyrlina, SCDI/SI Associate, Russia, Kursk State Pedagogical University, 305004 Russia, Kursk, Radishev Str., 56, Apt 6, Tsyrlina@aol.com.

Graham Clinton, Christian Liaison to International Mensa, grahamclinton@home.com www.intelligentchristian.org.

Scholars of the Institute:

Nancy Elizabeth Davis, Ph.D., 2608 Westbrook Way, Columbia, Mo 65203, ndavis@pppctr.org, 573-761-7766, Adjunct professor, University of Missouri-Columbia. 1991-present.

David Baker, seminarian, (The United Methodist Church), Institute for Ecumenical Theological Studies, School of Theology and Ministry, Seattle University, 206-353-7051 fixitguy@hotmail.com.

Appendix J

Stuart C. Dodd's Sample Papers

EpiDoc 400:3
Dec. 1974

by S. C. Dodd
Univ. of Wash.
Seattle 98195

A PREVIEW INTRODUCING AND EVALUATING THE "PAN-ACTS MATRICES"

64 EXHIBITS OF THE PAN-ACTS MODEL FOR THE <u>DIMENSIONS OF COSMOS</u>

in 16 Conspectuses of 64 pages

I. *What prompted this Exhibits booklet?*

At the age of 74, after two heart attacks in the last four months, I have decided to record this sixteen-year inquiry into the cosmos in preprint form so that, should I leave it unfinished, other cosmists can continue to explore and develop, to test and apply, this cosmic research. I intend to flesh out these skeletal outlines as far as time and health and assistance may make possible.

Such writing up of the Pan-Acts Modeling will use:

A. these 64 pages of exhibits as the gist of the modeling, supported by

B. 400 "EpiDocs" of some 2000± pages, which are mimeographed or Xeroxed studies preparing for fuller publication (Individual copies or whole sets are available at Xeroxing cost.);

C. 140 published research articles (and ten books) under contract with Gordon and Breach for republication in four volumes in 1975-76, entitled <u>Systemed Studies on Human Transacting</u>.

D. 30 notebooks, chronologically ordered, of my daily "Dawning Thots" (= "DT's"), hunches, memos, early drafts, etc., etc.

E. My 5-hour video-taped autobiography (from a seminar at Brown Univ. on "Masters of Sociology."

F. 6 systematizing monographs of some 4500 pages.

I plan a volume on <u>Dimensions of Cosmos</u>, comparing 4 versions in parallel columns on each two-page spread. The four versions, mutually enriching each other, would try to communicate to: (a) lay generalists; (b) scientists; (c) algebrists; (d) geometrists. All readers could enlarge their understanding of this World View by reading as most congenial and informative to them, while augmenting their knowledge by glimpses thru the other languages of science.

II. *What recent advances have helped deal afresh with the ancient questions of, Whence the universe! and Whither Mankind?* I list in partial answer:

A. Set theory, viewing every word or symbol as a name for the set of instances of its referent;

B. Systems theory, viewing complex wholes, with logarithms as the best algorithm;

C. Semiotics, studying systems of man x symbol x thing interactions;

D. The Zero exponent, $X_s^\circ = 1_s$, for every set, word, or qualitative entity (identified by subscripting) which enables man to deal with all things qualitative with mathematical rigor equal to current dealing with all things quantitative;

E. Computers, greatly simplifying complex calculating and checking of quantifiable hypotheses;

F. Stochastic processes, discovering continuous creation;

G. Combinatorics (or "Combics" for short), explaining increasingly large sections of scientific laws, processes, forces, formulas, etc., in simple terms of combinings, permutings, or repeatings (called "reiterings" here).

III. *What guiding principles helped most in this cosmic inquiry?*

My central quest was for better symbolizing (concepts, units, scales, formulas, hypotheses, law etc.) for analyzing the cosmos resynthesizably--to mirror its whole activity ever more simply and clearly to man. Mostly I used intuition, setting my subconscious to work while I slept to come up with my volumes or "Dawning Thots" on waking. But always I made explicit use of scientific methods when formulated as: "To so describe whatever is studied as to explain its past genesis, predict its future recurrence, and control its anytime changing better than hitherto."

IV. *What use of this cosmic Pan-Acts Model may be expected?*

For <u>philosophers</u>, I expect Pan-Acts Modeling will offer a more simple yet complete, a more explicit and exact, cosmology and epistemology than any present alternative theory.

For <u>theologians</u>, I expect Pan-Act-Theism to help solve ancient problems of the nature of God, God's Will, Good and Evil, the Creation of all things and the Destiny of man. (See EpiDoc 303.)

For <u>scientists</u>, I expect Pan-Acts modeling to prove a more comprehensive yet precise, more clear and operationally testable description and explanation of the whole cosmos than any current rival theory.

For <u>sociologists</u>, I expect the Transact submodel for Society gradually to be used as a societal supersystem or integrative framework within which more specific theories of human society can be expressed and tested.

For <u>people</u> universally, I expect the Pan-Acts model to provide a World View tending to help integrate nations and people, religions and ideologies, in One World Community.

3

· ·

PAN-ACTS CONSPECTUS #3 on PAN-ACT-THEISM
A Preprint Describing the Future FUNCTIONING of the Cosmos
page 3 --- by describing Things-Liked Most

EpiDoc 303,p.3
(Blue pages)

THINGS-LIKED MOST

This "Things-liked" theory of human behavior aims to so describe the probable acts of men as to explain and predict them increasingly and thus help to augment human self-control.

The theory starts by building, thru polls of humanity, a list of human wants which posterity now seems most likely to work and live for. This listing starts, in turn, on this page by inviting every reader to rank and revise the "Starting List" below so as will best express his own system of values.

Our Personal Present

0. We all, the <u>MEN</u> of Earth,
   want· life· of larger· worth·
   for Each, · and Now in time; ·
   we seek· ten· means· to climb; ·
   and thus fulfill· mankind.

Hygienic

1. We like <u>TO LIVE</u>· in health· --
   we seek· less sick· of any kind; ·
   we want· more whole· in heart· and mind; ·
   we strive· to grow· both safe· and strong; ·
   we yearn· for life· filled full and long. ·

Domestic

2. We like <u>TO LOVE</u>· -- be loved· --
   as mate; · or parent; · child; · or friend,
   as neighbor; · kin· or fellow men; ·
   as living; · dead; · or yet to be; ·
   each· in due· ways and due· degree. ·

Economic

3. We like <u>TO GET</u>· more wealth· --
   thru work· and trade· we're free· to choose·
   ourselves· to feed; clothe· and amuse; ·
   to fill· all needs· from high· to low·
   as we from child· to elder go.

Philan-thropic

4. We like <u>TO GIVE</u>· what's used·
   to help· men· climb; · those with least· health; ·
   those least· in other wants· like wealth; ·
   and those who long· have lacked· the most·
   of what· their own· groups· prize· the most.

Politic

5. We like <u>TO RULE</u>· by law· --
   thru rulers· picked· by vote· of all
   who let· no rights· nor· freedom· fall:
   with justice· and security·
   in small or world· community. ·

Religio-Ethic

6. We like <u>TO WORSHIP</u> well --
   our God, · our good, · our goals· in life, ·
   we march· in quest; · but with no strife·
   for what as holy· each· may see; ·
   while free· to speak· of what· should be. ·

Recreatic

7. We like <u>TO ENJOY</u>· life --
   each· day, · in work; or play; · or rest·
   on hill· or plain; · with more· of zest·
   and memory; · at cost· that's due, ·
   with fun for us· and playmates too. ·

Artistic

8. We like <u>TO BEAUTIFY</u>· --
   ourselves; · our homes, · and all around; ·
   thru music; · pictures; · gardened· ground·
   So what we touch· or taste· or smell
   makes· lovely feelings· in us· dwell. ·

Scientific

9. We like <u>TO LEARN</u>· the truth --
   to test out how· -- as science· tries -- ·
   things· move, · or breathe, · or symbolize; ·
   to learn· to curb· our fears· and war, ·
   to progress· fed by research more. ·

Scholastic

10. We like <u>TO TEACH</u>· what's wise --
    to each· child· here, · or not yet born·
    and all· who hope· from us· to learn·
    the best· of ways· to live· and grow· ·
    thru what we feel· and do· and know. · ·

Our Social Future

11. If we our <u>FUTURE</u>· Earth·
    plan· safe· from bomb· and dearth,
    then each· in roles one plays·
    must help· all win in ways·
    that best augment· man's· days. ·

This statement of a human value-system, or "things-liked," is intended to be highly:

1. <u>Comprehensive:</u> sampling somewhat typically all ten institutions of any culture;
2. <u>Universal:</u> satisfying men in most religions, ideologies, statuses, and periods;
3. <u>Exact:</u> specifying, in 400 words, 200 items of desiderata (between upper dots);
4. <u>Understandable:</u> words-per-syllable ratio = 400/440 = 90% of maximum simplicity;
5. <u>Important:</u> organizing 200 most preferred items into a standardizing hierarchy.

This base-line statement of values can help test such axiological hypotheses as:

6. <u>Personal Hypothesis:</u> If each reader substitutes his own more preferred items (keeping within 400 words) and rates them, then he can express his own value system.
7. <u>Group Hypothesis:</u> If groups, in controlled experiments, rerate each item after dis-
   cussion-with-intent-to-agree, then closer consensus tends to result.
8. <u>Human Hypothesis:</u> If people everywhere experiment thus, persistently from childhood on up, producing more consensus on more values, then a world value-system for
   humanity tends to emerge, that is democratically desirable, definitive and durable.

Project Value-systems.....S. C. Dodd....University of Washington, Seattle, USA   EpiDoc 138
This EpiDoc 138 expands the "Dimensions of Societal Planning" matrix, EpiDoc 314:1.

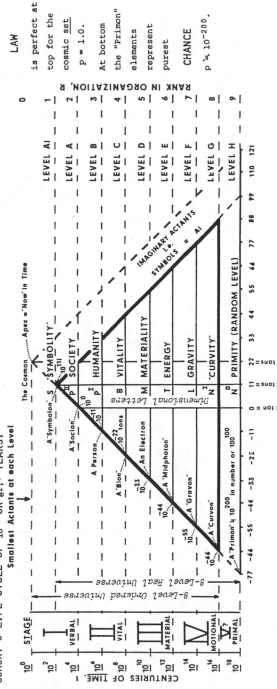

PAN-ACTS PICTURED

BY THE "MASS-TIME TRIANGLE" = MTT

Plotting Cosmic Activity (in Actants, A)
vs. its Level of Organization (in bits = lg A = O_r)
or Cohort Stage in Time (in cycles = $(2\pi r)t$) = $\Sigma |O_r|$

DEFINE COSMOS, (OR GOD_c), AS THE UNIVERSAL SET (= U^0 = 1)

OF ALL NAMABLE ELEMENTS, CALLED "ACTANTS," A.

THE EPICOSM HYPOTHESIS STATES FOR TESTING: IF ALL n ACTANTS (= THINGS-NAMABLE) INTERACT, RANDOMLY, CEASE-LESSLY AND REITERANTLY, FORMING AND EQUALLY UNFORMING IN THEIR OVERLAPPED COHORT LIFE-CYCLES, ALL THEIR n^n POSSIBLE COMBINATIONS, PERMUTATIONS AND REPETITIONS, THEN THEY ORGANIZE COSMOS AND ALL ACTANTS THEREIN AS HIERARCHIC NORMAL DISTRIBUTIONS, AT NINE LEVELS, BUILT BY VAST STOCHASTIC PROCESSES, AT AN OVERALL CONSTANT CREATANT RATE, c (= lg 10 ≏ 11), DURING EACH COHORT'S LIFE-CYCLE OF 10^{32} OR $e^{\pi I}$ YEARS.

LOG_{10} TONS OF MASS   (Extended at LEVELS F, G, H, and AI to LOGS OF ACTANTS, A)

THE EPICOSM EQUATION GRAPHED = U^0 = $a/c t$ = 1, THIS SAYS: ACTANTS AT t = CREATION RATE X TIME TAKEN.

by. S. C. Dodd, Univ. of Wash., Seattle 98195

EpiDoc 404:4. January 1975.

Appendix K

Futureum Grid, 46th Annual Creative Problem Solving Institute (CPSI) Reference Sheet.

46th Annual *Futureum* Homebase CPSI 2000*

Stages of Civilization Building

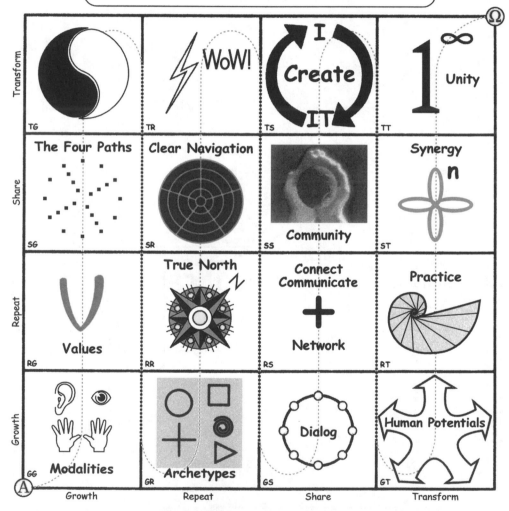

Let it be noted that CPSI pioneers ushered in the age of intentionality in June.

*Creative Problem Solving Institute
University of New York at Buffalo
June 18-23, 2000

Endnotes

1 "A Scientific Foundation for World Culture," Seattle, Washington, ©Burt Webb 1976.

2 The Rev. Joe Harding was arguably the best "preacher" in our conference. I was greatly privileged to work with him closely for three years. He retired in 1996 as co-author and former director of *Vision 2000*, General Board of Discipleship, The United Methodist Church in Nashville, TN. He lives now in Corvallis, Oregon.

3 Sponsors were East-Madison YMCA, the Seattle Rotary Boy's Club, and the Eastside Inter-Racial Clearing House in cooperation with: Seattle Public Schools, Bellevue Public Schools, University of Washington, Bellevue Area PTA Council, Seattle Human Rights Commission, Central Area Motivation Program, Bellevue Ministerial Association, United Central Area Ministerial Association, Seattle Opportunities Industrialization Center, Inc., Seattle-King County Economic Opportunity Board, Ind., and the Bellevue Chamber of Commerce.

4 Dick's Drive-In Restaurants in Seattle, which I co-founded and opened in 1954.

5 John Jacobsen—a doctoral student in semantics at the time who later accompanied me to Moscow as an interpreter to an educational conference organized by Tatyana Tsyrlina.

6 This was done at the University of Washington Academic Computer Center by the Church Council of Greater Seattle that had an account as a non-profit, charitable organization. The Church Council served as agent to UMCom, and I was the agent for the Church Council. It worked, and we all learned.(RJS)

7 Stuart Dodd was the only pollster who accurately predicted that President Truman would defeat Governor Dewey in the 1948 elections. He was called before Congress to explain how that happened.

8 The World Future Society, in Bethesda, MD, was founded in 1966 for the study of alternative futures and is a non-profit, tax exempt, scientific-educational association. It acts as an impartial clearinghouse for a variety of views and does not take positions on what will or should happen in the future. Many members are teachers, psychologists, and others in social science but there are also members in physical science. Most members are from government, industry, and religion, and I participate in the latter two camps. (RJS)

9 In 1999 I met Gus Jaccaci at the World Future Society General Conference in Washington, DC. He was a student and colleague of Stuart Dodd going back to 1972, when Stuart was a presenter at the Creative Problem Solving Institute (CPSI) conferences of the Creative Education Foundation in Buffalo, New York each year before his death. Jaccaci then came to Seattle for a conference in May, 2000 and introduced us to other Seattle-area students and colleagues of Stuart Dodd, notably Burt Webb, a cosmologist. I was then invited to attend as a presenter at the 46th annual CPSI conference held in Buffalo in June, 2000 where I met Rendle Leathem, a mathematical associate made known to me years ago by Stuart. It was at a session conducted there by Rendle that we both gained a new insight on the Unified Social Field Theory presented later in this book. It was as if Dodd's ideas have been incubating in Seattle all these years and now that all of us have gotten together, we are sparking new insights. (RJS)

10 Dr. Kirby was open to change—he wanted to come to the United States. He was a lecturer in the School of Business Administration at the University of Washington where he taught during 1997-2001.

11 I was a co-founder of the club in 1980 and held the active classification of "Futures Research."

12 My family originally came from Austria to Russia with Catherine the Great. My father was born in 1900 and came with my grandparents in 1904 to the United States. They settled in Portland, Oregon where I was born in 1923.

13 *The Book of Discipline* of The United Methodist Church, 1996, Page 74.

[14] Dr. Leroy Hood, "Foundation for the Future," Bellevue, Washington, Humanity 3000 Conference, Seminar #1 Proceedings, April 11-14, 1999.

[15] Joel A. Barker and Ray J. Christensen, "Discovering the Future—The Business of Paradigms," Video, 1989, produced by Infinity Limited and Charthouse Learning Corporation, and based on Barker's book of the same name.

[16] Richard J. Spady, Cecil H. Bell, Jr., and Gary A. D'Angelo, "A New View of Authority and the Administrative Process," *FUTURICS,* Vol. 4 No 2 pp 143-157, 1980 (Pergamon Press Ltd). "The Participative Heterarchy A>B>C>A; The Administration of Church and Society in the Future" by Richard J. Spady, was published by the Forum Foundation, 1984. The prepublication edition of the manuscript of this book titled, "Administrative Theory", was published in January 1986 as part of our research to get initial feedback and reaction of our general theories from scholars and leaders. (An article was also presented at session W3-13 on the theme "Reinvigorating Democracy" of the Seventh General Assembly of the World Future Society, June 27-July 1, 1993 in Washington, D.C. The article was titled, "A New View of Authority and the Administrative Process—Revisited.")

[17] (Old Testament) Leviticus 19:18 and (New Testament) Matthew 19:19.

[18] Gene Roddenberry, creator of Star Trek, "A Letter to the Next Generation," *TIME,* April 18, 1988, page 1.

[19] Rollo May, *The Meaning of Anxiety,* Revised Edition, 1977 (George J. McLeod Ltd., publisher; Toronto).

[20] Robert Putnam, a term referenced in *Bowling Alone* (Simon & Schuster, 2000).

[21] Erik H. Erikson, "Erikson, In His Own Old Age, Expands His View of Life," New York Times, June 14, 1988, page 13.

[22] Published in *Reader's Digest,* August 1978.

[23] Thomas Jefferson, The Declaration of Independence, July 4, 1776.

[24] Chester Barnard, *The Functions of the Executive* (Harvard University Press, 1938 and 1968), Chapter 12, pages 183 and 184.

[25] Alexander Leighton, *The Governing of Men* (Octagon Books Inc., New York), 1964, page 367.

[26] Thomas Jefferson, op. cit.

[27] Barnard, op. cit.

[28] Alexander Leighton, op. cit.

[29] New York Times national edition, November 28, 1989, "Unshackled Czech Workers Declare Their Independence," by reporter Esther B. Fein.

[30] The author had this learning experience in an advanced Air Force ROTC class given in 1949 at Oregon State University. (RJS)

[31] Rensis Likert, *The Human Organization,* 1967, page 142 (McGraw-Hill, New York, NY).

[32] Likert, loc. cit. p. 16.

[33] Likert, loc. cit., Authoritative, p. 46.

[34] Dr. Jacob Bronowski, *The Ascent of Man,* (Little, Brown and Co., Boston/Toronto 1973).

[35] From an address on "Human Relationships," given to state educators in 1970 in Seattle.

[36] Co-author of *Management and the Worker,* Roethlisberger and Dickson, Harvard University Press, 1939. This was in an address given in March, 1952 to Harvard alumni.

[37] Douglas McGregor, *The Human Side of Enterprise,* (McGraw-Hill Book Co; New York; 1960).

[38] Douglas McGregor, loc. cit. p. 45.

[39] Douglas McGregor, loc. cit., p. 246.

[40] Warren Bennis and Burt Nanus, *Leaders* (Harper & Row, New York); 1985.

[41] Dr. Arthur W. Combs spoke at the Seattle Center in Seattle, Washington in 1970 under the auspices of the Department of Administrators and Supervisors section of the Washington Education Association. He was the editor of the now classic 1962 yearbook of the National Education Association *Perceiving, Behaving, Becoming.*

[42] John W. Gardner, Leadership Papers, #2. The Tasks of Leadership, reported in *Future Survey* Annual 1987, XVIII "Methods to Shape the Future, A. New Thinking."

[43] This was a draft of an article personally given to the author by Dr. Combs when I went to Greeley, CO on November 16, 1985 in an effort to get Dr. Combs to co-author our book because one of the theories, Helping Professions, was based on his research. He subsequently decided not to be a co-author, but graciously approved our reference of his research. (RJS)

[44] Noted in a brochure by American Express. (RJS)

[45] Webster's *New International Dictionary,* Second Edition, Unabridged.

[46] "Prague Premier Sees Top Foes, Shares Platform with Dubcek; Party Calls Special Congress," New York Times, National Edition, November 27, 1989.

[47] Our colleague, Dr. Stuart C. Dodd, Director of the Washington State Public Opinion Laboratory at the University of Washington, was probably the leading authority on typical statistical polling in the Pacific Northwest. He was the only pollster who accurately predicted that President Truman would defeat Governor Dewey in the presidential election of 1948 and was called to testify before Congress as to how that all happened. It was an interesting story. He told us that the major polling services had been reporting a major lead by Dewey for weeks before the election. Because of this, they stopped their polling on the Saturday before the election the following Tuesday. Professor Dodd continued to poll right up to the election. He told us that the American people changed their minds in that short period of time and decided "not to change horses in the middle of the stream." The people probably changed the course of "future history" by the stroke of their pens.

[48] Eldon Byrd, scientist in an address titled, "The Transformation of Societal Institutions" given at a session of the "First Global Conference on the Future" and General Assembly of the World Future Society, Toronto, Canada, July, 1980.

[49] See Forum Foundation Fact Sheet in the Appendix H.

[50] Opinionnaire® and Viewspaper® are registered trademarks, U. S. Patent Office, of the Forum Foundation to assure use by participants in ways consistent with the theories provided in this book and to differentiate better between objective statistical (e.g., "Questionnaire") and objective participation (e.g. "Opinionnaire®") materials in theory and in practice.

[51] John W. Gardner, Godkin Lectures, Harvard University, reported in Christian Science Monitor, April 16, 1969.

[52] Peter Drucker, *Adventures of a Bystander,* p. 254, 1978.

[53] Elton Mayo, Harvard Professor sometimes called the, "father of the human relations movement," in the preface of the classic *Management and the Worker,* by Roethlisberger and Dickson, published in 1939.

[54] Howard Ellis and Ted McEachern, *Reflections on Youth Evangelism,* General Boards of Evangelism and Education, The Methodist Church, (1959).

[55] Thomas Jefferson, Declaration of Independence, 1776.

[56] The above paragraphs on "Peace" were first published in late 1985 in the prepublication edition of the manuscript of this book. Since that time the concept of *Glastnost* (openness) and *Perestroika* (re-structuring) proposed by Mikhail Gorbachev, General Secretary of the Soviet Union, became known. So, too, have the subsequent democratic movements in Poland, Hungary, East Germany, Czechoslovakia and elsewhere in eastern Europe. These examples are evidence of this trend we predicted.

[57] Elton Byrd, op. cit.

[58] Barnard, op. cit.

[59] "New Memes for the New Millennium" address by Barbara Marx Hubbard, co-founder, Foundation for Conscious Evolution, at the 1995 Annual Meeting of the World Future Society, "FutureProbe: Imagining Possibilities, Creating Opportunities," Atlanta, Georgia, July 18-20, 1995. Ms. Hubbard also received the "Earl Award" as the "Religious Futurist of the Year 1994" at the conference from the World Network of Religious Futurists.

[60] "Administrative Performance and System Theory" by Daniel E. Griffiths. Papers Presented at An Interdisciplinary Seminar on Administrative Theory, March 20-21, 1961 at The University of Texas, Austin, Texas.

[61] Abraham Lincoln.

[62] Margaret J. Wheatley, *Leadership and the New Science*, (1999).

[63] This diagram and a few other papers by Stuart C. Dodd are published in Appendix J. This book can be ordered initially from University Bookstore, Seattle, 1-800-335-READ and from Cokesbury Bookstore (Kirkland, WA, 1-800-605-4405. For Russian translations contact Dr. Tatyana Tsyrlina, Kursk State Pedagogical University, tsyrlina@aol.com.] For additional help, go online to www.ForumFoundation.org or phone (206) 634-0420; fax (206) 633-3561.

[64] Taken from a letter of August 14, 2000 by Presbyterian Ms. Lyn Fleury Lambert following her attendance at a "Theology of Healing" workshop August 12-13, 2000 by Rev. Richard S. Kirby at St. Peter's United Methodist Church, Bellevue, Washington.

[65] Todd Stedl (trstedl@u.washington.edu) and modified on 25 July 1996. See http://www-theory.chem.washington.edu/~trstedl/quantum/quantum.html.

[66] Hawking, Stephen, *A Brief History of Time* page 55-6 (Bantam, 1988).

[67] Daniel Liderbach, *The Numinous Universe* (Paulist Press, 1989).

[68] Liderbach, op.cit., p.85.

[69] David Bohm, *On Dialogue*, edited by Lee Nichol, 1996, Page 14.

[70] Stuart C. Dodd, *The Probable Acts of Man* and *The Probable Acts of Men* (State University of Iowa, 1963).

[71] Simmons, A. (1999). *A Safe Place for Dangerous Truths: Using Dialogue to Overcome Fear & Distrust at Work,* (American Management Association), p. 18.

[72] Jaideep Singh from *Administrative Theory,*1984, Ramesh K. Arora, Volume Editor, Indian Institute of Public Administration, Indraprastha Estate, Ring Road, New Delhi, India 110002. (Page XXII and Page 122 by Jaideep Singh).

[73] Robert Putnam, op. cit.

[74] *On Dialogue,* Edited by Lee Nichol. © 1996 Sarah Bohm, for the original material by David Bohm; Lee Nichol for selection and editorial matter, Reprinted 1997, 1998. Published by Routledge, 29 West 35th Street, New York, NY 10001.

[75] Assistance on developing this idea of Social Quantum Mechanics was provided by my co-author, The Rev. Dr. Richard S. Kirby, Theologian. Dr. Kirby's doctoral dissertation was titled "The Theology of Cosmic Disorder" (1992), King's College London. So Stuart Dodd in 1963, Richard Kirby in 1992, and ourselves, arrived independently at similar conclusions. I believe we are approaching "the truth." That is heartening, and it is—progress.

[76] Howard Ellis and Ted McEachern, op. cit.

[77] *The Crisis of Global Capitalism,* by George Soros (Public Affairs, Perseus Books Group); pages 96, 200, and 232.

[78] A.D. Ritchie, *Civilization, Science, and Religion*, page 9, (Penguin Books, New York); 1945.

[79] Jaideep Singh, op. cit.

[80] For more information see www.ForumFoundation.org or www.StuartCDodd.org.

[81] Robert Putnam, op. cit.

[82] This idea was postulated by John W. Gardner, Godkin Lectures, Harvard University, reported in *Christian Science Monitor,* April 16, 1969.

[83] John's major was: Interdisciplinary Studies; Applied Information Management at the University of Oregon. His master's thesis was titled, "A Selected Study of the Benefits of Dialogue in Small Groups and Implications for Symbolic Dialogue for Larger Groups." It was presented August 2000. The reference was from page 77. Dr. Linda F. Ettinger chaired his review committee. A copy of his study can be requested by E-mail at: jspady@aol.com.

[84] Although the functional, theoretical foundations were used in the Delphi Technique, they never used the term "Symbolic Dialogue."

[85] The explanation was published in my first book, *The Christian Forum or (Fast Forum), Why and What It Is!* (1969), page 3. (RJS).

[86] This research was developed during the Family Inter-Racial Dialogues of the Eastside Inter-Racial Clearing House, May, 1969. I was chair. (RJS)

[87] Demonstrated by Syd Simon, author of *Values Clarification* at a workshop given at the Bellevue Community College several years ago.

[88] Howard Ellis and Ted McEachern, op. cit.

[89] The National Computer Systems, 2125 4th Street NW, Owatonna, MN 55060, 1-800-533-0518, prints these forms. They are readable by NCS scanners that are utilized in many of the school districts of the nation.

[90] See also the Forum Foundation website (http://ForumFoundation.org/Partners/EveryWoman/) for further information. It contains an example of an Opinionnaire administered to women attending the United Nations Fourth World Women's Conference held in Beijing, China September 4-15, 1995. The Opinionnaire was administered in English, Chinese, French, and Spanish but was tabulated in a single "Language of Opinionnaire" Profile Report. This was a first for the Forum Foundation and a major breakthrough in communication and social science. It was administered in China by "Everywoman's Delegation of Seattle, Washington, USA; Jan Cate, coordinator. See Appendix D-2 for an example of the Opinionnaire used. (Dr. Cate was a member of the research team and is a board member of the Forum Foundation.)

[91] If you're not sure that a use of "Opinionnaire" or other copyrighted material is sanctioned as explained here, write to the Forum Foundation, 4426 Second Ave. N.E., Seattle, WA 98105-6191 explaining your situation and ask for permission.

[92] Ms. Virginia Balsley, an undergraduate at the University of Washington and a citizen of Redmond, evaluated the City of Redmond's Community Forum Program for a class project in 1997. Richard Kirby was her teacher. Some of her research findings are incorporated into this write-up.

[93] MiraMed Institute, Juliette Engel, See www.miramedinstitute.org; 1-800-441-1917; 206-285-0518.

[94] I was on the volunteer staff or the Church Council of Greater Seattle from 1971 to 1990 holding the portfolio of "Futures Research." The SMILE Syndrome paper was written in January, 1974. I posted it on the bulletin boards of all the University of Washington departments concerned with random-sample polling as a challenge; no one responded. Today this kind of data is often presented even on television. When used, however, it is always disclaimed, e.g., "The survey is not a scientific random sample, etc." That's progress. (RJS).

[95] Published in *Reader's Digest,* August 1978.

[96] Marshall McLuhan, *Understanding Media,* 1964.

[97] Gardner, op. cit.

[98] Lewis H. Lepham, author, *The Wish of Kings: A Democracy at Bay,* 1993; Editor, Harpers Magazine, was interviewed on C-Span, "Booknotes," August 15, 1993.

[99] Louis Harris was commissioned by Congress to poll the American people during the 1976 Bicentennial Celebration on how they felt about their democratic republic after 200 years. It was reported that the American people were highly alienated and felt they were not adequately involved in the decisions that affected their lives, public and private. It was also reported that a poll taken of public officials at the same time indicated that they felt they were doing a good job and that "the average American citizen was uninformed and not capable of making a positive contribution to the solution of my problems."

[100] Resolution adopted by the General Assembly: United Nations Year of Dialogue Among Civilizations (Homepage of United Nations) Available: http://gopher.un.org:70/00/ga/recs/53/res53-22.en (2000, July 24).

[101] *Webster's New International Dictionary,* Second Edition, Unabridged.

[102] (Emphasis added by Tarrant); Peter Drucker in *Drucker, The Man Who Invented The Corporate Society,* by John J. Tarrant, p. 50, (Warner Books, 1976).

[103] Alvin Toffler; Closing address, 2nd General Assembly, World Future Society, Washington, DC, June, 1975.

[104] John W. Gardner, Godkin Lectures, Harvard University, reported in *Christian Science Monitor,* April 16, 1969.

[105] John Naisbitt, *Megatrends,* 1982, (Warner Books, NY).

[106] In accord with *The 2000 Book of Discipline,* we recommend this research project to the General Board of Discipleship in accordance with ¶ 1102.10; to the General Board of Church and

Society in accordance with ¶ 1004; to the General Board of Global Ministries in accordance with ¶ 1302.12; to United Methodist Communications (UMCom) in accordance with ¶ 1806.16; to the General Commission on United Methodist Men in accordance with ¶ 2302.4 f); and to the General Council on Ministries in accordance with ¶ 906.17.

[107] Graduate seminarians first become deacons and are assigned a local church for a short probationary period. After serving satisfactorily as deacons, they are accepted by a Bishop as elders and become full members, not of their local church but of their Annual Conference (there are 72 Annual conferences in the United States with over 36,000 local United Methodist churches.) The Bishop can also assign laity as Local Preachers to provide limited services to local churches. Any lay person can become a Certified Lay Speaker by completing an initial training course; they can maintain their status each year by the completion of whatever training or course completion is required to remain certified. A Certified Lay Speaker can become a Local Church Lay Speaker without additional training each year with approval of the local church charge conference which meets annually. The primary responsibility of a lay speaker is not pulpit supply but is teaching. A lay speaker can "carve out" any lay ministry in which he/she wishes to serve as long as approval is given by the local church in support of that ministry. My lay ministry is the study of administrative and civilization theory and Zeitgeist Communication. I have been a Certified Lay Speaker or a Local Church Lay Speaker continuously since 1967. While I'm at the bottom of the totem pole, at least I am on the totem pole. The church is always on the lookout for "grassroot" solutions. They don't get much "grassier" than our Zeitgeist Communication research. But that is helpful because in the formulation of the scholastic and religious ideas in this book, they are all viewed simultaneously by a scholar (Cecil Bell), a layman (me), and a theologian and scholar (Dr. Kirby). That's progress! (RJS)

[108] Dan R. Dick and Evelyn M. Burry, *Quest, A Journey Toward a New Kind of Church,* page 79, 1999, (Discipleship Resources, Nashville, Tennessee 37202-0840), www.discipleshipresources.org.

[109] See "The Theory of Authority" in Section 1.

[110] Webster, op. cit.

[111] These questions were provided by Mr. Bill Wortman, retired Social Studies teacher from Interlake High School, Bellevue, Washington in a series of classes conducted at St. Peter's United Methodist Church, Bellevue, Washington USA in March, 1997.

[112] The "QUEST Forum" and "Converted Polarization-Consensus Rating" trademarks are pending, and "Opinionnaire," "PLAN Forum," and "Viewspaper" are registered trademarks, United States Patent Office, of the Forum Foundation. They can be used as long as they are used properly (i.e., don't label a random-sample Questionnaire as an "Opinionnaire" and don't provide questions or statements for response without allowing participants to abstain and object.) Just acknowledge the use, as appropriate, with:

"Fast Forum®", "Opinionnaire®", "PLAN Forum®", and "Viewspaper®" are registered trademarks, U.S. Patent Office; and "QUEST Forum™", "PC Rating™", and "CPC Rating™" are pending trademarks of the Forum Foundation, 4426 Second Ave. N.E., Seattle, WA 98105-6191, USA (www.ForumFoundation.org; (206-633-3561 Fax; 206-634-0420 phone); and are used by permission.

Other uses are not authorized unless written permission is obtained. Additional trademarks, United States Patent Office, of the Forum Foundation and which, when approved, may be used by those tabulating data through the Forum Foundation are: Citizen Councilor® and Fraternity Councilor® and "An Inspirational City in Pursuit of Happiness!®"

[113] The term was first used in *The Search for Enlightened Leadership, Many-To-Many Communication (A Breakthrough in Social Science),* Spady and Bell, 1998, page 82.

[114] Kuhn, T.S., *The Structure of Scientific Revolutions,* 1970 [2nd ed.] Chicago UP.

[115] Lakatos, Imre and Musgrave, M., *Criticism and the Growth of Knowledge.*

[116] Wick, David, *The Infamous Boundary: Seven Decades Of Controversy In Quantum Physics,* 1995, page 19, Boston: Birkhauser.

[117] Medawar, Sir Peter, *The Art of the Soluble.*

[118] President Abraham Lincoln, The Gettysburg Address, 1863.

[119] "The Discovery of the Future" was presented at the Royal Institution of Great Britain on January 24, 1902, and first published in the United States in The Smithsonian Report for 1902.

[120] John J. Tarrant, *Drucker: The Man Who Invented the Corporate Society* (Warner Books Edition, New York, 1976, Page 50).

[121] "Soaring CEO Salaries," *The Futurist,* November, 1999, page 9.

[122] "Chief Justice Marshall Takes the Law in Hand;" *Smithsonian,* November, 1998, page 170.

[123] Martin Crutsinger, Associated Press writer, "Massive Technological Changes Forecast," Journal-American, Bellevue, Washington, May 15, 1988. page A1.

[124] Eldon Byrd, scientist, "The Transformation of Societal Institutions," The First Global Conference on the Future, World Future Society, Toronto, July, 1980.

[125] Non-profit, tax-exempt, scientific-educational, and dedicated to the study of the future. It has nearly 30,000 members and subscribers to *The Futurist* magazine. There are three sections of the Professional Members Forum of the society: consultants, organizational futurists, and academics; Dick Spady and Richard Kirby are in the academic section and Richard Kirby is chair of the Youth Committee and co-chair of the Senior Committee with Norman Bakos.

[126] *The Christian Forum (or Fast Forum) Why and What It Means,* Richard J. Spady, 1969, Seattle, WA.

[127] The Forum Foundation has applied for a patent. If granted, we will license it to others to use without cost if they agree to give credit to the Forum Foundation, "used by permission," and reference our web site: www.ForumFoundation.org. Hopefully, we will be able to monitor and improve the process and expand its use.

Index

T

THEORY BUILDING and SYMBOLIC DIALOGUE

BT = Before Technology   AT = After Technology

The Leadership of Civilization Building
(Administrative And Civilization Theory, Symbolic Dialogue, And Citizen Skills For The Twenty First Century)

How to Order Additional Copies of
The Leadership of Civilization Building

5 Easy Ways to Order

1. Call Cokesbury Bookstore (Kirkland WA) at 1-800-605-9403 from 9–5:30 p.m., Mon–Fri; 9–2 p.m., Sat. $18.95. You can also order a copy of United Methodist *Book of Resolutions 2000.* A 20% discount will be extended to UM ministers on one or both titles. Major credit cards.

2. Call University Book Store in Seattle WA at 1-800-335-READ from 9 to 9 p.m., Mon–Fri, 9–6 Sat., 12–5 Sun. $18.95. Free shipping in U.S. Major credit cards.

3. For signed copies of *The Leadership of Civilization Building,* send $18.95 (checks only; WA residents add 8.8 per cent) to Forum Foundation, 4426 Second Ave. NE, Seattle WA 98105-6191. Free shipping in U.S. a limited number of hardback cover is available at $26.95.
Call 206-634-0420.

4. For volume discounts of *The Leadership of Civilization Building,* call the Forum Foundation at (206) 634-0420, or inquire online at FastForum@aol.com.

5. Translated copies of *The Leadership of Civilization Building* are also available in Russian. For details, contact the Forum Foundation at (206) 634-0420. In Russia, contact Prof. Tatyana Tsyrlina of Kursk State Pedagogical University at tsyrlina@aol.com.